PAULETTE

Other books by Joe Morella & Edward Z. Epstein include:

Jane Wyman: A Biography
Rita: The Life of Rita Hayworth
The "It" Girl: The Incredible Story of Clara Bow
Lana: The Public and Private Lives of Miss Turner
Lucy: The Bittersweet Life of Lucille Ball
Rebels: The Rebel Hero in Films
The Ince Affair (A Novel)

PAULETTE
The Adventurous Life
of Paulette Goddard

**Joe Morella
and
Edward Z. Epstein**

St. Martin's Press
New York

PAULETTE: THE ADVENTUROUS LIFE OF PAULETTE GODDARD.
Copyright © 1985 by Joe Morella and Edward Z. Epstein. All rights reserved. Printed in
the United States of America. No part of this book may be used or reproduced in any
manner whatsoever without written permission except in the case of brief quotations
embodied in critical articles or reviews. For information, address St. Martin's Press, 175
Fifth Avenue, New York, N.Y. 10010.

Design by Doris Borowsky
Editor: Toni Lopopolo
Managing Editor: Carol E. W. Edwards

Library of Congress Cataloging in Publication Data

Morella, Joe.
Paulette : the adventurous life of Paulette Goddard.

1. Goddard, Paulette.   2.Moving-Picture actors
and actresses—United States—Biography.   I. Epstein,
Edward Z.   II. Title.
PN2287.G56M67   1985   791.43′028′0924 [B]   85-11784
ISBN 0-312-59829-7

First Edition

10 9 8 7 6 5 4 3 2 1

CONTENTS

Sections of photographs follow pages 86 and 150.

Prologue

Charles Chaplin, Burgess Meredith and Erich Maria Remarque were three of her husbands . . .

George Gershwin was willing to forsake his wicked ways if only she would marry him (she happened to be Mrs. Chaplin at the time) . . .

Clark Gable, a gentleman who preferred blondes, found in her a brunette he preferred . . .

Diego Rivera was one of many celebrated artists who marveled at Goddard's "shimmering spirit . . . her inner fire," qualities he captured on canvas, canvases which she added to her collection.

An astounding array of gifted, powerful and creative men from many areas of life were drawn to Paulette Goddard, and she moved easily between their worlds of show business, art, politics and society. Whether it was H. G. Wells, Aldous Huxley, Harry Hopkins, Jock Whitney, the King of Yugoslavia, Jean Cocteau, Jean Renoir, John Steinbeck, William Saroyan, Stravinsky, Rachmaninoff or, in later years, Andy Warhol—she knew and charmed them all.

Paulette may not be aware of it but F.B.I. Director J. Edgar Hoover, although he never met Goddard, was for years kept personally informed of her exploits. F.B.I. documents, classified until now, reveal fascinating information about Goddard's political activities and her years-long relationship with Chaplin. Were they married or not? Were they divorced or had there been no reason for a divorce? The pair's coupling has remained one of the intriguing mysteries of Hollywood's golden years.

Goddard's life seems as if it were drawn from the pages of a Patrick Dennis novel or Margaret Mitchell's *Gone With the Wind*. In fact, Paulette was a prime contender in the "Who will play Scarlett?" chapter of Hollywood history.

Off screen, Paulette Goddard was the leading lady in the infamous "Ciro's affair," a legend that has haunted her image for years. Did she or didn't she? wondered the Hollywood gossip machine (then and now). The tale involves a romantic encounter in a nightclub. It is said that a version of the happening was the inspiration, more than thirty years later, for the hilarious under-the-table scene in a restaurant between Julie Christie and Warren Beatty in the hit film *Shampoo*.

Over the years the fallout from gossip and speculation about her private life extracted a price. Paulette Goddard's flamboyant life-style hardly encouraged people to take her seriously as an actress. But here, too, an unexpected picture emerges when the facts are revealed.

Chaplin's films *Modern Times* and *The Great Dictator* forever guarantee Goddard an unchallenged place in cinema history as the screen's quintessential gamine. Furthermore, Chaplin was not the only top filmmaker who had faith in Paulette's professional abilities. Cecil B. DeMille, George Cukor, Mitchell Leisen and Jean Renoir are other acclaimed directors who responded with enthusiasm to the Goddard persona.

Her co-stars are a virtual *Who's Who* of Hollywood's illustrious past: Gary Cooper, Charles Boyer, Fred MacMurray, Ray Milland and John Wayne, to mention a few. Paulette was leading lady to Bob Hope in three of his best pictures. And she also starred—and danced on screen—with Fred Astaire.

Paulette Goddard was the only one of the glamour girls of the time to win an Oscar nomination. But in typical Hollywood fashion it was her feud with co-star Claudette Colbert, not the recognition of her acting talent by her peers, that drew attention.

Goddard's career suddenly took a dismal slide in the late nineteen-forties. However, she subsequently proved in her middle years that the lively intelligence that had been the foundation of her success in her personal life was still operating. At forty-seven, she married a literary giant, Erich Maria Remarque. Time may have faded Paulette's physical beauty but her vibrant personality hadn't diminished and she embarked on yet another phase of life.

What, people wanted to know, was her secret?

"At social gatherings Paulette was like a bee, flitting from person to person, pollinating everyone with her charm," observed Hollywood wit Oscar Levant.

"There is so much more to Paulette than a camera can capture. The reverse is true of most other so-called glamour girls," said her lifelong friend Anita Loos.

"Here was a woman who could charm a rock," quipped Robert Benchley. He wasn't referring, of course—or was he?—to the rocks that are supposed to be a girl's best friend, many of which are owned by Paulette and all of which were gifts from admirers. Goddard's acquisitive nature is legendary. "I never give anything back," she was once quoted as saying. And her preference for nonperishable tokens of affection is also legendary.

But it has been Goddard's approach to life—her curiosity, her desire to be free, her joie de vivre—that qualifies her as one of life's genuine explorers. And her journey has not been the standard Hollywood-bound tale. It spans the globe. The playgrounds of Europe and the pleasure spots of the Orient are among the various settings where Goddard has lived—and continues to live—her sophisticated and adventurous life. Life for her has never been bordered by the walls of a soundstage or the pages of a script.

Indeed, the life of the little girl from Great Neck—"Plain Pauline Levy from Long Island"—is one that even the most imaginative screenwriter would be hard-pressed to invent.

PART

1

1

□□□□□

The birthdate and birthplace of Paulette Goddard are mysteries that even the F.B.I. hasn't been able to unravel. Although Miss Goddard claims she was born in 1915, and some sources indicate that the date might be as far back as 1905, the generally accepted date of her birth is June 3, 1911. She was born Pauline Marion Levy in Whitestone Landing, Long Island. Her parents were Alta Hatch, a beautiful, vivacious brunette, and Joseph Russell Levy (sometimes spelled Levee, other times LeVee).

Through the years, Paulette gave out conflicting information—that her mother's maiden name was Alta Goddard, or that her father was a man named J. R. Goddard. However, as events would determine, Joseph Levy could and did prove that he was her natural father.

Paulette has claimed that, as a child, she and her mother often traveled to Canada to avoid custody battles with her estranged father. One fact is certain: the Levys were divorced and Alta and Pauline moved around a great deal. At different times they lived in Brooklyn, Manhattan and Long Island.

One story is that mother and daughter were so poor that they often worked as seasonal farmhands in the Long Island potato and strawberry fields. Then Pauline looked up one day and said, "You know, I don't have to do this."

Life was not all bleak. Occasionally the young girl and her mother spent time in Great Neck, Long Island. Great Neck, then a posh suburb of New York City, was a town noted for grand houses and estates where successful people of the theater, such as George M. Cohan, Sam Harris and Arthur Hopkins, resided. It was only a three-quarter-hour train ride to Manhattan, and Great Neck had been the inspiration for the popular song "Only Forty-five Minutes from Broadway." Many movie people also came to Great Neck, since films were still being shot in nearby Fort Lee, New Jersey, and Astoria, Long Island.

How had a mother and daughter from the fields made their way into the beautiful homes of Great Neck? By visiting Charlie Goddard, whom Pauline later identified as her uncle.

Hedda Hopper (later the famous columnist) was then married to stage star DeWolf Hopper. Hedda, who was a young mother in those post-World War I days and lived in Great Neck, knew Charlie Goddard well. (Pauline's uncle is not to be confused with Charles Goddard, the playwright and scriptwriter who wrote *The Perils of Pauline*.) According to Hedda, the Charlie Goddard she knew "was president of the American Druggists Syndicate. He was president of the golf club, too, and had built a huge home on the clubhouse grounds, with a permanent dance floor on the lawn. Every Saturday night he gave the best parties on Long Island. Broadway stars came out after the show in droves. Marilyn Miller, Leon Errol, Raymond Hitchcock, Hazel Dawn, Francine Larrimore, Frank Craven, Oscar Shaw, Jane Cowl, Florence Moore—name 'em and they were there. They had Sunday and Monday to recuperate. The music was excellent, food the best, liquor ditto. Nobody thought of quitting till daybreak."

Miss Hopper continued, "One time, passing a front window of the house, I noticed a pair of enormous eyes peering from behind a venetian blind. I saw they belonged to a child, but thought nothing more about it. I went indoors, powdered my nose and returned to the party."

The girl Miss Hopper saw was Pauline Marion Levy. As an adult, Paulette Goddard recalled: "Those nights Charlie Goddard gave parties I didn't waste my time sleeping. I took in everything from behind the venetian blind—the merriment, the dancing, the champagne, the ones who stole away in the moonlight to the edge of the sound or tucked themselves up in the hedges. I made a vow to myself that someday I'd be more famous than any of 'em."

4

PAULETTE

For Pauline, someday was not such a long way off. Meanwhile, the girl was growing up and, despite their sojourns to Great Neck, she and her mother remained poor and Pauline's education minimal.

"By the time I was thirteen, I discovered things weren't coming to me on a silver platter. I wanted to attend Ned Wayburn's school of dancing. But that cost ten dollars a week—and it took all the money Mother and I had to run our little apartment on Ninety-fifth and Broadway. So I had to earn my tuition. I did it by quitting school in the first year of high and modeling."

Pauline was an attractive, bright and winsome teenager. She was not reed-slim—in fact, baby fat still clung to her bones. But through Uncle Charlie's connections she met men and women who saw her potential as a model. Her first job was modeling children's clothes at New York's fashionable department store Saks Fifth Avenue. She then switched over to Hattie Carnegie's.

With her mother's encouragement, the next step was from modeling to show business. These were the liberated, roaring nineteen-twenties, and fourteen-year-old Pauline bleached her hair bright blonde and adopted the look of a flapper. By fifteen, Pauline's measurements were those of a woman. She had learned to wear clothes well. "Ever since I was small I've cared about my clothes," she said.

Looking back on her youth, the adult Paulette later observed: "I think a background of poverty is good. You can always go back to living on twenty dollars a week."

Around 1926 cartoonist John Striebel began a comic strip that reflected the feelings and foibles of the day. The heroine of the strip was Dixie Dugan and one story line had Dixie trying to get a job in the fabled Ziegfeld Follies. "All there is to this Follies racket is to *be* cool and *look* hot," Dixie tells her cartoon-strip boyfriend.

This philosophy was apparently shared by young Pauline Levy and her mother. Certainly Pauline could get a part in the Follies. She not only had the physical qualifications but also the necessary introductions to the right people. Most important, she was a fearless youngster, unwilling to accept rejection.

Although later reports stated that the girl immediately appeared in the Ziegfeld Follies, it was in another Ziegfeld show that Pauline Levy made her stage début. And at this time she adopted the name Paulette

5

Goddard, a glamorization of her first name and a tribute to Uncle Charlie's help.

From this point on, she began referring to her father as a man named J. R. Goddard. It did not go unnoticed that the initials J. R. were the same as Joseph Russell Levy's.

The show that Paulette landed a bit role in was a revue. In the winter of 1926, Ziegfeld, encouraged by Florida interests to establish a permanent theater in Palm Beach, had decided to open his new theater, the Montmartre, with this revue. It was appropriately entitled *Palm Beach Girl*.

Palm Beach had been developed as a resort during World War I, when rich society folk could not travel to the resorts of Europe. By 1926 it had become a winter paradise. There was plenty of liquor, smuggled in from the Caribbean islands. There was gambling—and, of course, plenty of money. Palm Beach was the playland of the Eastern rich.

To accommodate their tastes while they were wintering in Florida, Ziegfeld had taken an old building, an assembly hall, and had hired architect Joseph Urban to redesign it into a spectacular new theater. Urban had refurbished the premises and installed a sliding glass roof; after all, people were in Palm Beach for the weather and now at the Montmartre they could enjoy theater under the stars. It was in this sumptuous setting that Paulette Goddard entered a world she had heretofore only dreamed of.

In the film *Some Like It Hot*, director Billy Wilder captured the visual aspects of what it was like when members of a touring show descended on an élite resort hotel in Florida in the twenties. Millionaire playboys eagerly awaited each fresh crop of gorgeous showgirls. The men would wine, dine and pursue the girls—and often marry them.

From the playboys' point of view, the girls were fair game. From the girls' point of view, diamond bracelets and mink coats were easily available to the beauties who were interested. (Perhaps the most famous playboy of them all was William Randolph Hearst. Only ten years before, he had taken teenage Marion Davies out of the chorus line and developed her into one of the silent screen's most famous stars. His obsession with Marion was the greatest success story that any Ziegfeld girl could imagine. And all the Ziegfeld girls had vivid imaginations.)

6

PAULETTE

The weeks in Florida were exciting for Paulette. The former Pauline Levy was at the threshold of a life-style to which she would quickly become accustomed. Plumes and pearls were far more satisfying than picking potatoes, as any girl would have to agree, and Palm Beach was merely the warm-up for what was in store.

The revue *Palm Beach Girl* starred the dancer Claire Luce. The musical numbers were lavish and one in particular had the chorus girls rise up as if out of the ocean. The costumes were designed so the damsels looked dripping wet, and the girls wore huge floor-length headdresses made of feathers that gave the effect of foamy waves on the ocean.

The Montmartre was inaugurated with an opening-night gala, at two hundred dollars a ticket. The dazzling audience included Ziegfeld's pals Edward F. Hutton (heiress Barbara Hutton's father) and millionaire Leonard Replogle. During the ensuing weeks in Palm Beach, Paulette was exposed to the crème de la crème of Palm Beach society.

After the sojourn in the sun, the Ziegfeld troupe returned to New York, where *Palm Beach Girl* was renamed *No Foolin'* and opened at the Globe Theater on June 24, 1926. The show's stars were now Luce, Gertrude Niesen, Ray Dooley and James Barton. It was Ziegfeld's summer show, and Paulette appeared in a sketch in which a notorious figure of the day, Peaches Browning, was spoofed. (Peaches was an underage nymphet who had caught the eye of a millionaire old enough to be her grandfather.)

The show was a respectable hit as a summer revue and ran for over a hundred performances. Although Paulette had only a small role, she did not go unnoticed by either the other chorus girls or Ziegfeld's publicity people. Ziegfeld's publicists were always looking for gimmicks to garner press coverage on the famed Ziegfeld girls. One stunt was particularly successful. Whether it was, as has been reported, Paulette's idea, or whether it was the brainchild of one of Ziegfeld's publicists, the blonde Paulette supposedly organized the other blondes in the chorus to picket Ziegfeld, protesting his preference for brunettes. Naturally, all the girls' pictures got in the papers.

The Ziegfeld girls were a worldly bunch, although most were not much older than Paulette. Louise Brooks—who, the year before, had been Ziegfeld's most prized Venus—has recalled that another showgirl,

Fritzi LaVerne, "seduced more Follies girls than Ziegfeld and William Randolph Hearst combined."

Spectacular Ziegfeld beauty Dorothy Knapp loved to admire herself in a full-length mirror while doing a provocative striptease. The fact that men like Gilbert Miller, Walter Wanger and Michael Arlen might be in the room at the time didn't discourage Miss Knapp from—in Miss Brooks' words—her ardent "love affair with herself."

While teenage Paulette was certainly not palling around with the likes of LaVerne and Knapp, it seems apparent that the ultrasophisticated environment of the backstage world of show business did not go against the grain of her sensibilities. Young Miss Goddard had a definite talent for not letting the coarseness that pervaded the milieu rub off on her. No one has ever described her, then or through the years, as hard-boiled, tough-talking or jaded.

"Ziggy" soon cast the sixteen-year-old in his big-budget musical for the 1927 fall season, *Rio Rita*. It was another role as showgirl. But *Rio Rita* was to be a *big* Ziegfeld production "glorifying the American girl" and starring the leading comedians of the day, Wheeler and Woolsey. It was a lavish, pull-all-the-stops-out extravaganza.

Ziegfeld, with the backing of Hearst, had built the Ziegfeld Theatre on Fifty-fourth Street and Sixth Avenue. *Rio Rita* opened the new Ziegfeld Theatre, and it was the outstanding event of the season.

Paulette later recalled there was little for her to do in *Rio Rita*. She sat in a cutout of the moon gazing at the baritone. "I was a sitter," explained Paulette. "Didn't say a word, didn't sing a note, just stood there while John Steel sang to me."

People who were there remember that Paulette, like many of the Ziegfeld girls, was scantily clad. Her dazzling smile and womanly body were displayed to perfection, and a few weeks after the show opened Paulette was approached by the successful Broadway producer Archie Selwyn, who promised her the lead in his new comedy, *The Unconquerable Male*.

Things were moving fast, and in the meantime Paulette had even made her début in the movies. Few people realize that Goddard appeared on film as early as 1927. She was in four short subjects for Ziegfeld and one for Paramount Publix. The shorts, all silent, were shot in New York City. With her film début and the offer from Selwyn, it

8

appeared that her career was about to take off—not bad for a girl who, just a couple of years earlier, was living in a tenement.

But then disaster. Paulette recalled: "I thought I was something wonderful when they put me in a play. They said, 'She looks beautiful.' They hadn't bothered to ask about my acting ability. Of course the play folded in a week."

Actually, *The Unconquerable Male* never made it to Broadway. It closed in Atlantic City after only three performances.

In a move that surprised many of her friends, Paulette Goddard chose a route that many Ziegfeld beauties took: marriage to an older, wealthy man. She had met him in Palm Beach and he had followed her to New York. He has been identified as either Edward, Edwin or Edgar James; he has been described as a playboy, a timber scion, a lumberjack, president of a lumber company, furniture company executive, businessman. Two facts are certain: he was rich and Paulette married him in November, 1927.

The newlyweds were a striking and visible pair in the speakeasies and jazz clubs that flourished in New York in the twenties. Irene Mayer, eldest daughter of movie mogul Louis B. Mayer, and a figure in Paulette Goddard's future, was aware of Paulette "when she was a dashing blonde in New York during the more adventurous days of her first marriage."

But then Paulette and her husband disappeared from the Broadway scene. Other chorus girls said that Goddard and her mother had moved to Asheville, North Carolina, where the James family lived. Over the years Ed James has remained a mystery man. There are no known photographs of him with Paulette and no reports about his age at the time he married her. In later years, when Paulette Goddard was clouding the issue of the date of her birth, she even denied having married James in 1927, since by her account she would have then been twelve. She did confess marrying him, but said, "I just don't know about that date."

However, the record of the divorce proceedings is clear about the marriage date. Paulette left James in 1929 and the reasons given were vague. "Her nightclub/playgirl attitude did not go over in provincial North Carolina society," said one account. "His staid relatives couldn't reconcile themselves to his marriage to an actress," said another. And another claimed that Goddard was simply bored to tears.

Writer Anita Loos, who became one of Goddard's closest friends, may have used Paulette's experiences as the basis for the decision of her fictional character Lorelei Lee to divorce her rich Philadelphian husband. Reason for divorce: "having to live with him in Philadelphia."

In any event, the time Paulette spent in North Carolina was not wasted. Goddard learned from every experience, and from this, one suspects, she realized that her personality and that of a businessman were not and would never be compatible.

It was agreed by all involved that Paulette, accompanied by her mother, would go to Reno and get a quick and quiet divorce. Paulette has never denied that the settlement, a healthy one for 1929, was $100,000 in cash.

The Levys were no longer poor.

After a trip to Europe with Alta, Paulette decided to head West again. They stopped briefly at a chic Arizona dude ranch, and then mother and daughter continued on to Hollywood. Although films were still being shot in New York, talkies had revolutionized the movie business and Hollywood was where everything was happening.

Paulette quickly landed a job, but not in films. It was as a chorus girl at the Cocoanut Grove nightclub, in the Ambassador Hotel in Los Angeles. Not long afterward, she met a talent agent who said he'd get her a screen test. It never materialized.

Years later, Paulette told a fanciful story of an incident in her first year in Hollywood. "My agent was beginning to get a little discouraged. But he sent me to one studio to see a new producer, who shall be nameless. I went into his office, with my head still whirling with all those tales about Hollywood wolves—and sure enough, there it was—*a couch!* Right in his office! And there was Mr. So-and-So, kind of leering up at me from his desk. . . ."

When the wolf made what Goddard considered a verbal pass, calling her "darling," she hit him. "He howled bloody murder—'Help!' She's mad! Lock her up!' And his secretary came racing into the office and said, 'What's happened, *darling?*'

"And then I began to catch on—all this 'darling' business didn't

10

mean a thing—it was just another friendly expression, like 'Bud' or 'Mac.' I wised up fast, but what could I do at that point—apologize? 'Course not—so I walked out, and I was barred from the lot."

Needless to say, this account is laughable. Paulette, although perhaps only eighteen, was already a seasoned showgirl-divorcee and knew how to handle herself. She remained in Hollywood and in 1929 appeared as an extra in two pictures. One was a two-reel Laurel and Hardy short, *Berth Marks;* the other, *The Locked Door,* a United Artists release directed by George Fitzmaurice and starring Barbara Stanwyck, William Boyd and fading silent stars Betty Bronson and Rod La Rocque.

For the wealthy young divorcee, however, extra work wasn't much better than picking potatoes, and Paulette's "I don't have to do this" philosophy clicked into gear. She retreated to the Arizona dude ranch, where she and her mother blueprinted a new plan to gain attention from the film crowd.

Hollywood, then as now, was a world of big cars, yachts, flashy clothes and jewels—in short: new money and totally conspicuous consumption. The Great Depression may have struck the rest of the country in 1930 and 1931, but tinseltown, for the time being, was immune.

Young Paulette zeroed in immediately on the concept that made Hollywood tick: you could *only* tell a book by its cover. The car you drove, what you wore, where you lived, the size of your diamonds—these *did* count in Hollywood society. The only commodity that was prized higher was talent. But that was something people would either recognize or not recognize in time. The more tangible items in life could and would receive Goddard's immediate attention.

Paulette bought a Duesenberg roadster. The deluxe German automobile was the ultimate in ostentatious luxury, costing $18,000 at a time when the Model T Ford cost $260. In her shining new chariot, Goddard confidently returned to the film capital for her second assault.

The citadel was still not an easy conquest. Only extra work continued to be available to the young woman. At Paramount she landed a small bit in *The Girl Habit,* a programmer (B picture) with Charlie Ruggles and Margaret Dumont. She played one of a group of lingerie salesgirls, and her efforts went totally unnoticed by the powers that ruled the studio.

Over at Warner Brothers, she got a walk-on in a picture starring Warren William, *The Mouthpiece*. Again, a meaningless appearance. But, like other hopefuls in town, Paulette made the rounds for more bit and extra work. Unlike other hopefuls, however, she did not have to worry about paying the rent, providing herself with a striking wardrobe or transportation to and from work.

Then, her first big break. She was signed on as a Goldwyn girl. The Goldwyn girls were little more than screen versions of the Ziegfeld girls. Producer Sam Goldwyn had transferred to the silver screen the concept of glorifying the American beauty, and he peopled his films, which were at that time mostly Busby Berkeley-choreographed musicals, with beautiful, scantily clad young women. He made sure that each film had several production numbers highlighting the Goldwyn girls. The girls rarely sang or danced, but just stood there and smiled as the camera moved from one to another.

On the Goldwyn lot, along with Paulette, were dozens of other ambitious, beautiful young women. Most of the aspirants would fade from the public's memory. A few of the Goldwyn girls of the early thirties— Lucille Ball, Toby Wing, Betty Grable, Jane Wyman—would eventually achieve stardom, or at least celebrity.

There were of course both advantages and disadvantages to being signed to a minor studio like Goldwyn. At majors, like Warners, Paramount or MGM, young players were given acting lessons and training and put into many tiny parts in the hundreds of films the studios made each year. At a small studio, however, only a handful of films were made per year, and the chance for development was slim. But the advantage was that the lot was physically small and a youngster didn't get lost in the crowd.

Reports claim that the independent-thinking Miss Goddard clashed frequently with Sam Goldwyn. He fired her many times and then rehired her. Goldwyn was not used to girls who did not *need* a job.

Paulette stayed on the lot long enough to appear in the Eddie Cantor vehicle *The Kid from Spain,* which was shot in 1932. Leo McCarey directed the film, and choreographer Busby Berkeley supervised the musical numbers.

By mid-1932 Goddard was off the Goldwyn lot. She had moved over to the Hal Roach studio in Culver City. Today Hal Roach, Sr., recalls the young blonde Miss Goddard and says, "I never knew her at the studio. Henry Ginsberg signed her." Ginsberg ran the operation for Roach.

The Roach lot, which was near MGM, was again a small operation. Roach made mainly two-reel shorts and every so often would produce a full-length feature. Although small companies like Roach weren't star-making machines like the major studios, Paulette had been promised a big buildup. The blonde starlet's picture began appearing in newspapers, and she was publicized as "a brand-new find" whom Roach was going to develop into a star.

"Life was very easy as a blonde," recalled Paulette of this period in her life. "I didn't have to think. I didn't have to talk. All I had to do was waltz around."

It was at this time that Miss Goddard began clouding the issue of her age. When the Roach studio sent her on interviews, the inevitable question arose. Paulette parried it with "Oscar Wilde and Goddard say that any woman who tells her age tells anything." The young starlet displayed not only her wit but her affinity for self-education. Not many high-school dropouts were quoting Oscar Wilde.

The publicity buildup was easier than most, since, being a young woman of means, Paulette was able to live like a star. There was an element of mystery. She intrigued the Hollywood crowd. Who was this rich kid? A society girl, of course, speculated some. A gold digger, said others. What was her *real* story?

Paulette wasn't talking. She drove her Duesenberg to the Roach lot every day, and that, in short order, supposedly caused problems. Goddard recalled: "One day an executive called me in and told me that the 'queen' of the studio was jealous. He begged me to buy a little runabout car to come to work in. And, of course, that made me angry. . . . Next morning a chauffeur drove me to the studio."

The queen of the Roach lot at the time was Thelma Todd, a blonde beauty who—along with Zasu Pitts and, later, Patsy Kelly—made highly popular comedy shorts for Roach. Paulette appeared in one of the Todd-Pitts shorts, *Show Business,* and then Roach cast Goddard as Charlie Chase's leading lady in a couple of other two-reelers, *Young Ironsides* and *Girl Grief*.

Another executive at the studio recalls that late one night, after work, Ginsberg suggested, "Let's go over to Paulette's." "But," recalls the executive today, "When Henry called her, she said 'No.' Henry was slightly embarrassed, since the implication was that he could stop by at Paulette's at any time he wanted."

Everyone on the lot knew that Goddard was uniquely independent. She later said, "I think everybody at the studio thought I had a boy-friend who owned a garage, because I used to go to work every morning in such big cars."

There was gossip on the lot that Paulette indeed had a boyfriend, but it was hardly a garage mechanic. In addition to her penchant for expensive cars and clothes, Goddard had a penchant for associating with well-to-do and influential men. While on the Goldwyn lot, she had become friendly with Joseph Schenck.

Schenck was the aggressive, tough president and chairman of the board of United Artists. (Sam Goldwyn was a partner in U.A.) Schenck was hardly an Adonis—Gloria Swanson has described him as "a squat, homely man who looked like a second-hand furniture salesman." He was immensely fond of beautiful women and had been married to Norma Talmadge, an important silent-picture star.

It was Hollywood lore that one morning when Miss Talmadge arrived at the studio hours late, she was asked, "Is everything all right?"

"A terrible thing happened to me on the way to work," answered Miss Talmadge. "I married Joe Schenck."

But Joe Schenck—or "Honest Joe," as he was known throughout the industry—was one of the biggest wheels in town. His brother Nick Schenck was even more influential. Nick was the head of the all-powerful Loew's Theaters circuit and its subsidiary, MGM. But Nick was an old-fashioned family man, while Joe was a mogul who loved to surround himself with women.

It was a source of amusement to many in Hollywood that Schenck's gorgeous young female friends on both coasts could often spot one another (and be spotted) because each sported a spectacular mink coat, courtesy of Mr. Schenck. The ladies unknowingly comprised what became known as the Joe Schenck Mink Club, and there were many new arrivals in Hollywood eager and willing to begin membership.

In the ways of the movie business, Joe Schenck was an acknowledged master. If you were willing to learn the ways of Hollywood, and if Joe Schenck liked you, you had the benefit of the best teacher in the business.

PAULETTE

Schenck liked Paulette Goddard. She has contended that when she defied the Roach studio's edict to drive less ostentatious cars and stop infuriating the queen of the lot, she was fired. But research proves that Goddard was not fired by Roach. Today Hal Roach says, "There was no feud between her and Thelma Todd. It was all publicity. Paulette was simply offered a better deal by someone else and Henry let her out of her contract."

Now Goddard signed with another studio, a smaller studio, a studio that made even fewer pictures than Goldwyn or Roach. But a studio whose head was the most famous moviemaker in the world: Charlie Chaplin.

It was through Joseph Schenck that Paulette Goddard met Charles Chaplin.

2

Charles Spencer Chaplin was forty-three years old in 1932 and at the very peak of his career. He was one of the most famous men in the world; his beloved cinema creation, "Charlie," was known even in remote regions of South America, Asia and Africa. Everyone adored "the wistful tramp"—"the little fellow" with the tiny mustache, the beat-up derby hat, the cane, baggy pants and too large shoes. He was a trusting, gentle and innocent soul. He loved the human race and therefore always found himself in trouble. The real-life Charlie Chaplin frequently found himself in trouble as well.

By this time Chaplin had had two disastrous marriages. In both instances he had been forced to wed very young women who were in no way equipped to understand or cope with an actor-filmmaker genius. Scandal had plagued him in his personal relationships. In 1919, Chaplin had married sixteen-year-old actress Mildred Harris when she claimed she was pregnant with his child. The pregnancy proved to be false, but Harris did give birth to a child fathered by Chaplin a year later. The infant died in a few days. Harris divorced Chaplin and received a huge settlement.

Once again a bachelor, Charlie's career hit new heights in the early

16

twenties with the success of *The Kid* and then *The Gold Rush*. But during production of *The Gold Rush* Chaplin was again forced to marry a teenager, whom he had made pregnant: his leading lady Lita Grey. Chaplin married sixteen-year-old Lita in November, 1924, and a son was born to them the following spring. For years Charles Chaplin, Jr.'s, real birthdate was kept a secret. Everybody—even the boy himself— thought he had been born on June 28, 1925. It was only years later that his actual birthdate, May 5, was revealed. Charlie Chaplin had been powerful enough to have the records changed.

A second son was born to Chaplin and Lita less than a year later, on March 30, 1926. This boy was named Sydney, after Charlie's older half brother. The Chaplin-Grey marriage, however, was doomed and shortly after Sydney's birth the couple separated.

The ensuing divorce was hostile, headline-making and scandalous. "When Lita Grey divorced him, she put out vile rumors that he had a depraved passion for little girls," recalled Louise Brooks, with whom Chaplin had had an affair. "He didn't give a damn, even though people said his career would be wrecked. It still infuriates me that he never defended himself against any of those ugly lies, but the truth is that he existed on a plane above pride, jealousy or hate. He lived totally without fear."

Chaplin had many brief affairs with worldly women like Miss Brooks. Clare Sheridan, Winston Churchill's cousin, and heiress Peggy Hopkins Joyce were two of his other amours. But the comedian was always strongly attracted to very young, innocent maidens. Chaplin's close business associates, and even Torachi Kono, his valet-butler-secretary, would endeavor to keep underage girls from his path.

After the acrimonious split with Lita Grey, Chaplin eventually settled out of court for a whopping $625,000 because, unknown to the public, Lita was prepared to name in court five famous actresses with whom Charlie had been committing adultery. The most famous of the five was William Randolph Hearst's mistress, Marion Davies.

No sooner had Lita and her mother moved out of the Chaplin mansion than his new leading lady, Georgia Hale, and her mother moved in. The affair with Miss Hale was short-lived and soon Chaplin was again a roving bachelor. But though the private life of Charlie clashed with his wistful screen image, the public still flocked to his films. He followed

The Gold Rush with *The Circus,* another silent classic. Chaplin's pictures were the most consistent and biggest moneymakers for United Artists, the distribution company that he, Mary Pickford, Douglas Fairbanks, Sr., and D. W. Griffith had founded. Chaplin, however, was the only star-filmmaker who literally owned his own studio. He had built his own facilities, in 1918, on the corner of La Brea Avenue and Sunset Boulevard.

In 1931, Chaplin had defied all advice that no one could make a silent picture in the new era of sound. His latest film, *City Lights,* was a silent and a smash. It starred his newest discovery, blonde Virginia Cherrill. But *City Lights* had totally drained Chaplin's creative energies and, as he did after each of his films, he decided on a long, recuperative trip. He went abroad. In this period, just before he met Paulette, Chaplin confided that the reason for his trip was that "the disillusion of love, fame and fortune left me somewhat apathetic." He said that he needed emotional stimulus. And that he "wanted to live in my youth again."

City Lights was still packing them in in June, 1932, when Chaplin returned from his travels around the world. His ship docked in Seattle, and he proceeded on to Hollywood. He was still going through a difficult emotional period. Charlie's beloved mother, who had been in a sanatorium for years, had died while the comedian was mired in production of *City Lights.* It was a devastating blow on the heels of his divorce from Lita and the withdrawal of his children from his life. All that, combined with the always present fear that he might not be functioning at the top of his creative capacities, brought an unhappy and confused man back to American shores.

City Lights had already netted $3 million, and more revenue was flowing in at the rate of $100,000 a month. But Charlie was nettled by the opinion of a young critic who stated that *City Lights* was a fine picture but it verged on the sentimental and perhaps Chaplin should try to approximate realism. "I found myself agreeing with him," Chaplin later conceded.

The filmmaker was also depressed that his close friends Doug and Mary had separated. The Hollywood that Chaplin knew was fast disappearing.

Joe Schenck phoned one afternoon. "Save the weekend, Charlie. I'm having a yachting party."

PAULETTE

Chaplin liked Schenck's huge, luxurious 138-foot boat, the *Invader*, which accommodated more than a dozen guests. Schenck rarely sailed farther than Catalina, an island off the coast of Los Angeles. He would usually moor there, near the quaint town of Avalon, where the party guests would enjoy a pleasure-filled visit.

Chaplin at first declined Schenck's invitation. He knew that Schenck's guests were not his sort; they were usually poker-playing cronies. But in Chaplin's words: "There were other interests. Joe usually embarked with a bevy of pretty girls, and being desperately lonely, I hoped I might find a pretty little ray of sunlight. That is precisely what happened. I met Paulette Goddard."

Although Chaplin implies there was a bevy of pretty girls on board this particular trip, sources quoted in F.B.I. files claim there were only two young women: one for Schenck, and one for Chaplin.

Chaplin and Goddard's attraction for each other was immediate. Some say that Chaplin, in addition to being attracted to Paulette's youth, beauty and vitality, was impressed with her interest in business matters. She was obviously no simple chorus cutie seeking a role in a picture. She was a young lady of means, and asked Chaplin's advice on investing $50,000 of her own money in a movie company.

"She had brought aboard all the documents, ready to sign. I almost took her by the throat to prevent her," recalled Chaplin. He told Paulette that the enterprise she was considering was a phony, and he cautioned her that even an expert like him found it risky to invest in films. It was certainly no game for a novice.

"Look at Hearst," said Chaplin. "He's lost seven million investing in movies. What chance do you have?"

Although Chaplin later claimed that Paulette had just arrived in Hollywood from New York and didn't know anyone, this was not so. It may, of course, have been the story she told him. Chaplin later said, "The bond between Paulette and me was loneliness."

From Chaplin's point of view, Paulette Goddard was a miraculous discovery. She was young but there was no doubt that she was worldly for a girl of twenty-one. She was intelligent but not abrasive, smart but not conniving, and she had the ability to fit into any social situation. She was refreshing, and genuinely charming. And Chaplin has given insight to the fact that at this time of his life he was very vulnerable to a new relationship: "I had had in Europe a vague hope of meeting someone who might orient my life, but nothing had come of it. Of all the women I met, few fitted into that category—those who might have done were not interested." It appeared that Chaplin had found in Paulette someone who could orient his life and was interested in doing so.

Paulette was becoming involved with a complex man whose sexual appetites and preferences were well known on the Hollywood scene. Lita Grey has told of the books in Chaplin's house—medical manuals with explicit directions about intercourse, and copies of novels such as *Memoirs of a Woman of Pleasure* (*Fanny Hill*). According to Lita, Chaplin had underlined passages in all the books that had to do with sex.

"There were nights after our marriage when Charlie was good for as many as 'six bouts,' as he called them, in succession—with scarcely five minutes' rest in between." He told Lita, "I'm a stallion, Lita, and you'd better resign yourself to it."

Chaplin appreciated imagination in lovemaking. He was a very strong, passionate lover, according to Miss Grey, with absolutely no inhibitions and he expected the same from his partner. He liked oral sex as foreplay.

Supposedly, Chaplin liked to experiment with *ménage à trois,* and later F.B.I. reports stated: "Rumor has it that Chaplin is unnatural in his sexual relations, and it has been said that he is a homosexual." The F.B.I. based this spurious assumption on reports that "Charlie, though essentially normal himself, could not be the creative person he is and not have an understanding that it had been the exponents of the intermediate sex who have dominated art through the centuries."

Assumptions about Chaplin's sexual preferences, pecadilloes and "performances" had been buzzing around Hollywood for almost two decades (and would continue to be mythified to the present day). When Paulette Goddard met Chaplin, everyone naturally assumed that she knew Chaplin's reputation. However, as is often the case, the person belies the reputation. And it seemed that Chaplin had found he had much more in common with Paulette Goddard than mere physical attraction. They discovered a deep emotional tie.

They began seeing a great deal of each other, especially on weekends. Chaplin introduced Paulette to his two sons, seven-year-old Sydney and eight-year-old Charles, Jr. The boys would visit Chaplin's house on alternate weekends, since they attended private school during the week. Their mother was usually off on a vaudeville tour, and the boys became close to their father during these years.

Charles Chaplin, Jr., has recalled that up to this point he and his brother thought of their father as stern and their father's house as forbidding. But with the entrance of Paulette Goddard into the lives of the Chaplin household, Chaplin's sons felt the house no longer seemed austere.

Charlie, Jr., has vividly recalled the day he and his brother first met Paulette. Chaplin, Sr., brought her to the house where the boys were living with Nana (Lita's mother, Lillian). The boys were waiting on the porch as they saw their dad pull up, jump out of the car and run around and open the door on the passenger side.

"He helped out a beautiful platinum blonde. Syd and I were so thunderstruck we could only stare. Her pale, shining hair framed a piquant, heart-shaped face alive with sparkling blue-green eyes."

The visual impact of Paulette on the Chaplin boys lived in their memories for years to come. According to Charlie, Jr., "We lost our hearts at once."

Although the general public did not immediately learn of the Chaplin-Goddard romance, in Hollywood they were an item. When Paulette flew to New York, Chaplin was at the airport kissing her goodbye, leading to speculation that Charlie had found another cute young thing to nurture and mold into his next leading lady.

That fall, *The Kid from Spain* was released, and all the shorts Goddard had made for the Roach studio were also in the theaters. By the end of the year, Chaplin had bought her contract from Roach and Paulette Goddard was now a player with the Charles Chaplin studios.

Their affair continued but it was not at all typical of the affairs Chaplin had known. Paulette was a woman of independent means. She could and would travel, leaving Charlie to contemplate what life without her might be like.

Although Paulette Goddard was under contract to Chaplin's studio, there was no picture to put her in—indeed, there was no picture for anyone on the Chaplin lot. The Chaplin studios made only Chaplin pictures, and he made one film every three or four years.

Physically, Chaplin's was unlike any of the other studios in town. It was like a pleasant private playground. There were the stages and the necessary prop and costume rooms, of course, but they took up less than half the lot. Most of the small area was parklike. There was an old house, which used to be Chaplin's residence before he built his Beverly Hills mansion. There was a tennis court and a swimming pool. And there were many trees. Instead of barnlike buildings, there were many cottages, which housed the offices. The atmosphere was pleasant; it was almost a cottage industry rather than the factory-warehouse setup that typified other studios.

Everyone was kept on full salary while waiting for the muse to strike the boss. Chaplin continued to be plagued by depression over his lack of creative inspiration, but at least now he had Paulette to help ward off his feelings of loneliness.

On weekends, they took long drives up and down the coast of California. (Chaplin was not a good driver.) They often visited San Pedro, the harbor section of Los Angeles. In the thirties, most of the stars and millionaires docked their yachts at San Pedro. Occasionally, Charlie would borrow Schenck's yacht and he and Paulette would go sailing, alone or with friends.

One day Paulette noticed a yacht that was for sale. "Now if you had something like that," she told Charlie, "we could have lots of fun on Sundays and go to Catalina."

The yacht was owned by a manufacturer. It was a 55-footer with three staterooms, and could accommodate a small crew. Chaplin wasn't buying. But he *was* a shopper. He took Paulette to look over the yacht a number of times. The owner, knowing who Chaplin was, said they could come look at it as often as they liked. However, after they had visited the boat three times within a single week, Paulette became embarrassed.

On one particular Sunday, Chaplin picked Paulette up for their usual drive. When Paulette realized they were heading for San Pedro, she said, "You're not going to look at that boat again?"

"I'd like to go over it just one more time before I make up my mind," Chaplin said.

"Then you'll have to go alone," Paulette answered. "I'll sit in the car and wait for you but I'm not going on board again. It's too embarrassing."

Unbeknownst to her, he had bought the boat as a surprise. He had had it stocked. He had sent his own cook to the boat and had hired David "Andy" Anderson, a pal and ex-Keystone Kop, now a licensed boat captain, to head the crew.

When Charlie and Paulette got to the dock, no amount of urging from Chaplin could get Paulette out of the car. "I told you, Charlie, you'll have to go alone. Hurry up, though. We haven't had breakfast yet."

Chaplin boarded the boat and several minutes later came back to the car. "Come on, Paulette, Just one last time."

It finally became obvious to Paulette that they would never get any breakfast unless she boarded the boat again, so reluctantly she agreed. When they got on board, Paulette noticed that the table was set.

"The captain has kindly invited us for breakfast," Chaplin said. "We have wheat cakes, bacon and eggs, toast and coffee."

Paulette glanced into the galley and instantly recognized the cook from Chaplin's house. "What's going on?"

"Well, you wanted someplace to go on Sundays," said Charlie, delighted. "So after breakfast we're going to Catalina for a swim."

Chaplin was always one for practical jokes and he liked to surprise people with his bursts of generosity. When it became obvious to Paulette that he had bought the yacht, she jumped up and rushed back to the dock, yelling over her shoulder, "Wait a minute!" Chaplin recalled that she ran about fifty yards along the harbor, where she covered her face with her hands.

He called her back to the boat. When she was again on board, she told him, "I had to do that to get over the shock of it." He had bought the yacht she wanted. And although Chaplin never conceded that he had bought the boat for her, events would prove that indeed he had.

They had a glorious breakfast that morning and then sailed to Catalina. They moored off the coast of the island and remained there in seclusion for nine days.

Chaplin and Paulette continued their affair. They "did all the witless things." They went nightclubbing, to the horse races, to premières and parties. "Anything to kill time," Chaplin later recalled. "I did not want to be alone or to think."

Charlie and Paulette took the boys fishing, to the beach, to amusement parks. In retrospect, what many people don't realize about Charlie Chaplin is that although his name was world famous, and his screen character would be recognized around the globe, in the thirties he could for the most part go unnoticed along the streets of California. The Chaplin character that people knew from the screen was "the little tramp," the fellow with a black mustache, black eyebrows, curly black hair and a derby hat. In private life, Chaplin had let his hair go gray, he had no mustache, his eyebrows were light and he was a dapper, immaculate dresser. So in the early years of his dating Paulette, he, she and the boys could often go on jaunts looking just like any well-to-do family from Pasadena.

Although it has been reported that Chaplin was by now at work on a script, he later denied this. He said that at the time he did not have any idea of what his next film would be. He credits Paulette with inspiring him to write the script of what would become his next picture.

The couple had been together for some time when one day they went to the racetrack in Tijuana. There Paulette was asked if she would present the silver cup to the winner. Since the horse was from Kentucky, Paulette was requested to give her speech with a slight Southern accent. Always eager and willing to participate in such activities, she readily agreed.

Chaplin later recalled: "I was astonished to hear her over the loudspeaker. Although from Brooklyn, she gave a remarkable imitation of a Kentucky society belle. This convinced me that she could act."

Chaplin envisioned Paulette as a gamine, and he hit upon the idea of his own character, "the tramp," encountering the gamine in a paddy wagon, where the tramp would be ultra-gallant and offer her his seat. Chaplin's method of working was to take an idea, such as this, and use it as the basis for building a plot. He now had "the tramp" and "the gamine" meeting, and began searching for a story to build around this little gag.

Chaplin reveled in being a mentor; he had already suggested books for Paulette to read and took great pleasure in helping to educate her. He now arranged for her to have dancing lessons, singing lessons, acting lessons.

Paulette, under Chaplin's spell, followed every bit of his advice. During this time, a woman who had known Goddard back in New York marveled at the transformation of the former chorus girl into a studious person.

Although reports were that Chaplin and Paulette were already married or at least living together, if Paulette was indeed sleeping over at the mansion, it was done in a very discreet fashion. She certainly never stayed overnight on the weekends when Chaplin's sons stayed with him. But, in the words of one of his sons, "Paulette would sometimes be a guest on those weekends." And her presence brightened the youngsters' stays, which were otherwise still rather stern and formal.

The Chaplin mansion was situated on an estate of over six acres in the Bel Air section of Beverly Hills. Chaplin had been persuaded to buy the property and build the house by his friends and partners, Fairbanks and Pickford. Their fantastic estate, Pickfair, was nearby. Also nearby was the Harold Lloyd estate. It was larger and more lavish than Chaplin's, but not quite as large as Pickfair. Other immediate neighbors included Ronald Colman, Western star Tom Mix and glamorous actress Kay Francis.

There were gardens around the Chaplin house and the trees surrounding the property had not been cut, so the effect of a woods remained. There was a circular driveway leading to the two-story building. Naturally, the mansion had a screening room, along with a huge living room with fireplace, a grand piano and an elegant formal dining room. On the first floor there was also a large kitchen and the servants' quarters. The second floor contained only three massive rooms, all bedrooms, each with its own bath.

Chaplin told Paulette that he led a very orderly and organized life when he wasn't working on a film. She learned that he liked to stay up late and usually rose around noon. That he would stay in his bedroom most of the afternoon reading and writing. Then, in the late afternoon, he'd join her on the tennis courts. He taught Paulette how to play tennis and she eventually became, according to Anita Loos, a "championship-caliber player."

In the evenings, after Chaplin had taken a steam bath, he would dress formally to dine, either in or out. When Paulette first entered Chaplin's life, Kono was still on the scene. He had been Chaplin's man Friday from the comedian's earliest days in Hollywood. But in 1932, after

Chaplin had returned from a trip to Japan, his relationship with Kono seemed to have changed.

Some contend that Paulette did not get along with Kono and eased him out of Chaplin's life. Others say that Kono was ready to retire and wanted to return to his native land. In any event, another Japanese servant, Frank, who had been chauffeur under Kono's reign, now became head man at the house, and two other Japanese servants—a cook, George, and a new chauffeur, Kay—completed the staff.

These men waited on Chaplin silently and efficiently, and were devoted to him. Frank's duties were literally to anticipate Chaplin's every need: to lay out his clothes, to keep his schedule, to screen people.

Charles Chaplin, Jr., later said that the devotion of these three Japanese "was something no Occidental could understand." They even traveled with Chaplin when occasionally he went to New York, or when he cruised on his yacht.

"The Educating of Paulette" continued. Charlie was fascinated by her inquisitive mind and felt that for once he had found a most unusual young woman—one who could be as young in spirit as he, but who was mature in outlook. Paulette might be twenty-two years his junior, but she was no child in areas where it counted.

Her acting lessons, diction lessons, singing and dancing lessons continued. Chaplin also knew just how he wanted her to look, and the blonde hair had to go.

"When I went back to being a brunette, I had to learn how to live all over again," exclaimed Paulette, adding, "Take it from me—being a brunette makes life a lot tougher!"

While Chaplin was busy working on the new script—called *Modern Times*—he and Paulette spent all their free time together. She would occasionally convince him to take time to spend a day, or at least an afternoon, with her and the boys.

The Chaplin-Goddard romance bloomed. There were more rumors of marriage. A French newspaper reported that Chaplin had married the young woman who was to be the leading lady in his next film. Chaplin neither confirmed nor denied this, and in the spring of 1934 there were additional stories that Paulette had married Chaplin aboard their yacht, *The Panacea*.

Chaplin was too engrossed in writing the script of *Modern Times* to

26

pay attention to these rumors. He loved to write almost as much as he loved to act, and for him fashioning the script of a movie was always creatively satisfying. (In production, he would often change his mind about the script, and, like most auteurs, spontaneously go off on some creative tangent.)

He had, of course, had ideas for a film about mechanization and its effect on the masses before meeting Paulette. Now he combined the two plots: little fellow meets gamine, and little fellow's problems with the mechanized world.

One point intrigued the industry: surely Chaplin's new film would be a "talkie."

There was always much speculation about the latest Chaplin venture. Like Woody Allen today, Chaplin insisted on complete secrecy on any film prior to and during production. The press and the public needn't know anything, as far as Chaplin was concerned, until the film was on the screen. He was, however, interested in one piece of information being publicized about this production: that he had discovered and was developing a new leading lady.

For her upcoming role in *Modern Times,* Charlie rehearsed Paulette in the house, on the tennis court, almost every waking moment. He made her do a scene over and over. "Try it again, try it again," he coaxed her. He never shouted, and seemed to have infinite patience, but his intensity wore her down.

She was often reduced to tears. "Oh, Charlie, I'm not an actress, I'm just not an actress." But Chaplin was determined to make her one. He wanted her to be proficient in the part long before they did it at the studio, long before the cameras started to roll. The part had been written for her, she would be perfect in it. There was no rush to begin filming; he would take all the time necessary before even thinking of starting the cameras turning.

Finally, after endless writing and revising, and revising again, the script was completed and a starting date was scheduled for the coming fall. It came not a moment too soon for Paulette, whose patience and understanding were severely strained. It was hard to believe, but it had been two long years since the idea had first taken hold of the genius.

Paulette's life had not exactly been one of hardship during that period—although there are differences of opinion on this subject. Certainly the physical life-style Goddard experienced was, to the average person, glorious. A mansion, servants, beautiful clothes. And all at the height of the Depression! But few girls Paulette's age, with her gift for enjoying life and attracting men, would have had the emotional strength or the intellectual ability to weather the mercurial temperament of Charles Chaplin on a long-term basis. Women like Louise Brooks spent very limited time with the man; Paulette spent *all* her time with him.

Even so, there were those in Hollywood who would have gladly changed places with her and who wondered why Paulette bothered to pursue a career in films at all. But Paulette was indisputably a career-minded girl and no one was happier than she that the Chaplin studio was at last humming with activity.

At first the director had seriously considered making *Modern Times* a talking picture. But he ultimately realized this would be foolish because of two considerations: first, his little tramp character should never talk; second, Chaplin's timing as a comedian was dependent on the noise made by the gears of the silent-film camera.

Always the perfectionist, Chaplin continued to be especially demanding of Paulette. She was his responsibility, and his alone. If she didn't deliver the goods, *his* reputation was at stake. He went on tutoring Paulette night and day.

Modern Times finally began filming in October, 1934. At the studio Paulette discovered that Chaplin's perfectionism extended deep into every aspect of moviemaking. The most minute details of costume design and makeup were of concern to him. He was insistent on getting just the right "look" for Paulette. She was, after all, to be the female counterpart for his "little tramp." While she was to be a beguiling gamine, she was also a street urchin and had to be dressed in rags.

According to Chaplin, "Paulette's outfit in *Modern Times* required as much thought and finesse as a Dior creation." He insisted that all aspects of the costume be authentic, and did not want the "rags" to look "theatrical." In Chaplin's mind, the goal in creating any costume was to "create a poetic effect, and not detract from the actor's personality."

The first day she was scheduled to shoot, Paulette had appeared on the set with her hair, as she thought, properly coiffed for the role of the urchin.

"It's not right, it's not right," Chaplin said.

28

She was desperate—what did he want? Nothing was easy with Charlie Chaplin. Did he want her to look ugly? She had gone back to being brunette, as he desired, but still he was unsatisfied. He pointed out to her that a street urchin would hardly have a glamorous coiffure. Chaplin had a solution.

"Sit still, Paulette. This will work, I promise."

Once again the young woman complied. Her mentor poured a bucket of water over her head. "Now dry that off," he instructed, "and run your fingers through it. The effect will be perfect."

In *Modern Times,* the urchin also had to have smudges on her face, but Paulette strenuously objected. After all, this was the era of glamour and perfection on screen, not realism. A girl wanted to be in the movies because she would be beautiful, not sloppy and dirty!

"Those smudges are beauty spots," Chaplin said, humoring her. Needless to say, Paulette did not go along with the theory, but she had no choice; the master had spoken.

Paulette's acting in *Modern Times* was not the director's only concern. He had other problems. As an actor, there was his own creative inspiration—or lack of it—to deal with. Some evenings the great genius came home wearily, drained of any confidence. "I just couldn't make anyone laugh," Chaplin would complain. "I had a very bad day. Very bad." Often he would say, "You know, it's so hard trying to be funny when you have to be and you don't feel like it."

To complicate their already hectic lives, Chaplin and Paulette had to contend with an unexpected personal development. Well-to-do people all over the country had become frantic about the possibility of kidnappings since the recent Lindbergh case. The children of movie stars were prime candidates, and now the set of *Modern Times* became even more tense when Chaplin and Paulette learned that there were kidnap threats against his sons.

Chaplin immediately took elaborate security measures, hiring bodyguards for the boys and announcing that special equipment and arms had been installed both at home and at the studio. Of course the Chaplin sons spent the major part of their time not at the studio or the Bel Air estate but at the Black Fox Military Academy. And at Nana's home in the San Fernando Valley. (One assumes the military academy had its own precautions against kidnapping, since the sons of many famous and rich people attended the school.)

Although this kidnap scare proved false, it left a lingering paranoia in Chaplin for years. He would often explode if the boys came home late or he didn't know where they were. Paulette would patiently explain to them in less emotional tones that their father was only showing concern for their welfare.

Chaplin, however, was so immersed in *Modern Times* that he had little spare time for Sydney or Charlie, Jr. But Paulette made time to spend with them. She often took them on trips to the zoo or to sports activities, sometimes to lunch at the Brown Derby. She shopped for their Christmas presents that year—Chaplin had no time.

Those who were there at the time remember that, as always when Chaplin was in production, his personality changed. He became tense and moody. People closest to him attributed this to what they called his fear of failure. In any event, it was a side of him Paulette had not seen before; they had met and fallen in love when Charlie was between pictures. Now the carefree days they had spent together were replaced by grueling work sessions, followed by more grueling work sessions.

Since *Modern Times* was a silent, Paulette did not have to act with her voice. But Chaplin, always the perfectionist, demanded that she produce exactly the right effect in her facial expressions and body movements. Years later, when she could look back on this period with some detachment, Goddard said of her role in *Modern Times:* "It was absolutely me. There is something in my character of the barefoot gamine. Charlie *understood* me."

And she added: "The pantomine helped me a great deal because I was lacking in stage experience. I was glad my first picture was a silent one because it gave me a chance to find myself."

But she wasn't talking that way when she was living through those arduous days.

Modern Times posed many difficult technical problems for Chaplin, its producer, director, writer and star. On top of everything, Chaplin had to contend with distribution contracts as well, an almost overwhelming responsibility. After a few weeks of shooting he suddenly stopped production and left for New York to discuss business matters.

By this time, Paulette had completely taken over the role of surrogate mother and sister to the Chaplin boys. "When Paulette moved in, she adopted the boys, not as a Mama but as someone much more fun; the French term 'copain' is a better description of their relationship than that cold and sexless term of 'pal,'" observed Paulette's friend Anita Loos.

Copain is not readily translatable, but it connotes comradeship, one who is a "co-conspirator, a comrade-in-arms type of buddy."

"Most people in Hollywood couldn't comprehend Paulette's genuine interest in Chaplin's children," noted Miss Loos. "But that facet of personality was what made Paulette truly unique."

As an adult looking back on his childhood with Paulette, Charles Chaplin, Jr., said that he felt he and his brother meant as much to her as she did to them. And he suspected that they satisfied some need in her life, as well.

By Christmas, Chaplin was back from New York and Lita Grey had returned from a vaudeville tour to spend the holidays with her family. She had not seen Chaplin since their bitter divorce. Lita was staying at the Ambassador Hotel, and decided to throw a party for her sons. Boldly she asked the father of her children to the party. She was shocked when he accepted.

When Chaplin arrived at the party, he was cordial to Lita, but after a few minutes grew restless. Lita was making polite conversation. When she complimented him on his youthful appearance, Chaplin answered: "Blame it on Paulette. She's a fresh-air fiend—has me out sailing and playing tennis from dawn to dusk. Which reminds me—I can stay only a minute. Paulette's waiting in the car downstairs."

"In the car? Why didn't you bring her up? I'd love to meet her."

According to Lita Grey's recollections: "He telephoned down and had the doorman deliver the message. Five minutes later Paulette entered the suite, a dark-haired, buoyantly alive vision in black velvet." Lita had been prepared to despise the new woman in Charlie's life, but instead: "I liked her instantly, liked the aura of vitality and genuineness about her, and we hit it off together right away . . . as if we'd known each other all our lives."

In typical Goddard fashion, Paulette immediately made Lita feel comfortable. In Miss Grey's words: "She informed me she was plain Pauline Levy from Long Island. I informed her I was plain Lillita McMurray from Los Angeles."

31

They talked of the children, Paulette complimenting Lita on what wonderful boys Charlie, Jr., and Sydney were. Lita was captivated by the young woman, who was only three years younger than she. Miss Grey later described Paulette as "disarming, a wonderful, wonderful girl with a good sense of humor. I'll never forget how beautiful she looked."

Miss Grey also observed: "She had class; it was obvious in every word and gesture. Yet Paulette was utterly without affectation or guile. She put me at my ease by ignoring herself, bypassing mention of Charlie and telling me what a colossal performer I was."

The two women gossiped until it was time to go. Paulette told Lita: "I like you, plain Lillita McMurray from Los Angeles. I'd love to see you again."

Although Paulette occasionally kept in touch with Lita through the years, the women never did see each other again.

Christmas Day festivities at the Chaplin home were an institution. Chaplin had the custom of serving Christmas brunch at noon. There was always a large white Christmas tree in the hallway, a tree tall enough to touch the ceiling. The holiday was a special one for Chaplin, for it reminded him of his Dickens-like childhood in the London slums and orphanages. Now that he was a millionaire, he compensated by making Christmas the most glorious and lavish holiday imaginable. He was generous with gifts to his children, to Paulette, to his friends, to his servants.

Charlie, Jr., and Sydney were thrilled by their gifts that year—most especially with the toy Paulette had chosen for them: an electric cart. They couldn't wait to get it outside and take turns speeding along the circular drive. Later on, Paulette, and even Charlie, Sr., had fun driving around in the cart.

But such carefree moments were short-lived because after the new year Chaplin resumed his tense involvement with *Modern Times*. Paulette, however, decided that she and the boys needed a vacation. She arranged to take them on a long weekend up at Lake Arrowhead, where the three romped in the snow and had a memorable time.

"Paulette might have been our older sister up there," recalled Charles Chaplin, Jr. The first night, when it was time for bed, the boys begged to be allowed to stay with Paulette.

32

"Paulette laughed, 'Okay, ten minutes,'" remembered Charlie, Jr. "And Syd and I jumped into bed with her. It was restful lying there with her arms around us, listening to her tell us a fairy tale. Soon we were drifting off to sleep.

"Then, from a long distance away, we heard Paulette saying, 'Okay, come on now, back to bed you go.' And she shook us gently, and shoved us out, and Syd and I wandered off to bed."

Unfortunately, the weekend ended and the boys had to return to school. Paulette had to return to work.

The weekend with Chaplin's children, of course, did not go unreported by the press. There was further speculation that Goddard *was* married to Chaplin. After all, how many women took their lover's sons on a vacation?

Through the entire filming of *Modern Times* there were frequent items in the press that Chaplin and Goddard were married. But Chaplin remained oblivious to such comments. He had no time for his personal life while he was obsessed with his latest—ergo his greatest—project.

While doubtless there were many actresses envious of Paulette Goddard's seemingly glamorous, career-launching opportunity, few would have survived the grind. Chaplin required endless retakes in his quest for perfection on *Modern Times*. Goddard had to do take after take after take and Charlie never seemed satisfied. Often, in front of cast and crew, he would act out her role himself, and discuss what she was doing wrong and how she should correct it.

She would try again, and be criticized for her efforts yet again. It was nerve-racking and emotionally draining, and director Chaplin didn't leave his work on the set. As before, the training of Paulette the actress continued at home.

By the summer of 1935, shooting was finally completed and for the first time in months Charlie and Paulette had time to socialize. One of the parties they attended was at the home of writer Donald Ogden Stewart. Beatrice Kaufman, wife of playwright George S. Kaufman, attended the party too, and Mrs. Kaufman wrote home: "My evening was made for me when Mr. Chaplin sat down beside me and stayed for hours. . . . He is very amusing and intelligent and I enjoyed talking to him a great deal. Pauline Goddert [sic] was there too—very beautiful; everyone says they are married." They weren't.

33

PAULETTE

Although the cameras had stopped rolling on *Modern Times,* work on the picture was far from over for Chaplin. He still had to compose the musical score and supervise all postproduction. But Chaplin had begun to emerge from his trance of complete dedication to work. As usual when this happened, he soon discovered that many of his personal relationships were severely damaged.

There was no doubt that the months of intense work had taken a toll on the Chaplin-Goddard relationship. Whether or not the couple had mutually agreed on a separation, it appeared that Chaplin and Paulette decided they needed other people and other activities in their lives. Soon she began dating other men.

Paulette did not, of course, lose contact with Charlie, Jr., and Syd. She still took the boys on weekend jaunts, and by the time fall came Chaplin and Paulette had reconciled. She once again became the hostess at the Chaplin house.

People in Hollywood did not fail to notice that it was Paulette, as Chaplin's representative, who was at the airport in Glendale to meet H. G. Wells on his widely publicized arrival in Hollywood. Wells and Chaplin had become friendly on Chaplin's trips to England, and now Chaplin was entertaining the famed British writer in California.

The middle-aged Wells was a notorious womanizer. Many ladies who crossed his path subsequently expressed their shock—and, in some cases, amusement—at the grabs and passes this renowned man of letters was capable of. One can imagine Wells' reaction on seeing the beautiful and vivacious Paulette. However, the young woman was adept at fending off unwanted attention from the opposite sex without alienating the interested party.

"Many ladies knew how to say no," observed Anita Loos, "but to do so without offending or making an enemy was a definite talent!" It was another remarkably useful resource that Paulette Goddard possessed and it was an invaluable one in the libido-oriented world in which she functioned.

Through Wells she met writer Hugh Walpole, and on at least one occasion she accompanied Wells and Walpole on a trip to San Simeon, where they were guests of Hearst and Marion Davies.

The Chaplin studio geared up to introduce its new star. As was often true in the nineteen-thirties, the studio publicists conveniently forgot that a player had appeared as an extra and a bit player. The performer's first major role was always considered to be his or her screen début. And so it was with Paulette Goddard in *Modern Times*.

Stills of Paulette were sent to newspapers and magazines. It was obvious from these photos that the gamine quality Chaplin had perceived was indeed evident. No matter what her real age, in these shots Paulette looked fifteen.

However, Chaplin's leading lady wasn't the only news about *Modern Times*. Before anyone had even seen the film, the press, based upon synopses of the plot, began denouncing the picture as "Communistic" and "anti-American," and a cloud of controversy surrounded the production's impending release.

Because Chaplin had been vocal about his political views, which were socialistic, because he had entertained Soviet filmmakers such as Sergei Eisenstein, because he considered himself "a citizen of the world" rather than an American or a British—as he was—subject, the press had already begun to turn on Chaplin and refer to him as "a Communist sympathizer."

Modern Times was about social problems during the Depression and included scenes of workers' strikes, the mechanization of assembly-line workers and their oppression by industrialists. But the real plot of *Modern Times* dealt with the little fellow encountering his perfect counterpoint, the gamine, and with her discovering a reason to continue living. *Modern Times* is more Paulette's picture than Charlie's in the sense that he needed a reason to make the film and he found it in her.

The plot of the film has the little tramp in prison but, owing to unusual circumstances, he is leading a very comfortable life. He is unhappy when is released and forced to return to the world. He gets himself arrested again so that he can be sent back to prison. In the paddy wagon he meets the gamine. When they have an opportunity to escape, she says, "Come on!" He hesitates, then decides to join her. They encounter many difficulties. She becomes discouraged but by now he has regained his spirit. He soothes her and says, "We'll get by." The film ends with the gamine and the little fellow walking off into the sunset, determined to stay together and survive the cruel world.

In real life, Chaplin's prison was his success. It was a comfortable prison; he had luxury, wealth and fame. But he did not have a raison d'être—a reason to keep going. In Paulette he had found someone who had given him a reason to re-enter the real world, which, for him, was filmmaking.

Other aspects of the *Modern Times* script were autobiographical as well. There is a classic scene that both explains and spoofs the labeling of Chaplin as a Communist. In the picture, the little fellow is innocently walking down the street when a passing truck carrying lumber accidentally drops its red flag. The little fellow picks up the flag and, waving it, begins chasing the truck to tell the driver that he's dropped his flag. Suddenly a parade of disgruntled workers turns a corner and is marching directly behind the little fellow. Police on the scene quickly arrest the bewildered little fellow as the leader of an insurgent mob!

Shortly after the new year, a print of *Modern Times* was ready for preview. It was shown to a few of Chaplin's friends and business associates, and then to a paying audience. The results were not what Chaplin had anticipated, and the nervous director made several revisions in the final print before the film's première. Everyone was happy with the musical score Chaplin had composed, especially with the haunting theme, "Smile."

In February, 1936, *Modern Times* premièred in both New York and Los Angeles. Although there had been a great deal of negative press about the film's so-called "Communistic overtones," the public did not care about alleged political implications. The first week's grosses were tremendous.

Although the grosses fell slightly in the second week, nothing could dampen Chaplin's and Paulette's spirits. Reviews were excellent, including Paulette's personal notices. The aggravation, the hard work, the tears—it had all been worthwhile.

"Paulette Goddard, a winsome waif attired almost throughout in short ragged dress and bare legs above the knees, is naturally introduced," observed *Variety,* adding: "She registers handily." Frank Nugent described her, in his *New York Times* review, as "a winsome waif and a fitting recipient of the great Charlot's championship."

Even if Paulette Goddard never made another motion picture, her place in film history was assured. She was the female counterpart to "the little fellow." And, in Chaplin's words, the theme of the picture was simple: "Two nondescripts trying to get along in modern times."

A few days after the picture opened, Chaplin applied for a re-entry permit from the Immigration Department, leading to speculation that he was planning another trip abroad. Since he had never become an American citizen, each time he left the United States he had to apply for a re-entry permit.

On February 5, 1936, Paulette, her mother and Chaplin left Los Angeles and headed toward San Francisco en route to Honolulu, where they were going to vacation. While they were on the dock in San Francisco, Chaplin happened to spy some crates that were stamped "China." He suddenly blurted out, "Let's go there."

"Where?" Paulette asked.

"China."

"Are you kidding?"

"Let's do it now or we never will," Chaplin said.

"But I haven't any clothes."

"You can buy all you want in Honolulu."

Charlie, who liked Paulette's mother (she was, in fact, a woman his own age), suggested to Alta that she accompany them on the adventure. Someone who knew Alta Goddard well says, "She was very much like Paulette in many ways. Alta and Paulette had the same sparkling eyes and the same infectious laugh. And they shared a spirited sense of humor." Most people thought Alta was Paulette's older sister, and she and Chaplin had a warm, friendly relationship. She happily agreed to join Chaplin and her daughter on the trip.

The trio, accompanied by Chaplin's servants, continued on to Hawaii and later embarked for Tokyo. Chaplin was a huge favorite in Japan. In fact, all Chaplin films made back their negative cost from the Japanese market alone.

From Japan the group continued on a cruise through the China Seas. If the trip to China had been a spontaneous decision, Charlie and Paulette made another spontaneous decision while they were in the Orient. It was not one that they shared with their public—and now is when the "mystery" began.

37

3

Chaplin had said that this was going to be his honeymoon voyage—that he intended to marry Paulette somewhere along the way. These statements had been dutifully noted by the press. After docking at Yokohama and Shanghai, the couple stopped in Hong Kong and then headed for Singapore. Chaplin had sent a wire to the United Artists representative in Singapore: DO YOUR UTMOST TO ARRANGE FOR OUR MARRIAGE.

Singapore at the time was a British colony. And suddenly the question of the validity of American divorces under British law was raised. Chaplin of course had been divorced twice, Paulette once. Since the Anglican Church was the official church of Singapore at the time, additional questions were raised. The Archdeacon of Singapore, Graham White, announced flatly that he would refuse to perform any wedding between divorced people, Charlie Chaplin included.

In mid-March, the United Press sent a message over its wire: CHARLES CHAPLIN AND PAULETTE GODDARD WERE REPORTED MARRIED IN SINGAPORE TODAY. The story gave no other details and, as was usual in those days, local papers picked up the story from the wire service, embellished it as they saw fit and printed it.

Everyone concerned assumed that since the couple couldn't have been married on land in Singapore, they had been married at sea. All that was really known was that they finally docked in Singapore.

Also in Singapore at this time was Hollywood director Tay Garnett. He was traveling with his wife, Helga, and producer Bert Friedlob and his wife. Garnett learned from reporters that Chaplin and Goddard were arriving aboard one of the liners.

"I had never known Charlie, but Paulette was a friend," recalled Garnett. "I respected her quick mind, and in addition she was, from north to south, a landscape to refresh the eye."

Garnett asked the reporters, "Where are they staying? The Raffles?" The Raffles was the famous British hotel in Singapore where everyone who was anyone stayed. The reporters told Garnett, "No, they're not staying at the Raffles. The word is out that they're checking into a little dump on some side street to avoid all the crowds."

Garnett decided to go to the dock and meet the ship. He would invite Paulette and Chaplin to join his party at the Raffles. Garnett remembered, "I was refused permission to go aboard, and the Chaplins remained in their cabin until all other passengers had disembarked. Finally a mountain of handsome luggage was brought down the gangplank. Stenciled all over the luggage was, in huge letters, *Charles Chaplin*. The porters loaded the bags and trunks into—and on top of—a cab."

Garnett told his driver, "Follow that taxi!"

Eventually the luggage-laden cab stopped in front of what Garnett has described as "a down at the heels hotel, with hot and cold running rats on the veranda." Although the luggage stood there for half an hour, Charlie and Paulette did not appear, so Garnett returned to his own hotel. When he got to the Raffles, he discovered that Paulette and Charlie had already checked in. The luggage ploy had served its purpose—the reporters and fans had been misled.

In Singapore, Chaplin stayed to himself but Paulette joined the Garnetts and the Friedlobs on some of their sightseeing ventures. One of the nightclubs the group visited was The New World. "It might be lively," the desk clerk at Raffles warned them.

"It was lively," according to Garnett's recollections. It was like something out of a South Seas B movie, complete with sailors and ruffians of all nationalities; dime-a-dance girls; and frequent brawls, with the police arriving in force.

"I want to get out of here fast," said Garnett's wife.

"Just a moment," interjected Paulette. Goddard had noticed a beautiful Eurasian girl who was one of the taxi dancers and pointed her out to Garnett. The girl was a knockout and Garnett had the manager of the club bring her to their table. Then and there the director offered her a Hollywood contract.

"Oh no," the young woman answered in a rather haughty fashion. "I couldn't do a thing like that."

"Why not?" asked Paulette, dumbfounded.

The girl looked at them and with all seriousness said, "I've heard about Hollywood. It's a very, very wicked place."

It was that "wicked place" that Chaplin and Paulette were returning to as they now continued their journey enroute back to the States. On the ship home, they met the famed French writer Jean Cocteau. Paulette's association with Chaplin gave her many opportunities to meet intellectuals like Cocteau, and even to associate with heads of state. In every port of call on their trip, they were treated royally by local government officials and dignitaries.

While most people assumed this style of life would be overwhelming to an average—indeed unschooled, uneducated—girl, Paulette had the ability not only to take it in stride but to deal easily with the kind of people Chaplin drew to him. She often contributed to the conversations.

Cocteau, like many others aboard the luxury liner, was fascinated by Paulette. She was truly a scintillating female, and Cocteau told Chaplin he was certain Paulette had some French blood. "She *must!*" he exclaimed.

"Why?"

"Because only a Frenchwoman can combine such intellect with such beauty. You must do a film in which she would play Madame Du Barry!"

"I will think about what you have said," answered Chaplin.

Paulette's recently acquired wardrobe of Oriental silk creations dramatically enhanced her beauty, as did the glittering bangles of rubies and diamonds that she'd also acquired on her "honeymoon trip." When they docked in San Francisco, Chaplin had a limousine waiting, and insisted on giving Cocteau a ride to Los Angeles. The geniuses vowed to see more of each other, and Cocteau again expressed his admiration for Paulette.

Back in Beverly Hills, both Paulette and Charlie refused either to confirm or to deny that they had been married. While through the years people have assumed it was Chaplin's desire to keep the matter secret, there is another possible explanation. Paulette Goddard knew the value of publicity. She knew that if she confirmed the story it would lose its publicity value. Being Charlie Chaplin's wife would be news only once. Chaplin went along with this for any number of reasons.

He undoubtedly felt victimized by the press and found it fun to keep everyone in suspense. His point of view was, "It is none of their god-damn business." He had been treated so badly in print in connection with his previous marriages that he was simply not going to provide the fourth estate with *any* information. He was indulging his ability to be contrary because he could afford to. Unlike other stars of the day, who had contracts with morals clauses to contend with, Chaplin worked for no boss or studio. He was his own man. For years he had not even given interviews.

But now Paulette, to promote her own career, did consent to interviews. What actress in that era didn't speak to the press? Only one— Garbo—and Paulette knew she was no Garbo. Furthermore, when it came to publicity, Goddard was exceedingly adept. When she spoke to the press, she was as skillful as a high-level diplomat.

A sample of Paulette's typical repartee with reporters:

"Are you and Mr. Chaplin married?"

"It's never been announced officially."

"But is it so?"

"It's been rumored so much! Sometimes the rumors have us married, sometimes they have us not married. Back and forth."

"Would you deny you are Mrs. Chaplin?"

"I never discuss my private life. I feel that my private life is one thing and my career another."

Her career was certainly off to a good start. *Modern Times,* which had cost an astronomical $1.5 million to produce, had already made back its cost and a substantial profit.

Gossip, however, centered on not what was on the silver screen but whether or not "the little fellow" and "the gamine" were in real life man and wife. One fact was certain: while Goddard may not have been a permanent resident in the Chaplin home before their trip to China, on their return she moved into Chaplin's house and assumed all the duties and privileges of a wife.

There was a distinct change in the household regime. Paulette brought a Scandinavian maid with her. And she introduced pets into the domicile—she loved dogs. Chaplin didn't, but he endured them for her sake. (Over the next few years, Paulette often presented the Chaplin sons with puppies. They adored the animals and loved her for giving them the pets.)

Determined to brighten up what she considered the dreary Chaplin household, Paulette soon found a glamorous ally. Shortly after she and Charlie were settled back in Bel Air, Chaplin's best friend, Douglas Fairbanks, Sr., and his extravagant new wife, Lady Sylvia Ashley, a porcelain-skinned blonde beauty (and former chorus girl who had married a title), threw a welcome-home party for the couple. Paulette was impressed with Sylvia; she admired her exquisite taste and impeccable style, and the women became good friends. Sylvia's talent for spending money on the finest clothes, jewels and furnishings had even Hollywood's "A-group" green with envy.

At the welcome-home party, Chaplin played one of his most successful practical jokes. Fairbanks had a Chinese houseboy, and when Chaplin arrived that night he took the boy aside.

"Look," he said. "I'm going to pretend to be talking Chinese to you all night. Even if you don't understand a thing I'm saying, answer me."

The houseboy understood the spirit of the joke, and all evening, as Chaplin spouted ersatz Chinese, the houseboy answered in the real tongue. The two pulled it off so convincingly that for days afterward Hollywood was abuzz that Chaplin's genius went beyond filmmaking. He had only been in China one or two months and he could already speak that difficult language.

Paulette shared this sense of fun that Chaplin had. He had the spirit of a youngster, and she knew how to appreciate it and keep it bubbling.

It was Frank, Chaplin's majordomo, who told the Chaplin sons that their father had gotten married on the boat while in Hong Kong. The boys were eager for details. The Japanese manservant laughed, "I didn't see them get married. But they told me so."

Later that afternoon, when the boys were reunited with their father and Paulette, Chaplin himself told his sons that Paulette was their new stepmother. He cautioned: "This is information for your ears only."

The boys' real mother, unfortunately, was having problems. Although Paulette did not visit Lita, she was concerned. Miss Grey has recalled, "When I entered a hospital for an operation more than a year after our short, single meeting, my room was flooded with baskets of flowers and other gifts. The card read, 'Get up and get out of there fast. Love, Plain Pauline Levy from Long Island.'"

Plain Pauline Levy from Long Island quickly assumed her position as the wife of Hollywood's—indeed the world's—most celebrated actor. To those who were still skeptical that the comedian and the actress were really married, it was pointed out that no woman who wasn't Chaplin's wife could have taken command of his household with such authority.

In the ensuing weeks, Paulette moved into the middle upstairs bedroom and had it elegantly decorated to suit her taste. Her closets were a reflection of her love of beauty and luxury. There were dozens of evening gowns in bright colors, countless dresses, suits, matching shoes and handbags, scarves, gloves, millinery. There were jewels for daytime, for evening, for every imaginable occasion. It was a toilette worthy of a young Marie Antoinette. She insisted on fresh flowers everywhere. And she interfered in the workings of the kitchen and the staff.

Now that she was Chaplin's wife, she wanted to be a real hostess— like Sylvia Ashley. She wanted to entertain. At first Chaplin balked, but when it became evident that Paulette would handle details and all he had to do was show up and play host, he relaxed and assumed his place as one of Hollywood's most elegant partygivers.

Hal Roach, Sr., who knew Paulette and Charlie socially during this period (and often played tennis with Chaplin), contends that the Chaplins became more social due to the influence of a man who ran the Los Angeles office of E. F. Hutton, the brokerage firm Chaplin used.

According to Roach, the broker encouraged Paulette to throw lavish dinner parties because he liked to impress famous and wealthy clients by introducing them to Chaplin when they were visiting Hollywood. In turn, Paulette wanted to hobnob with the crème de la crème of the business and society worlds. Thus, with the broker as an ally, Paulette wore down Charlie's resistance to entertaining. And of course Chaplin liked meeting noted and/or influential people.

At various parties and dinner parties in their home, Chaplin usually ended up performing. Sometimes the other guests, famed comedians themselves, would join in the revelry, and the gathering would turn into an incredibly star-studded show.

On some occasions when they had people in, Chaplin would entertain simply by rehashing thoughts he had for a new script or retelling and acting out scenarios he was contemplating. According to a close Goddard friend, when Chaplin acted out proposed scenarios for his guests, Paulette often "used to sit on the floor behind Charlie's big armchair, under which she stashed a bottle of Dom Perignon champagne to keep her alert. Even so, these recitals were frequently interrupted by the snores of Mrs. Chaplin."

But it was being Mrs. Chaplin that enabled Paulette to continue meeting the leading artists, intellectuals and musicians who visited Hollywood. Men like Aldous Huxley, Rachmaninoff, Hanns Eisler, Horowitz, Schönberg—even Albert Einstein—came to the Chaplin home.

Paulette, being young, also thrived on the Hollywood social whirl. After an evening of nightclubbing, Chaplin was heard to remark: "Well, that's it for another year." Paulette responded in horror, "What do you mean, another year? What are we supposed to do, stay home and read Ph.D. theses?"

The social scene was, more than ever, old hat to Chaplin. He had lived the high life in its heyday, with Valentino, Swanson, Fairbanks and Pickford. He was one of Hollywood's 400. Hollywood society of the thirties, though it might dazzle a youth like Paulette, left Chaplin unimpressed. She conceded that there had to be a balance in their social lives together.

Thus Charlie and Paulette alternated between going out and spending quiet evenings at home. Both were fond of reading. Often he worked on scripts for future projects and she worked on her petit point or knitted. But on other evenings she insisted that they go to a nightclub or entertain.

Paulette was also anxious to return to work. *Modern Times* was a success, but even a Chaplin film could not stay on the screen forever. She knew she had to follow *Modern Times* quickly with another successful picture, and no doubt her Hollywood so-called "friends" encouraged her to be dissatisfied. But, along with everyone else in Hollywood, Goddard also knew that Chaplin did not make more than one picture every three years. How could she stand the wait?

Chaplin assured her, however, that he was working on a script expressly for her, and her alone. It would be her talkie début and a film that he would write and direct but not co-star in.

For the time being, she was patient. Not to be overlooked was the fact that Paulette, like all Chaplin employees, was kept on full salary, even though she was not working. In her case, this was not an inconsequential sum. She was reportedly receiving $2,500 a week while waiting for the genius to create. Thanks to Chaplin, Paulette continued to be independently wealthy.

Meanwhile, it seemed that life for Paulette Goddard was as close to a fairy-tale existence as possible. She and Charlie spent many days sailing on *The Panacea*. One October afternoon, they encountered Chaplin's old friend Stan Laurel and his wife, Ruth. Stan and Ruth's little fishing boat was dwarfed in the presence of *The Panacea,* but neither man made any comment about it. The two old buddies from music-hall days in London reminisced for many hours. They performed their old routines as their wives looked on: Chaplin and Laurel, two of the greatest talents in the world, delivering impromptu performances that no producer could afford to buy.

The Chaplins were able to spend more than the usual amount of time with Charlie, Jr., and Sydney. The boys' lives were disrupted momentarily when their mother eloped with a young dancer, Henry Aguirre, Jr. It was a whirlwind courtship and marriage—and, within months, another disaster. Although the boys might have been confused about the instability of their mother's life, they were comforted by the stability of their father's life with Paulette.

From this point on, as Lita Grey's life was plummeting downhill, Paulette was an anchor in the emotional lives of the Chaplin youngsters. Lita would be plagued from now on by health problems and nervous breakdowns. Referring to Paulette, Lita noted: "In the years that followed I was to admire her even more and be in her debt for the endless kindnesses she showed my boys when I became helpless as a mother and as a human being."

Christmas, 1936, was an especially happy time for the Chaplin children. It was the first year that Paulette served as hostess in an official capacity at the Chaplin mansion, and the Christmas brunch and afternoon festivities were more lavish than ever.

Charlie's other half brother, Wheeler Dryden, and Dryden's young son Spencer were on hand. Sydney Chaplin and his wife were also present, along with Charlie's great friend, brain surgeon Dr. Cecil Reynolds. Chaplin's oldest friends, Alf Reeves and his wife, Amy, were also in attendance. Reeves, who had known Charlie since his London music-hall days, had been running the Chaplin Studio from the beginning.

Doug Fairbanks and Sylvia dropped by, along with other old Chaplin pals, Constance Collier, King Vidor and Anita Loos. Chaplin's new friend Tim Durant, a New England Yankee who remained a lifelong buddy, was there too. Durant was a great tennis player, a passion he and Charlie shared.

Paulette's mother was of course on hand. That year Paulette's gifts to the Chaplin boys were two terriers, which they named Punch and Judy.

Since Paulette and Charlie seemed to enjoy family life so much, some Hollywood observers were surprised when Paulette hadn't become pregnant after four years of intimacy with Chaplin. According to Lita Grey, Chaplin in his marriage to her had "refused to take precautions—not on moral grounds but on the ground that contraceptives were aesthetically hideous." One must assume that Chaplin thought birth control was the woman's responsibility.

There are many speculations about why Chaplin and Goddard did not have children. The obvious one is they did not want them. Someone who knew them at this time states: "Charlie did not marry Paulette to have children."

Although he was a virile forty-eight, Chaplin was slipping into middle age. He was content being the father of two growing boys.

However, although Chaplin seemed content, Paulette's adventurous nature simply couldn't abide a stay-at-home regimen, and often she and Chaplin went their separate ways. For example, after Christmas she went to a six-day house party at King Vidor's mountain retreat near Big

Bear. (Paulette was friendly with Vidor's daughter Marjorie.) Chaplin did not accompany his wife. He said he was immersed in writing his new script for her.

When instances like this occurred, there were immediate rumors of the Chaplins' impending split. But then, cynics would ask, what exactly were they splitting from? After all, it had still never been clearly established that they were officially married.

And so the legend of Paulette Goddard continued to flourish. If Paulette's aim was to keep her name in the papers, it certainly worked. Speculation on her marital status was not just a matter of gossip-column innuendo; it was also the subject of off-the-movie-page news stories. Even other celebrities became embroiled in the "vital question."

Randolph Churchill, the son of Winston Churchill, was quoted as saying: "I am not at liberty to quote Mr. Chaplin directly, but I can definitely say that they are married. They have been married for more than a year."

However, statements like this only clouded the issue. If they had been married "more than a year" at this juncture, it meant that they had been married months before they left for the Orient. So back into the news came the stories of Paulette Goddard marrying Charlie Chaplin on a yacht off the coast of Catalina. And at the end of each story appeared the inevitable tag: "Neither Miss Goddard nor Mr. Chaplin has any comment."

Early in 1937, Paulette began to lose patience with Charlie's interminable indecision about the script he was writing for her. She understood his creative paranoia. He was a genius, after all, and each of his projects had to top the last one. Nevertheless, she fretted.

As in the pattern of his creative past, Chaplin was faced with dozens of ideas. He would work feverishly on one for days, then discard it. He longed for one idea to grab hold of him and hang on and force him to see it through to completion. But the inspiration he had felt with Paulette as the gamine and him as the little fellow was no longer there. He had proved what he wanted. And now ideas that revolved around Paulette no longer really intrigued him.

Theirs seemed the classic case of a relationship serving its function and working until it was sealed with a marriage vow. They had been together for years, but Chaplin later admitted that within a year after they married they began to drift apart emotionally. His creative moods continued to drive a wedge between them.

Paulette began to have a sinking feeling regarding his professional plans for her, because although he kept talking about ideas for her, he continually got sidetracked. She later confessed, "Millions of situations, when it's something he's interested in, pop out of him as if he had the hives. But for me . . ." And she began to entertain the idea of working for other producers.

Across the street from Charlie's mansion on Summit Drive was the home of producer David O. Selznick and his wife, Irene Mayer Selznick. The Chaplin and Selznick driveways faced each other.

David was the wonder-boy producer who was every bit as enamored of films and filmmaking as Chaplin, but Chaplin was not fond of Selznick. He kept their relationship on a cool, distant basis. His dislike of Selznick was based on both business and personal reasons. Selznick had recently bought into United Artists and was now distributing his films through U.A. Chaplin had opposed the deal.

Fuel had been added to the fire when, on the home front, there had been an unpleasant incident. Chaplin's children, in a youthful prank to make money, had decided to sell their dad's costly collection of imported liquor and liqueurs. The boys had set up a stand outside their house—a lemonade stand—and their first and only customer was their tall, curly-headed, bespectacled neighbor, Mr. Selznick. He was indeed happy to buy all their expensive Scotch, bourbon and liqueurs for around fifty cents a bottle. The boys were delighted when he bought the whole boodle, and noticed that he rushed away quickly as though fearful someone would stop him.

Naturally, when Chaplin found out the liquor was gone, he was incensed. What really irked Charlie about the entire incident was the fact that Selznick gave him such a hard time about returning the liquor. Apparently the producer didn't want to let Chaplin off the hook so easily. He had bought the liquor in good faith and he was going to keep it. Selznick's sense of humor wasn't appreciated by the screen's foremost comedian. It is fascinating that two of the world's most famous and successful men were such children at heart—and unforgiving ones at that.

Charlie's anger was unabated even after the liquor had been returned, and he decided to punish the boys severely. The incident had occurred early on a Friday afternoon, and Chaplin immediately sent his sons to bed with no supper. His decision on their punishment was similar to what he might have experienced himself in the workhouse and the London orphanage of his childhood. The boys were confined to their rooms—in fact, to bed—without food, and would have no dinner for the next three days.

As the first long evening progressed, ten-year-old Sydney and eleven-year-old Charlie, Jr., became hungry but they knew they daren't get up. Then, in the dark, they saw the door open and a hand reach for the light switch. When the light went on, there was Paulette carrying a tray of food. She closed the door quietly. "Sh-h-h," she warned them conspiratorially. And she told them that, against their father's edict, she had sneaked the food up because she felt sorry for them.

She did the same thing over the next two nights, always shushing them and saying their father didn't know she was bringing them food. In retrospect, however, the boys had to admit that Chaplin undoubtedly knew what Paulette was up to, and had sanctioned it because he could not lose face by rescinding his punishment. Chaplin had agreed with Paulette that perhaps he had overreacted in demanding that the boys go without food for three days.

Unlike Charlie, Paulette did not dislike David Selznick, and was friendly with Irene. Goddard often dropped in at their home. Irene Mayer grew fond of Paulette, but she had no illusions about the young woman's *modus operandi*. In fact, Mrs. Selznick has remembered an amusing—and very character-revealing—incident that involved her, Paulette and a bathing suit Irene owned.

The suit was a favorite of Irene's; it was a one-of-a-kind possession that was extremely flattering and attractive. At the Selznicks' one afternoon, Paulette expressed not only her admiration for Irene's bathing suit but her desire to have it.

Mrs. Selznick had no intention of parting with the suit. She ignored Paulette's playful hints. Finally, one day, the beauteous Mrs. Chaplin, not at all accustomed to being denied something she wanted, just took it.

In the words of Mrs. Selznick: "I never put anything past Paulette."

PAULETTE

When she found that the suit was missing, she phoned Paulette. Without discussing anything else, she simply said: "Send it back, girl."

Goddard sent back the suit, but, as Mrs. Selznick has described the ensuing weeks: "Back it came, only to disappear again shortly thereafter, right out of the pool house. She offered me certain swaps: no dice. We negotiated. Finally we compromised: Paulette was permitted to borrow it for very special occasions provided she returned it on her own. That would be the day!"

As Paulette's friendship with the Selznicks progressed, Chaplin was irked because it became clear that Selznick was willing to give Paulette a contract with his studio. Chaplin was furious at the thought.

"I am writing a script for you, what more do you want? I've launched you in the most spectacular fashion."

"But it was a silent picture, Charlie," she retorted. "I want to prove that I can act."

The relationship was becoming very strained. However, Paulette maintained her ability to gracefully stay out of Charlie's way for a day, a week, or however long it took when he was in one of his creative moods and unwilling to socialize, even with her. She would spend time with her mother or the boys, or resume her acting and dancing lessons. She became a close friend of Constance Collier, who was not only a great actress but a great acting coach—and a woman who was helpful in explaining Chaplin's creative moods to Paulette. "My dear, you must expect this kind of behavior when dealing with genius," she said. "He is not like other men. You are one of the few women who seem to understand this."

Paulette understood, but that didn't make Charlie's behavior any easier to live with. Although Paulette had made headway in changing the life-style at the Chaplin mansion, one thing she could not change was her husband's style of shoes. For years, since Chaplin had become well-off and successful, he had been in the habit of wearing on formal occasions old-fashioned high-button shoes—a type of shoe that had been worn by gentlemen of England when Chaplin was an impoverished youth. To Chaplin they represented the height of status. Though they had been out of style for years, he clung to this fashion, and had the shoes custom-made for him in England.

Getting Charlie to change his shoes became one of Paulette's ardent campaigns. When her hints about their being hopelessly old-fashioned fell on deaf ears, she tried another tactic.

In the words of one of Chaplin's sons: "Paulette had a way about her. She could wheedle a lot of things out of Dad. But she wasn't successful with the shoes."

"Honeybun, just for me, please wear your other shoes tonight," she would plead. Eventually the shoes became the basis for a dramatic confrontation one evening as Paulette and Charlie were dressing for a party. Chaplin discovered all three pairs of his high-button shoes were missing.

"Where are my shoes, Frank?" he called out.

"Aren't they there, Mr. Chaplin?" Frank was as shocked as his boss.

"Charles! Sydney! Have you seen my shoes?"

The youngsters didn't answer. They were as stunned as their father and Frank. Who would have dared tamper with *the shoes?*

"Damn it, where are they?" Chaplin demanded.

Paulette was in her room dressing. She pretended unconcern for the scene that was taking place.

"Do you know where my shoes are?" he asked her.

She gave a noncommittal answer. It was a device she'd mastered with reporters' direct questions on her marital status, her age, or just about any topic.

Chaplin's rage was building. His Japanese valet quietly continued to help Chaplin try to locate the shoes, but Frank, the children and Charlie, of course, all knew who had taken them. Moments later Paulette had finished dressing and casually said, "Come on, Charlie. We're going to be late. Aren't you ready yet?"

He stared at her. "I'm not going without my shoes." His voice was harsh. "Some goddamn bloody bastard has stolen my shoes."

All present knew that if Charlie Chaplin was using the word "bloody," he had reached the point of no return. Paulette gave it one more try. "They'll turn up. For the time being, put your other shoes on." She started walking toward the stairs. "Come on, it's getting late. You know how I hate to be late."

"I'm not going without my shoes," Chaplin stated once again.

He and Frank began another frantic search. A few minutes later,

Paulette found the shoes—all three pairs seemed to be in the same place.

There was deafening silence. Chaplin said nothing in front of the boys and Frank. He merely chose a pair of shoes and donned them, and he and Paulette went off to the party.

Social life continued to divert Paulette's attention from her career and became her main activity through much of 1937. Celebrity tennis tournaments were a popular pastime. At one such event, at the Los Angeles Tennis Club, Paulette encountered a stunning-looking young would-be actress, Jinx Falkenburg.

"I was teamed with Paulette Goddard, whom I'd never met before, and we managed to win the tournament," recalled Miss Falkenburg. "All through the afternoon, she and friends of hers took pictures on her little movie camera and after the match she invited me out to her place to see the results. That was my first trip to the palace of Mr. and Mrs. Charles Chaplin, the first of many."

According to Falkenburg, since Paulette was waiting for Charlie to finish a script for her, Paulette "had lots of free time on her hands. He wouldn't let her appear in any pictures but his own, so we took out our current dramatic frustrations on the Brontë sisters. Coached by Constance Collier, Paulette, Tilly Losch and I wrote a script about them; Paulette was the symbol of the artist. We thought it was just marvelous and, after tennis games at the palace, we made everyone sit down and watch it. We even forced our efforts on H. G. Wells, their houseguest."

Jinx also recalled, "I *think* I played Charlotte, and I *know* it was just awful. We started out like a bunch of high-school nitwits, just performing it for ourselves, but we ended up doing it at all the Chaplin parties."

Jinx and Paulette had much in common. Both young women were unusually energetic. Goddard looked on Jinx as—in Falkenburg's words—"a symbol of organized energy . . . but I'll bet I learned it from her in those days. She never stopped. She's the only one I know besides Gussy [Moran] and Mary Martin who can talk quite as much as I can."

Falkenburg has fond memories of these early years of their friendship. Paulette encouraged Jinx's acting ambitions, and when Paulette visited Jinx at her home, "we all treated her like a big movie star. We all waited on Paulette, set the stage for her, and she coached me because she thought it would be good for *me* to teach *me* how to act like a star. But she never carried her 'star' role too far."

Every Sunday the Chaplins would host an informal tennis party on their courts adjacent to their house. Tim Durant, who was recently divorced from one of the daughters of E. F. Hutton, became a regular. Chaplin, always a friend of the underdog, befriended tennis star Bill Tilden, who had been ostracized by the sports world when it became public knowledge that he was homosexual. Chaplin gave Tilden the run of his courts.

Around this time, Chaplin met a writer named Konrad Bercovici and they began knocking around ideas about a story in which Chaplin would play Hitler. But then Charlie tired of the notion and, as was his way, eliminated Bercovici from his life. One of his sons later explained that Chaplin had "an incurable enthusiasm" and that people got the impression "they were indispensable to him" but "once they are out of his sight he forgets them completely." This happened, for a time, to Bercovici.

One of Chaplin's friends was Greta Garbo, a person who understood Chaplin's form of creativity. If Chaplin suddenly discussed an idea for a movie he wanted to make with Garbo, she recognized that it was an idea of the moment and the moment would pass. She would become wrapped up in the enthusiasm but did not expect any follow-through, which Paulette and others *did* expect.

Chaplin enjoyed women like Garbo and Dietrich; with them he could discuss the creative aspect of making pictures and also music, art and ballet—subjects close to his heart. In the main, however, he found most actors boring and preferred to associate with writers and musicians.

Other Chaplin acquaintances of this period were Alexander Korda and actress Merle Oberon. Chaplin later said it was Korda who suggested to him that he do a film about Hitler. Chaplin's films were now banned in Germany because of the striking physical resemblance between the madman who was frightening half the world and the little tramp Chaplin had created.

Chaplin did not think too much about the Hitler movie idea at the time; he filed it away in his memory as a possible idea for the future. He claimed he was still grappling with a story for Paulette, and was even considering remaking *A Woman of Paris* (a film he had directed years earlier with Edna Purviance) as a talkie starring Paulette. But he was worried about his work, or his trying to work, and the breach was widening between him and Paulette.

Through Elias Berger, a wholesale jeweler in Hollywood, Chaplin bought Paulette a magnificent diamond bracelet, inches wide, set with large, fine white marquise-shaped and round gems. Berger delivered the bracelet to the Chaplin home and was in Charlie and Paulette's presence when she opened the gift and literally screamed with surprise and delight. The jeweler later told friends that it was a wedding-anniversary present from Chaplin to his wife.

Paulette made an amusing comment to Berger that she still didn't have a wedding ring. So, on his next visit to the mansion, Berger brought with him a platinum wedding band set with marquise diamonds.

"She was like a child, laughing one moment, crying the next, as she slipped the ring on her finger," recalled Berger.

Obviously, Chaplin's romantic bursts of generosity could be endearing. But just as he treated his children generously, and then expected them to retreat when he was immersed in his work, he expected the same of Paulette.

In March, the Chaplins were invited to a dinner party in honor of the famed composer Igor Stravinsky. Charlie was not altogether happy about attending this dinner. It appeared that Stravinsky thought he'd recognized one of his compositions in the score for *Modern Times*. He had written Chaplin about it and his lawyers were also trying to get in touch with Charlie. But the director had avoided the matter successfully, and would continue to do so in the future.

But Paulette was eager to meet Stravinsky and she accepted the dinner invitation. It wasn't Stravinsky, however, but another musical genius at the party who would affect her life and offer her a dramatic choice.

Edward G. Robinson and his wife were considered intellectuals on the Hollywood scene. They were art collectors, and socialized with writers, artists and thinkers of the day. At the dinner party for Stravinsky, at the Robinsons' home, Paulette and Chaplin, Doug Fairbanks and Sylvia, Frank Capra and his wife, and Marlene Dietrich were among the guests. It was a brilliant affair, and one of the other guests was the renowned composer George Gershwin.

Gershwin was to the world of music what Chaplin was to films: an innovator and a genius. The dynamic composer-musician had successfully combined the structure and sound of classical music with jazz. In the twenties, Gershwin's compositions were lauded as musical landmarks. *Rhapsody in Blue* appeared in 1924; *Piano Concerto in F* in 1925; *An American in Paris* in 1928. The thrilling rhythms and poignant, plaintive melodies of these American classics clearly revealed the composer's inner self—a man of intense passion and stunning creativity.

Gershwin was ambitious for great popular success as well as artistic acknowledgment, and for Broadway—with his brother Ira, the lyricist—he had written, among other successes, *Lady Be Good, Funny Face, Strike Up the Band, Girl Crazy* and *Of Thee I Sing*. The last won the Pulitzer Prize in 1932. By the mid-thirties many Gershwin brothers songs were already standards: "Swanee," "The Man I Love," "I Got Rhythm," to mention only a few.

In 1935, the controversial Gershwin opera, *Porgy and Bess,* had premièred. It was the first American opera that would eventually become an international staple. At the time of its début, however, it was considered highbrow, not commercial—especially by Hollywood. In the opinion of the film moguls, it was Irving Berlin, not George Gershwin, who was one hundred percent *commercial.*

As the spring of 1937 approached, the Gershwin brothers had been in Hollywood for a couple of years writing for films. They had just finished doing the score for the Astaire-Rogers film *Shall We Dance?* and were working on Astaire's next picture, *A Damsel in Distress.*

The Gershwin brothers were very close and family-oriented. George lived with his mother and his brother Ira and Ira's wife, Lee, in a splendid house on North Roxbury Drive. Sunday brunches at the Gershwin home became popular and fashionable. Usually attending were members of the New York set such as Lillian Hellman, Dashiell Hammett, Vincente Minnelli and Rouben Mamoulian.

George Gershwin, at thirty-eight, was considered one of the most eligible bachelors on both coasts. Although he was a tennis fanatic, and in Hollywood style had bought himself a dashing convertible—a Cord—most of his other tastes were strictly New York. He was a nightclubber, a dapper dresser and a ladies' man.

When he had first come to the West Coast, he had told his friends that the women of Hollywood didn't attract him, but soon he was dating screen actresses. Elizabeth Allan and Simone Simon, both beautiful brunettes, were among his acquaintances. And now, at this dinner party for Stravinsky, Gershwin met another dazzling brunette.

In a letter Gershwin wrote to his friend Mabel Schirmer, dated March 19, 1937, he noted: "Dined at E. Robinson's the other night at a party mainly for Stravinsky. Many celebs were there. Sat next to Paulette Goddard. Mmmmmmm. She's nice. Me Likee."

It was more than "likee." Gershwin was instantly captivated by Paulette. Men usually were. Constance Collier used to call Paulette "a natural-born honey pot," and often said: "Adulation to her is as normal as breathing." Paulette's friends of the time state that while this is true, she reacted to such attention without dramatics.

Within days Paulette and Gershwin began a romance. According to Anita Loos, Gershwin "fell hopelessly in love. He used to follow Paulette everywhere, came to life in her presence as nobody had ever seen him before."

Gershwin's friends agreed; his pal Oscar Levant affirmed that the composer "fell madly in love with Paulette. He was more in love than I'd ever seen him."

The lovers had to be somewhat discreet. If they wanted to go out in public, they had to resort to the old "beard" ploy. Levant explained: "George would take his mother and Lillian Hellman to the Troc. Then he'd leave them and join Paulette at her table. It's an old trick." Although playwright Hellman went along with this several times, Levant also noted that she was "quite annoyed at being made a shill for George."

Since many men paid court to Paulette, George's attentions did not seem any more obvious than the others. Writer Charles Lederer was also at the time pursuing the married Paulette.

Paulette's fast-moving life, however, included family obligations. Chaplin came in and out of his moods and Goddard of course had to schedule her social life around him. That Easter, Chaplin, the boys and Paulette celebrated the holiday together. Chaplin enjoyed playing family. At Eastertime he often colored eggs with his sons and liked to hide the eggs himself, delighting in watching Paulette, Charlie, Jr., and Syd find them.

But poignant holiday get-togethers could not overcome the fact that all was not well between Charlie and Paulette. The more she night-clubbed and socialized, the less happy he was. And the more obvious it became that he was not ready to start a new production, the more they would wrangle over her working for Selznick or others.

Chaplin retreated to his creative cocoon and Paulette resumed her gadding about. Her relationship with Gershwin intensified, and they arranged to be in Palm Springs at the same time.

Like Chaplin, Gershwin was multitalented. Although he had had little formal education, he was a brilliant musician and his interest in art collecting led him to painting, where he also displayed unusual abilities. According to Levant, "George also had an instinct for good manners, and he was thoroughly original in everything he did. He was the toast of elegant society. They loved him and he in turn adored them."

Gershwin had visited Mexico and he described to Paulette his meeting with the famous Mexican muralist Diego Rivera. (Gershwin had even sketched Rivera.) George delighted in telling Paulette about his extensive art collection, his travels, his music, his Broadway successes. (Chaplin, the world would have been surprised to learn, owned virtually no important paintings. Spending the kind of money necessary to accumulate a collection simply was not on his list of priorities.)

Soon the Goddard-Gershwin relationship had become serious, at least from Gershwin's point of view. Gershwin's friend composer Harold Arlen states: "You know, he wanted to marry Paulette Goddard. We sat by his pool talking about it. She was a great girl, but George's life-style was very freewheeling. I knew that marriage would tie him down, so I told him that he would have to give up some of the freedom he had. He didn't say anything, because I knew—all of us knew—that he wanted to get married. But George was the kind of guy who would go first to one house and play a few songs, then go on to another house and play some more, then to another, and so on. He knew he couldn't do that if he were married. Yet there was that warmth and wistfulness in him too, and it all made for great internal conflicts. So it would have been hard for George to change his life-style from work, partygoing, tennis, golf, long fast walks in the mountains. He always was so goddamned excited, and the glory road had to be his."

What Arlen didn't mention was that George was also fond of frequenting call girls, and this was another activity he would presumably have to discontinue if he married. In any event, there is little evidence that Goddard, though charmed and intrigued by the sensual, dynamic Gershwin, ever seriously considered leaving Chaplin.

The Goddard-Gershwin relationship was further complicated by Gershwin's ill health. The composer was tense and quixotic, not the person his friends had known back in New York. Harold Arlen recalled, "During the last year he was very often unhappy and uneasy. Lots of other people were writing well—Rodgers, Porter, others—and, of course, George liked to be kingpin. I felt that something was wrong with him one day when after a lot of us had played the piano, George said to me, 'No you don't. I'm not going to follow you.' I was shocked with surprise. Since we were always together in one bunch trying to help one another, there was little show of jealousy. When he acted that way, I felt uneasy. I knew something was wrong with him, and I thought it was Hollywooditis."

What most of his friends did not know was that Gershwin was suffering from severe migraine headaches. Earlier in the year, in February, Gershwin had had a complete physical checkup and had been pronounced okay. Many thought his headaches had to do with his intensity toward his work. *Porgy and Bess,* although later recognized as a brilliant piece, had not been received well. In late 1936, Gershwin had embarked on a rigorous concert tour. Now in Hollywood the Gershwin brothers were working hard to finish the Astaire film at RKO while simultaneously working on *The Goldwyn Follies* for Sam Goldwyn.

Gershwin had undergone psychoanalysis. But the first symptom of his problem being a physiological one came at a concert he performed early in 1937. While playing the last bar of a concerto, Gershwin missed one of the last four notes. Since they were slow, easy notes to play, this was quite startling. Still the doctors could find nothing wrong.

There are many accounts of the pain Gershwin suffered in the last months of his life. Stories were published through the years that Paulette, via Chaplin, was instrumental in getting Gershwin to Dr. Reynolds, who diagnosed a brain tumor and instantly rushed Gershwin into surgery. But the stories were not true. Paulette had broken with Gershwin weeks before he submitted to a spinal tap. (This was decades before the brain scan, and a spinal tap was the method of diagnosing a brain tumor.)

PAULETTE

Numerous famous doctors were sought to operate on Gershwin. His family and friends were in shock. The intrusion of horrifying reality into the lives of Hollywood's chosen was always earthshaking. In a society where almost everything could be bought, it was staggering to realize there was still something money couldn't buy.

Gershwin's brain tumor was deemed inoperable. But an operation was performed. He died on July 11, 1937. He was only thirty-nine years old. His body was returned to New York. On July 15, two lavish simultaneous funeral services were held for George Gershwin, one in New York City, one in Hollywood. And all the studios in the film capital observed a moment of silence at the exact minute the services were scheduled to start.

Some claim that even before Paulette knew he was ill, she made it clear to him that there could be no marriage between them. Elsa Maxwell later said, "Paulette, I'm sorry to say, after leading George on and on, abruptly called it quits."

Oscar Levant: "George and Paulette broke off their romance two months before he died. I never knew why."

Bernard Drew, a writer and longtime observer of the Hollywood scene (he was a protégé of Dashiell Hammett's), was an acquaintance of Goddard's in later life. Drew was of the opinion that Goddard was in love with Gershwin and had permitted herself that romantic fling. Drew believes that Paulette had to make her choice between geniuses, and the ever-practical side of her won out. Chaplin was the known quantity. Others, less charitable, contend that Paulette made her choice knowing that there was no future with Gershwin because of his illness.

It should be remembered that the entire Gershwin-Goddard romance was very brief. There were only four months between the day they met and the day he died. But Gershwin, like Chaplin, was a legend in his lifetime, and since Paulette was the last and most celebrated of his love affairs, a mythology evolved around it.

Part of the mythology is that Gershwin wrote one of his last songs, "They Can't Take That Away from Me," for Paulette. Of course it was brother Ira who wrote the lyrics, and actually the song had been written before George met Paulette. But it was more romantic to think the dying composer had written the plaintive ballad for his last love.

(As Paulette's acquisitive nature fast grew in Hollywood lore, a snide parody of the lyric became "They Can't Get That Away from Me.")

4

▉□▉□▉

After the tragedy, Goddard focused with a new intensity on her career. She wanted Chaplin's attention—shopping sprees, dinner parties and other social activities simply weren't enough. She was weary of his promises that her script would be ready soon. It seemed he would never complete the script.

It was time to take things into her own hands. Goddard's attitude was understandable. This was the era when actresses made two, three, often more pictures in a year. The major studios had rosters of stars under contract, and the stars were not only on screen but on magazine covers, on billboards, on radio. Girls with far less impressive connections than Paulette's were being given buildups by the studios. At the rate Chaplin worked, Goddard would be ready for character roles by the time she had a few films under her belt.

Around this time Paulette signed with the Myron Selznick talent agency. More to the point, she signed with Myron Selznick (David's brother) directly. He was the top agent in Hollywood. His associate, Leland Hayward, handled most of the clients. Myron personally handled only a select few—and Paulette was among them.

There are accounts of a little game Paulette and Myron played. When she visited his office, she would sit gracefully on the corner of his desk, cross her legs seductively and coo: "What have you got for me today?"

"What do you want?" Selznick would ask. The story is that Myron often took Paulette to one of the Beverly Hills shops (Billy Seymour's jewelry salon in Saks Fifth Avenue was one of Paulette's favorites) and bought her a costly bauble or two. These tales seem somewhat exaggerated. Although it might have happened once or twice, Selznick was hardly the kind of man who would allow himself to be used in such a flagrant fashion, even by a charmer like Paulette Goddard. And Paulette was, after all, still married to Charlie Chaplin, and was much too smart to hold herself and Chaplin up to ridicule.

At the start of their association, Myron undoubtedly enjoyed squiring Paulette around to the various studios and introducing her to producers. However, the producer who owned the property that contained the most coveted female role of the day was David Selznick.

Although his company, Selznick International, produced two movies a year, David Selznick's major concern at this point was the preparation of, and the casting for, the celebrated film of the decade. Selznick had bought, in galleys, Margaret Mitchell's now enormously successful best-seller, *Gone With the Wind,* and he was determined to transfer it to the screen in the most lavish yet faithful adaptation.

From the onset, the public wanted Clark Gable to play Rhett Butler. And Selznick was in negotiation with his father-in-law about the possibility of borrowing Gable from MGM for the picture. But the part of Scarlett O'Hara was up for grabs, and every major star in town was reaching for it.

Paulette was no exception. She told Myron she wanted to play Scarlett. In the words of Irene Mayer Selznick: "At first, we treated it as a joke."

Paulette was dead serious, and she began rehearsing for the role. Constance Collier coached her; George Cukor, set to direct *Gone With the Wind,* playwright Sidney Howard, who had adapted it for the screen, and Selznick all attended Paulette's rehearsals for her screen test.

Suddenly, what had seemed to be a dream was now a possibility. Paulette obviously fulfilled Scarlett's physical qualifications, but she had little acting experience. This was a part that would require enormous technique; the actress would be on screen almost the entire epic running time.

David Selznick was willing to put Goddard under contract, give her experience in other films and build her into a real contender for the role of Scarlett. Paulette had not been on the screen since 1936. It was now 1938. A major decision had to be made, and Paulette made it.

Soon into the new year, Paulette Goddard's name hit the headlines across the country as Louella Parsons announced an exclusive: "The longest search for a screen heroine ended today when Paulette Goddard was signed on a long-term contract by David O. Selznick, producer of *Gone With the Wind,* which, of course, only means that she will play Scarlett O'Hara . . ."

Legally, Paulette was free of her contract with the Chaplin studios and could sign with Selznick. But inside the Chaplin household there were fireworks. She had not only defied her mentor, the man who had developed her into a name; she had defied her husband.

Chaplin's wrath was instant. The Chaplin studios announced that Paulette Goddard was "a Chaplin star." She was *not* at liberty to sign with Selznick or any other studio.

Paulette retorted that there was no legal contract in force between her and the Chaplin studios. Obviously, however, there was a verbal agreement and it had been understood that Paulette's next film, her "talking début," would be for Chaplin.

Now Paulette began stating publicly what she had been brooding about for months. "He said my first talking picture had to be with him, in a story he was writing for us both, but I have no faith that the story will ever be completed. He's told me dozens of times that he had a story ready—only later he tears it up and says it wasn't right. He gets so enthusiastic over an idea and then, before it's completed, he starts another entirely different one."

There was much consternation, and Paulette, in a frenzied attempt to keep Chaplin on her side *and* work for Selznick, persuaded Selznick to obtain Chaplin's approval of her new contract. Selznick assigned the duty of dealing with Chaplin to his right-hand man, Daniel O'Shea. It was a thankless assignment.

After many days, O'Shea finally reached Chaplin on the phone. Charlie did not hide his anger. He was blunt, suggesting that Selznick was only after Paulette and had offered her a contract as a means of getting her. In addition, Chaplin fumed that he had not built Paulette Goddard into a star so that others could exploit her.

Mr. O'Shea somehow stemmed the tide of Chaplin's anger. He was emphatic that Selznick's interest in the actress was legitimate. Chaplin questioned the pitfalls of her signing a long-term contract. But then Chaplin's tone suddenly changed. "It's all right. Miss Goddard has left the room now and I'm alone."

In an unemotional manner, Chaplin and O'Shea now discussed terms and conditions. Chaplin insisted on a clause in Paulette's contract that would ultimately be known as the Chaplin clause—to wit, he (Chaplin) would have the right to use Paulette Goddard in Chaplin films whenever he wanted to.

No sooner had O'Shea concluded the conversation than his phone rang. It was Paulette. "I'm so glad it's all worked out," she said with a sigh. She expressed her relief that the terms and conditions had been met. O'Shea sensed she knew all the details.

"Has Charlie briefed you?" he asked.

"No, no," Paulette said. "I was hiding in the closet. I heard the whole thing."

Although Chaplin had capitulated from a legal point of view, his anger toward Paulette had not abated. As he often did, Charlie decided the only way to avoid further argument was by flight. He disappeared one weekend. The explanation Paulette gave to her friends was that Charlie and his pal Tim Durant had gone to Pebble Beach, near Monterey, to play golf.

But soon it was clear that Chaplin's weekend jaunt was extending into weeks. He had sent for his Japanese manservants, and he and Durant had rented the home of socialite Estelle Monteagle.

Friends chuckled because Paulette and her mother were ensconced in the Chaplin mansion on Summit Drive and weren't leaving. Obviously, Chaplin wasn't coming back until they did leave.

To confuse the situation further, it became known that both Paulette and Chaplin were seeing other people. Again rumors flared—some said Goddard and Chaplin couldn't be married if they were now dating others. (Paulette was seen with Spencer Tracy—also married—and David

Niven.) Other friends said Paulette and Charlie were certainly married but divorce was apparently imminent.

Louella's "exclusive" that Paulette had the role of Scarlett had, of course, been supposition on Miss Parsons' part. The search for Scarlett would continue for a year. But Paulette was and would remain a leader in the contest, and Selznick saw in Goddard a girl with tremendous potential. She was already famous, thanks to Chaplin, and yet she had not yet made her début in a talkie! Selznick's publicity genius, Russell Birdwell, could squeeze a great deal of mileage out of a new star like Goddard and keep *Gone With the Wind* and Scarlett in the news.

The Selznick studio announced that Paulette would make her talking début in the Selznick International picture *The Young in Heart*. In confidential memos between Selznick and director Richard Wallace, the producer discussed other actresses up for the role: Margaret Lindsay, Pat Patterson, Dorothy Hyson. Selznick had also screened the British-American co-production *A Yank at Oxford* to check out a new young British actress, Vivien Leigh. He noted, "While I think Vivien Leigh gave an excellent performance, and was very well cast, I don't like her for the part in *Young in Heart*."

The film would star Janet Gaynor, fresh from her triumph in Selznick's *A Star Is Born*. Douglas Fairbanks, Jr., had the male lead and the supporting cast was to be headed by Billie Burke and Roland Young. Other cast members included Richard Carlson, Lucile Watson, Minnie Dupree and Henry Stephenson.

Working for Selznick wasn't too different from working for Chaplin. Both men were perfectionists, and quality in performance and production were prime considerations. Selznick, however, didn't literally direct his pictures (although many in Hollywood, pointing to his incredible interference in all aspects of production, said he might as well be directing). And, most important, Paulette didn't have to go home with Selznick after work and spend the evening listening to him rehash the problems of the day. Nor did she have to endure an unending critique of her performance.

Russell Birdwell lost no time in publicizing Paulette. She was on the cover of *Life* magazine in April. After she completed *The Young in Heart,* Selznick announced that he was lending his new star to MGM, where she would star with two-time Oscar-winner Luise Rainer in a film titled *Dramatic School* (Metro's answer to RKO's *Stage Door*).

Meanwhile, Chaplin's absence from his estate on Summit Drive was becoming almost a *cause célèbre*. Although the outside world might believe he was merely vacationing while Paulette was working, insiders knew better. Chaplin would not even accept his wife's telephone calls, although she would phone, weeping hysterically, and beg to speak with him.

Ostensibly, he was still working on the script for her film. In reality, Paulette had hurt him and the time Chaplin spent in Pebble Beach was used to rejuvenate his spirit. Chaplin himself described the Pebble Beach of that era as "wild, baneful and slightly sinister. I called it 'the abode of stranded souls.'"

Others living in Pebble Beach and its environs (Monterey and Carmel) included the poet Robinson Jeffers and the novelist John Steinbeck. Chaplin always felt at home associating with writers. Jeffers especially was a fascinating person to know; he and his wife lived in a castle-like house that was a frequent visiting place of writers and intellectuals from the international set.

Wherever Chaplin went, in Pebble Beach and Monterey, he soon became the darling of society. He met Peggy Brokaw, of the prominent New York family, who had married into the Crocker family of West Coast bankers. Through Peggy, Chaplin and Tim Durant traveled in the highest social circles, and Chaplin's name was soon linked romantically with that of Geraldine Spreckels, the sugar heiress. (The Spreckels family owned C & H Sugar.)

Shortly afterward, Miss Spreckels was dogged by reporters who wanted to know when *she* was going to marry the famed comedian. The young heiress obviously had a sense of humor, and, like Chaplin (and Paulette), tended to lead the press on. "We've never exactly discussed marriage," she said. "I think it would be nice for anyone to be Mrs. Chaplin. Yes, I like Mr. Chaplin very much." Like Paulette, the lady neither confirmed nor denied her relationship with Chaplin, nor did she discuss Chaplin's marital status.

Geraldine Spreckels was not the only woman Chaplin was involved with. He later revealed that a very attractive married lady had decided on an amorous affair, and although he had every "adulterous intention," when the lady disclosed the fact that she had not had sexual relations with her husband in some years, and grew emotional, Charlie was sympathetic and their affair became platonic rather than physical. "The whole thing became cerebral," said Chaplin. "Later it was rumored she had turned lesbian."

Chaplin was not at a loss for playmates, either in or out of bed. Within a few months, Chaplin and Durant knew so many people that Charlie threw a spectacular party for his new friends at the Pebble Beach Lodge. He spared no expense and society columns were full of the doings for weeks afterward.

Meanwhile, back in Hollywood, Paulette wasn't exactly sitting by the fireside. She was out visiting nightclubs with men closer to her own age—Anderson Lawler, Michael Brooke and David Niven. Paulette and her mother continued to inhabit the mansion on Summit Drive and by this time Goddard had assembled her own support system. A business manager, Arthur Taylor, handled her investments. Two young attorneys, Greg Bautzer and Bentley Ryan, handled her legal affairs. And of course Myron was allegedly in charge of her career. When Paulette was mentioned in the press, she was referred to as "Scarlett O'Hara Goddard."

Chaplin and Paulette had been separated for so many months that rumors of their divorce now began in earnest. Hollywood gossips chattered that Paulette had been ordered to sell the yacht Charlie had given her, and all other personal possessions, so that their lawyers could begin negotiating a community property settlement. Some investigative reporting turned up the interesting fact that she had put the yacht up for sale.

But Paulette spiked the divorce rumors: "If Charlie wants a divorce, let him get it. But I'm too grateful to him for everything, and love him too much, to cause him a moment's anguish. Besides, I'm satisfied with my present status."

Chaplin's attorney, Lloyd Wright, labeled the latest rumors "preposterous. I don't know Mr. Chaplin's plans for divorce, but I'm certain he would never ask his wife to sell her jewels and furs in order to make a community property settlement."

It was obvious that Paulette had crossed the line when she had signed the Selznick contract. The one thing Chaplin could not abide was being made a fool of. Years before, his ardent and long romantic relationship with Edna Purviance had turned sour over a far less publicized incident. He forgave her and they continued to work together, but things were never the same.

PAULETTE

And now, again, Chaplin felt that he had been betrayed. The story of his estrangement from Paulette broke nationwide. Since, throughout these Depression years of the thirties, strikes were always front-page news (Lillian Hellman had written a play about strikes, *Days to Come*), Louella Parsons now delighted in informing her readers that "the film capital's first husband-and-wife strike is in full swing today." Front pages across the country told fans that Hollywood was involved in "a sit-down strike. Paulette Goddard and her mother were 'sit-downers' in Charlie's Beverly Hills mansion. . . .

"Charlie, meanwhile, announced he wouldn't return to Hollywood as long as the 'sit-downers' were occupying his domicile.

"And there it stands—or is it sits?"

Chaplin truly loathed "cheap" publicity such as this. Paulette tried to telephone and explain, but he wouldn't accept the calls.

She had to take action. Paulette had started up to Pebble Beach to talk over, as she said, "many things" with Charlie. But she got only as far as Santa Barbara. Her studio needed retakes for *The Young in Heart* and summoned her back.

On the Selznick International lot, Paulette was hounded by the press. They wanted to know if the ski club she was opening in Reno had anything to do with establishing Nevada residency for a quick divorce.

"I'm simply going to Reno next week to establish the ski club. It's a good spot to make money."

Reporters reminded her there was no snow in Reno this time of year. "Are you going to get a divorce?"

Paulette smiled.

"Are you married?"

Paulette frowned.

"Let's talk about skiing," she said.

Meanwhile, up at Pebble Beach, writer Konrad Bercovici and his friend Melvyn Douglas came to visit Chaplin.

Again they discussed the story idea about Hitler. The comedian told the writer: "I really can't think about that now. I'm still concentrating on the script for Paulette."

Chaplin was in the process of completing his adaptation of the novel *Regency* and an original script, *White Russian*. Even though he had not taken any of Paulette's telephone calls and their relationship seemed to be at an impasse, he had proceeded with the script.

No one could predict what would happen next in the unpredictable lives of Charlie and Paulette. Goddard realized she would have to eat humble pie. She decided to go to Pebble Beach, and she took Charlie, Jr., and Sydney with her.

Chaplin, Sr., was delighted to see her and the children. According to the recollections of one of the boys, "Almost immediately, he and Paulette were back in the same close relationship."

Paulette stayed with Charlie, and everyone at Pebble Beach accepted her as Chaplin's wife. Naturally, reporters had followed her from Hollywood and the big news of the day occurred when she entered a golf tournament under the name "Mrs. Chaplin." The news was flashed around the world: "Paulette Goddard, who has never confirmed or denied reports that she is married, registered for the Cypress Point Golf Tournament as 'Mrs. Charles Chaplin.'"

While in the nineteen-eighties this preoccupation with marital status seems ridiculously overblown, it must be recalled that, in the thirties, forties and fifties, if a woman lived with a man without proof of marriage, all sorts of moral issues were at stake. She was no more than—in the jargon of the day—"*that* kind of woman."

Obviously, that kind of woman would never be accepted in Pebble Beach society, so the newspapers duly reported that placecards at various dinner parties designated Paulette as "Mrs. Chaplin." And that "socially prominent visitors at the hotel introduce her as 'Mrs. Chaplin' and have 'accepted' her as the wife of the famed comedian." Confirmation at last that the couple was married.

Although Charlie, Jr., and Sydney returned to Hollywood, Paulette remained in Pebble Beach with Charlie for the entire month of July. Then the couple returned to the Summit Drive mansion together as if nothing had happened. As if Charlie had never been away.

5

Chaplin's script was ready. Gary Cooper was the obvious choice for Paulette's leading man. Chaplin was going to direct the picture but not appear in it. He was going to do for Paulette what he had done for Edna Purviance in *A Woman of Paris:* build a film around her and star her opposite a dashing, handsome romantic leading man of the day.

Cooper was at the very peak of his career and was adept at both straight drama and light comedy. As was Chaplin's way when he wanted someone, he just picked up the phone and called Gary Cooper. He had a film ready for production. Would Cooper like to see the script?

The actor was elated. Of course he would be happy to meet with Chaplin to discuss the project. And the two men did meet. It seemed that Paulette at last would have her wish.

Meanwhile, *Dramatic School* had completed shooting at Metro and both it and *The Young in Heart* were being readied for release. *The Young in Heart* would première at Radio City Music Hall.

At the same time, Paulette was still a front-runner for the role of Scarlett. The Selznick studio sent her to New Orleans to work on her Southern accent. Jeffrey Lynn, a new player at Warner Brothers, was to be tested for the role of Ashley. He and Paulette were placed under the tutelage of dialect coach Will Price. Goddard and Lynn were scheduled to film a screen test under George Cukor's direction. They would play two scenes from the completed screenplay: the encounter between Scarlett and Ashley in the library of the Twelve Oaks plantation, when Scarlett blurts out to Ashley that she loves him; and the scene in the woodshed at Tara, after the war has devastated their lives, when Scarlett again declares her love for Ashley.

Both scenes were emotion-charged moments in the story, and Selznick had to know if the actors were capable of delivering the goods. The screen tests were to be costumed, lit and photographed as if the mounted full-scale production were being shot. Jeffrey Lynn, who was used to the Warner Brothers "grind 'em out" technique, was impressed.

Selznick was more than impressed with the second test of Goddard. He wrote a memo to Dan O'Shea: "I saw the Paulette Goddard-Jeffrey Lynn test and thought there was an enormous improvement in her own work—so much so that I think she is still very strongly in the running as Scarlett."

However, Russell Birdwell brought one and all down to earth when he pointed out to Selznick that if he announced Paulette had the part, they were going to have to have a press conference, and if they had a press conference, Paulette was certain to be asked *when* and *where* she had been married.

Confronted with this fact, Paulette retorted: "It's none of their goddamn business."

Birdwell was against Goddard playing Scarlett. "Strictly from a publicity standpoint, I cannot go too strongly on record in opposing the proposed selection of Paulette Goddard for the role of Scarlett O'Hara," he said. Birdwell warned his boss "of the tremendous avalanche of criticism which will befall us and the picture should Paulette be given this part . . ."

The press agent, who was one of the few men who would argue with David Selznick, wasn't subtle about his reasons for not thinking Paulette a good choice. "It will throw us under the shadow of such a resentful press that all of our good public relations work of the past will be completely dissipated. I have never known a woman, intent on a career dependent upon her popularity with [the] masses, to hold and live such an insane and absurd attitude toward the press and her fellow man as does Paulette Goddard . . ."

Birdwell also offered the opinion that the girl who got the role "must be prepared to have her life laid bare in cold black type. This, Goddard is neither willing nor able to do. Briefly, I think she is dynamite which will explode in our very faces if she is given the part."

Around this time Paulette and Charlie were grouped together with a half-dozen other couples in a widely read and highly controversial *Photoplay* magazine article. The piece stated: "To the outside world Clark Gable and Carole Lombard might as well be married. So might Bob Taylor and Barbara Stanwyck. Or George Raft and a minor actress, Charlie Chaplin and Paulette Goddard. Unwed couples, they might be termed." Constance Bennett and Gilbert Roland were also named in the piece. One blatant omission was Marion Davies and William Randolph Hearst.

The *Photoplay* piece continued, "But they go everywhere together, do everything in pairs, no hostess would think of inviting them separately, or pairing them with another. . . . They build their houses near each other, take up each other's hobbies, father or mother each other's children. Yet to the world their official status is 'just friends. No more.'"

Today, with divorce, illegitimate children, sexual preference and other intimate details of stars' private lives accepted as casually as junk mail, it's hard to realize that an article in 1938 about a few celebrity couples living together could create such a furor. The article does indeed seem tame by today's standards. And though it never specifically stated the couples lived together, newspapers of the day seized on the idea, and suddenly the nation's moralists were incensed.

Photoplay discovered that its reporters had instantly been barred at the major studios. The fan magazine ran a public apology the following month, but the damage had been done. The Hays Office, creator of a self-regulatory code of ethics for the motion-picture industry, brought pressure on studio heads: "Get those characters married!"

With the exception of George Raft and Virginia Pine, all the couples eventually married. The irony, of course, was that Chaplin and Paulette already *were* married.

At this point Paulette was a hot property in town, although her two films had yet to be released. Universal wanted to borrow her from Selznick to play a dance-hall girl in a Western comedy the studio was preparing, *Destry Rides Again*.

Selznick told Dan O'Shea, "I think we ought to take the chance that if she doesn't play Scarlett, we will be able to find other engagements for her besides the Universal job." In the Hollywood of that time, there would always be work for a beautiful girl who, although not wildly talented, had screen personality.

In November, *The Young in Heart* opened at the Music Hall. Paulette's rendition of a young secretary in love with an ex-con man (Fairbanks, Jr.) received pleasant reviews. Very little was said of her acting ability, and most reports concerned her beauty and screen presence. *Variety* noted: "She's an eye-filler and possesses an exciting screen personality."

The ads for the film prominently featured Goddard, pointing out that this was "Her Talking Début." She was billed third, after Gaynor and Fairbanks and above the title.

A month later, *Dramatic School* followed *The Young in Heart* into the Music Hall. This was interesting because MGM pictures usually played Loew's theaters. Paulette Goddard had been responsible for the booking—although she didn't know it. It seems that Jock Whitney, prime backer of David Selznick's company, had financial connections with the Music Hall. So MGM, which was still negotiating with Selznick for a percentage of *Gone With the Wind,* and the Selznick studio, interested in building up Paulette, made a deal for *Dramatic School* to go into the Music Hall.

Goddard and Luise Rainer shared star billing on the picture, a lightweight story of girls at a Parisian drama school. Mervyn LeRoy, MGM's new fair-haired boy, had produced it. Robert Sinclair directed.

"Paulette was a lovely girl," recalled Sinclair. "She was very nervous and I think working with Chaplin had made her insecure about her ability. She was accustomed to the director telling her *every* move to make. She wasn't the kind of actress who came to the set with her own ideas or her own way of doing things. You were supposed to tell her how you wanted her to perform."

Maxine Marx, daughter of Chico Marx, had a bit role in the picture. She has recalled saying to Paulette one day on the set, "You have such incredible posture!" Paulette replied: "You would too, if Charlie was behind you all the time with a stick saying, 'Sit up, sit up.'"

One critic noted of Goddard in *Dramatic School,* "Paulette handles the role of a sophisticated, sharp-tongued student admirably." (Also in

72

the cast, in an inconsequential role and billed below the title, was Mervyn LeRoy's fast-rising protégée, a seventeen-year-old whom he had brought over from Warner Brothers: Lana Turner.)

Paulette's two recent films had been well received and she was eager to begin the comedy for Charlie. But she learned that Charlie had had an abrupt change of mind. He couldn't bring himself to film the project. It didn't compel him enough. It could be conjectured that he had forced himself to finish the script merely to prove to Paulette that he, not Selznick, had her best interests at heart. But at this point in his career Chaplin was really not interested in creating a light romantic comedy. As the title of an upcoming S. N. Behrman play read, this was No Time for Comedy. Certainly no time for a frivolous comedy that made no social statement. With *Modern Times,* Chaplin had produced a comedy, a hit, and had made social commentary. He had to top it with a picture that would do the same thing.

He abandoned the project for Paulette and began earnestly working on a script for "the Hitler story." "How could I throw myself into feminine whimsy, or think of romance, or the problems of love, when madness was being stirred up by a hideous, grotesque Adolf Hitler," he later explained.

However, he placated Paulette. They could always shoot her picture later. Besides, in any script he was writing there would certainly be a part for her.

Since their return from Pebble Beach, the Chaplins had had a more placid relationship. Chaplin's sons continued to spend weekends with them and Paulette often took the boys with her on trips to Arrowhead.

Chaplin's eldest son has recalled that as he and his brother grew to manhood, their relationship with Paulette changed. In his words: "It was Paulette, though, who really made me aware that I was leaving childhood behind. One night in the mountains I went to climb into her bed with her as always. But she just threw back the top cover for me.

"'What's that for?' I asked her.

"'You're an older boy now, Charlie,' she said.

"'What do you mean?' I insisted.

"Paulette laughed. 'You! Really, Charlie! You'll be just like your father when you grow up. I can see it now.'

"So I had to be content with sitting on the bed with the top blanket around me," bemoaned young Chaplin, adding: "And the next day Paulette told Dad and they joked about it."

Humor was one of the common denominators between Goddard and Chaplin. They often kidded each other to defuse potentially explosive situations.

Someone who was privy to their personal conversations recalls that after being at a party or a nightclub Chaplin might remark: "An awful lot of men were looking at you."

"The women weren't ignoring you, honeybun," Paulette would retort.

They were both experts at the art of indirect communication. Also, their relationship was less tense in this period because Paulette's professional attention was totally focused on obtaining the part of Scarlett O'Hara.

On a personal level, it would be impossible to point to a more open marriage involving two celebrities than the one that existed between Paulette Goddard and Charlie Chaplin. Paulette had made a trip to New York for the openings of *Young in Heart* and *Dramatic School*. And just as Chaplin had instantly become the sought-after glamour boy of Pebble Beach society, Paulette easily captured the attention of sophisticated New York café society. Pre-jet-set New York was the focal point of glamorous nightclubs and restaurants where formality was the order of the day. Men always wore black tie, women evening gowns and jewels. Luxury was the byword in appearance and no woman was more deluxe than Paulette Goddard. "She is so deliciously *expensive*-looking," wrote Cholly Knickerbocker, one of the leading New York society columnists.

Paulette made further social news when, through David Selznick, she met Jock Whitney and, through Whitney, his English cousin Lord Wakefield. Her name was romantically linked with Wakefield's and she made a trip with him and the Whitneys to Bermuda that fall. When they returned from their holiday, Paulette was sporting a spectacular new bracelet set with fine cabochon stones and diamonds.

Back in Hollywood, the actress was scheduled to make a final screen test for the role of Scarlett. Katharine Hepburn and Jean Arthur were still in the running, and Selznick, while discussing Hepburn's current negative box-office standing and Arthur's identification with other roles, noted: "Paulette Goddard also has plenty against her in the way of the public's attitude, but I think that when it comes time for a final decision, she at least has in her favor that she is not stale. For this reason, I think George [Cukor] ought to devote particular attention to the dramatic sections of the Goddard test."

As usual, Selznick was also thinking of his stars as assets to be used in his business dealings. He told an aide, "Warners have so far definitely refused to consider letting us have [Olivia] de Havilland for Melanie, but I think they might be persuaded, especially if we offer Goddard in trade, since I understand Jack Warner thinks well of Goddard."

By late November, 1938, others were still being tested but Goddard was high on the list. Selznick wrote to Dan O'Shea: "I have looked at the new Goddard test . . . practically daily since it arrived to see whether my first impression of the great improvement in her remained; and I must say that each time I see it I am more and more impressed. As much work as possible should be done with her. Incidentally, the point in her contract about which I have written you, concerning Chaplin's rights, should be straightened out immediately if it needs straightening out. It might be wise for you to make clear to Goddard that unless this point is straightened out (provided you feel it needs straightening) and unless we get a further extension of the contract to a full seven years, she is not going to play Scarlett."

Irene Selznick confirms that Goddard's tests were good, and she has remembered: "David called her in one day and told her it was no longer a joke. 'My God, I may really be stuck with you!' (They were rather inclined to bait each other.) But he said he had to clarify her legal status; was she actually married to Charlie? She turned quite haughty; how dare David ask her a question like that?"

Their dialogue went something like this: "I've got to ask a question like that," said Selznick. "There's too much riding on *Gone With the Wind*.

"We were married on a ship off the coast of China."

"Yes, I've read that too," Selznick shot back. "But what's the real story?"

"No one's ever dared talk to me that way," snapped the fiery Miss Goddard.

"No one's ever offered you the part of Scarlett O'Hara," said Selznick.

Paulette burst into tears. She told him that she was going to reveal a secret that she had been sworn never to tell. "Charlie and I were married by the mayor of Catalina."

Naturally, Selznick had his staff check this. It turned out that Catalina was an unincorporated section of Los Angeles County, and had no mayor. It was clear to Selznick that Paulette was not going to be able to produce a marriage license.

Although in later years it has been stated as fact that Paulette's marital status was the reason she lost the role of Scarlett O'Hara, it is not true. The proof: additional screen tests were made with Paulette. It was down to the wire. Production had to start in January, 1939. MGM had made it clear to Selznick that he had Gable for twenty weeks and not one day longer.

There was a last-minute burst of confusion and excitement when the New York *World-Telegram* announced that Paulette Goddard was "the definite choice": "Bang the fieldpiece, twang the lyre, for they've at last settled the Scarlett O'Hara question. It's Paulette Goddard whether you like it or not, the *World-Telegram* learned exclusively today.

"Thus ends two and a half years of frenzied speculation and argument over the greatest casting headache Hollywood has ever experienced.

"David O. Selznick . . . has made up his mind definitely this time."

But a day later there were retractions and apologies. The Selznick publicity department implied that MGM was behind the erroneous announcement, in an attempt to get extra publicity for their current feature, *Dramatic School*. MGM publicists countered that the Selznick people had "sacrificed Paulette" and that Jock Whitney may have been trying to force Selznick's hand.

In any event, there was an official denial on December 3: "No decision has been reached. . . . However, we don't deny that it might be Miss Goddard."

As late as December 20, 1938, George Cukor was filming an all-day test with Goddard. He was also filming tests with Jean Arthur, Joan Bennett and a newcomer to the Scarlett sweepstakes.

Paulette Goddard's version of the story years later: "Selznick had as good as decided on me. I gave a tennis party to celebrate. Laurence Olivier turned up with his girlfriend, Vivien Leigh. And that was that."

That was Paulette's version. But the real story was more complex.

Myron Selznick handled Olivier. The actor insisted that the agent meet his lover, Vivien Leigh, who wanted a crack at the Scarlett role. David Selznick and Cukor had already screened Leigh's film *A Yank at Oxford,* and had dismissed her. But Olivier prevailed on Myron to meet Leigh.

Some thought the reason Myron agreed to consider Vivien Leigh was that he expected her to be unsuitable and that might make Paulette an even stronger candidate. Myron told Olivier, "I warn you, Larry, I'm still pushing Scarlett O'Goddard, as Louella is calling Paulette."

But Myron liked what he saw when he met Leigh in the flesh; he forgot his allegiance to Paulette and arranged for a test for Vivien. He also introduced Leigh to brother David in a very dramatic fashion. He had brought her, along with Laurence Olivier and other dinner guests, to the shooting of the spectacular burning-of-Atlanta sequence on December 10. But David Selznick did not, as myth has it, decide then and there on Vivien Leigh for Scarlett merely by looking at her in the firelight.

He scheduled tests. In a letter to Irene regarding Vivien Leigh, Selznick wrote, "Shhhh: she's the Scarlett dark horse, and looks damned good. (Not for anybody's ears but your own: it's narrowed down to Paulette, Jean Arthur, Joan Bennett and Vivien Leigh.)"

Goddard and Leigh were the only two to receive Technicolor tests. "The day that I tested for it," recalled Vivien Leigh, "I remember the costumes being taken hot off somebody else's body and put on mine. It was quite unpleasant."

Around Christmastime, since Jock Whitney had given an ultimatum that shooting with the principals *had* to begin in two weeks, Selznick made his decision. It was based strictly on the obvious: the tests proved that Vivien Leigh was a superlative actress and the best choice for the role.

Losing the role of Scarlett was a heavy blow. In private Paulette cried her eyes out. But publicly she kept a philosophical, witty facade. She "forgave" Selznick. "Poor David," she quipped. "He was down to his last Whitney."

6

Chaplin was feverishly completing the Hitler script, now titled *The Dictator*. *Dictator* would be a sound film and presented enormous creative problems for Chaplin. He had never made a sound film. Writing the script was a challenge—there would have to be dialogue, not just titles and stage directions.

As for Paulette: "Although we were somewhat estranged," Chaplin said, "we were friends and still married." And Goddard's disappointment over losing Scarlett was to some degree offset, for surely *The Dictator*, Chaplin's first film in four years, would be as eagerly awaited as *Gone With the Wind*. But who was kidding whom? This wasn't the role of a tempestuous, strong-willed, gorgeous Southern belle. The *Dictator* character for Paulette was a little Jewish waif, Hannah (Chaplin's mother's name).

It would be months, however, before shooting would start on *The Dictator*, and in the meantime Paulette was anxious to keep busy. Myron got her the lead in an episode of the highest-rated radio series of the day, Cecil B. DeMille's "Lux Radio Theatre." On January 15, 1939, Paulette starred with Fred MacMurray in a radio adaptation of the movie *Front Page Woman*. Myron was fielding many offers from the major studios, all of whom wanted to put Goddard under long-term contract. And George Cukor signed her for a film he was unexpectedly doing at Metro. Cukor had been fired after only a few weeks as director of *Gone With the Wind*. He had allegedly been replaced because Gable felt he was favoring the female stars.

David Selznick had seen to it that MGM immediately signed Cukor to direct their film of Clare Boothe Luce's hit play *The Women*. It would be an all-woman, all-star cast. And only the industry's leading "women's director," Cukor, could be counted on to handle the assignment.

But while working at Metro was fun, the *Women* set was fraught with tension. The stars, Joan Crawford and Norma Shearer, disliked each other intensely and were rivals in real life just as they were in the film. It appeared that almost every actress in the production—Rosalind Russell, Paulette, Joan Fontaine, Mary Boland, Marjorie Main—was typecast, but especially Shearer, who played the ladylike society matron. Crawford played the hard-nosed shopgirl who steals Shearer's husband and "makes it" in society, and Paulette was cast as the likable but *very* knowledgeable showgirl.

Paulette had made concessions to be in this picture. She was not billed as a star; it was Shearer, Crawford and Russell who were on the top line. Paulette was co-starred, and her name came after Mary Boland's. Many of Paulette's contemporaries feel that the role Goddard played in the film was very revealing of her true self.

An extremely clever and effective sequence was devised for the opening credits of the picture. Each actress was, in turn, represented by a particular animal: Shearer's character was a doe (which was how many of the actress's fans would have mistakenly perceived her in real life); Crawford's a tiger; Roz Russell's a cat; and Paulette's, most appropriately, a fox.

When showgirl Goddard encounters bitch-wife Rosalind Russell at a Reno divorce ranch, Roz is furious when she learns Paulette is the other woman responsible for the breakup of her marriage. Roz threatens to get even by demanding a walloping divorce settlement from her unhappy husband. Goddard counters coolly, "I made Howard pay for what he wants—you're making him pay for what he doesn't want."

Cukor was the perfect director for Paulette Goddard—very creative, intelligent and articulate. There was no doubt in a performer's mind about what bits of business and nuances of performance this director wanted. And he never made an actress feel she couldn't deliver.

Cukor liked Paulette: "She had great personal charm and humor but was very nervous about not being good enough to hold her own with the other actresses. She realized they all had great experience. But Paulette had what they all had—the camera was her friend. Her eyes registered brightly on film and her face 'moved' in the right way, and that's what being a film star is all about."

The pace on *The Women* was fast and exciting. "On a Cukor picture, there's no rest. He keeps you so busy, you're spinning," noted Roz Russell. "You're rehearsing, you're running lines, you never get to go to your dressing room, or to the bathroom, somebody comes out and combs your hair right in the middle of the set, and it's great, it's stimulating."

While Shearer and Crawford clashed off the set, and Russell and Shearer had several near collisions, Paulette, in typical Goddard fashion, got along with everyone. She even endeared herself to the crew by arranging for platters of sandwiches to be on the set on days she was filming. And she was not a person who feared competition.

According to Joan Fontaine's recollections, on the set of *The Women* she and Paulette shared a hairdresser, a girl named Betty, a very attractive young woman. "Betty told me that Paulette had looked up at her from the makeup table, turned around, and said, 'You're pretty—why are you a hairdresser?' Paulette then told Betty that she, too, had had to work as a young girl, picking strawberries in the fields. One day, she straightened up and said to herself, 'I'm pretty, why am I doing this?'"

At this point in her career, Paulette was not reluctant to discuss her humble background—or to impart what she considered sage advice. After all, *she* had never had to pick strawberries again.

Paulette's pal Hedda Hopper, the woman who "knew her when," was now a famous columnist. But Hedda still occasionally worked as an actress and had a small role in *The Women*. Hedda's observation: "Paulette was a natural for a role in the picture. The cast wouldn't have been complete without this goddess." And Hedda noted that "while the picture was in production, life on the soundstage was as rugged as the lines being spoken." According to Hedda, all the stars, including Paulette, "carried their little sharp razors."

The sparks flew on the screen as well. At one point, Paulette's character asks Shearer's: "You want me to spit in Crystal's [Crawford's] eye for you? Where I spit, no grass grows."

At another point, Goddard's character states matter-of-factly: "Where I come from, women *have* to come out ahead."

Of the Adrian-designed costumes for all the stars, Paulette's were the least likely to become dated; they were simple, clinging dresses and tennis togs, for the most part, and one remarkably classic sari-style evening gown (in which her nipples were very clearly outlined by the filmy fabric). Some of the spectacular Goddard jewels (a diamond-and-ruby brooch and bracelet) glitteringly accented another outfit.

Cukor waited until all the other scenes had been shot before he scheduled the climactic fight scene between Paulette and Roz Russell. "The fight had to be realistic and you never know if someone will sprain something—or *really* anger the other actress and get carried away," noted Cukor. "That kind of thing, when someone gets hurt, can hold up production for days."

The fight scene was a highlight of the picture. It took three days to shoot. The two women, at a dude ranch, engage in physical combat, culminating in Russell biting a chunk out of Goddard's leg. Paulette was dressed in shorts, a blouse and boots, Roz in a formal, tailored suit and hat. There were several duplicate outfits for each actress, since the scene would have to be shot from different angles over the course of some days.

Russell threw herself into the fray, and she and Paulette "really roughed it up." It was worth it. The rushes on the scene drew guffaws and applause in the executive screening room. There was no doubt about it, *The Women* was a top production. But the role wasn't Scarlett O'Hara. Now decisions had to be made, and Paulette made them.

Paulette left Selznick International and signed a long-term contract with Paramount. It was obvious to her that she had no future with the Selznick studios. The producer would only lend her out and make money on her—as Chaplin had predicted.

Paulette's agreement with Paramount carried the same clause that her Selznick contract had: that she could make films for Chaplin. Charlie was still preparing *The Dictator,* and having his own problems with

Paramount. They owned the title, and did not want him to use it. So Chaplin ultimately changed the title of his film to *The Great Dictator*. Although the script was completed, he was now, in typical Chaplin fashion, having second thoughts about actually making the picture.

Paulette and Chaplin did make the social scene together: The Tropics Café, Sardi's, The Brown Derby (there were actually three Brown Derbies—a mini-chain before the term "restaurant chain" had been coined), the intimate Café Lamaze, Victor Hugo's. These were the elegant restaurants where stars and celebrities were supposed to be seen and photographed. One can imagine Chaplin's annoyance at being peered at and photographed constantly, but Paulette was in her element on these occasions, her arm entwined in Chaplin's as she smiled her dazzling smile for the cameras. Every outing called for Paulette to wear a different fur coat: silver fox, ermine, mink or sable, and all, of course, in the latest fashion. (When Paulette learned Jinx Falkenburg was going East to appear in a revue with Al Jolson, Goddard—generous to her friends, folklore to the contrary—lent Jinx three fur coats and insisted on wiring Jules Glaenzer, a vice president of Cartier, asking him to call Jinx when she arrived in Gotham.)

During this time, Garson Kanin met Chaplin, and Chaplin had taken a liking to the young actor-director-writer. One night, Chaplin, Paulette and Kanin were out having dinner together. Chaplin was wrestling with his usual dilemma—what to do about the *Dictator* project.

Kanin, of course, thought the project a brilliant one. But Chaplin kept saying, "I don't know. I just don't know. It's such a risk. Such a risk."

"Everything's a risk," Paulette said.

The conversation continued. Kanin kept urging Chaplin to proceed with the project. Finally, Chaplin told the young man, "Go away, leave me alone."

"No, no, don't go away," said Paulette. "I'm paying for dinner tonight, so sit still."

Kanin has recalled, "Chaplin began to eat, unhappily. Paulette winked at me, egging me on." And Kanin continued to expound on why the master should make *The Great Dictator*. His arguments were persuasive. And then, in Kanin's words, he told Chaplin: "It's inevitable, a foregone conclusion."

Kanin remembered, "There was a long pause. We finished dinner.

"'You may be right,' said Chaplin.

"The following day he called the picture off for good. The subject became taboo for several weeks."

Kanin's anecdote is interesting because it illustrates three points: one, that Chaplin endlessly discussed the ideas for his films with friends and associates; two, that even after he had a script he would continue to discuss the pitfalls of actually making the film: and three, at this point in their relationship, Paulette occasionally picked up the checks.

In March, Paulette appeared on Bob Hope's network radio program. It was no secret in the industry that Paulette (and many other actors and actresses) was uncomfortable doing radio, which was performed in front of a live studio audience. One report claimed that for the Hope broadcast Goddard seemed so petrified the comedian "had to nudge her to wait for laughs."

It was announced that Paulette would make her first film at Paramount with Hope: *The Cat and the Canary,* a mystery-comedy—the remake of an old Universal silent. The screenwriters had added lots of gags to accommodate the personalities of the two stars.

Working on the picture was fun for Paulette: no tension, as in *The Women*; no artistic problems, as in working with Chaplin. Director Elliott Nugent elicited just the right balance of light comedy and necessary fright from Paulette, who had to do a lot of screaming on cue. Basically, her role consisted of traipsing around in attractive outfits displaying her shapely legs, and expressing fright. Hope was playing the first of what would become his trademark character—a coward with false bravado.

One Saturday afternoon, Paulette and Chaplin were at the Santa Anita racetrack—the couple frequently went to the races. Bob Hope was there, and he went over to say hello. Paulette made the introduction: "You know Charles, don't you?"

Hope was starstruck. He wanted to babble about how he had idolized the genius and had won amateur contests doing imitations of Chaplin. He had even once stood on a street corner in New York for an hour and a half, waiting for Chaplin to come out of a restaurant. But at this meeting Hope "controlled himself." He didn't want to gush and be "just another fan."

"I really enjoyed *Modern Times,*" he told Chaplin enthusiastically.

The men briefly discussed that film, and then Hope, of course, noted, "And it's been great fun working with Paulette!"

"Young man," said Chaplin, "I've been watching the rushes of *The Cat and the Canary* every night. I want you to know that you're one of the best timers of comedy I have ever seen."

It was a compliment the thirty-five-year-old Hope would always remember. And it came at a crucial point: Paramount was not thrilled with Hope's potential as a screen star. The studio felt he was too much like Jack Benny. *The Cat and the Canary* would have to be a hit or Hope's film career was in trouble.

Besides the fun involved, being on the Paramount lot and being a contract player was for Paulette a new and exciting experience. The lot hummed with activity and other stars. It was at Paramount that Paulette soon came to know Fred MacMurray, Bing Crosby, Dorothy Lamour, Ray Milland and Joel McCrea. There were almost as many producers, directors and writers under contract as there were actors. People like Mitchell Leisen, Elliott Nugent, Preston Sturges, Billy Wilder, Don Hartman and Arthur Hornblow, Jr. DeMille, of course, had his own unit and was somewhat removed from the others. Edith Head was the studio's costume designer, and over the years she would design most of Paulette's on-screen wardrobe.

Miss Head was one of the people on the Paramount lot who were not charmed by the vivacious Miss Goddard. Edith has recalled the Goddard of this period as a rather callous young woman who taunted the young workers in the wardrobe department.

"She would carry around a cigar box filled with jewels. And then open the box and pass it around for the girls to see." But Head felt that Goddard's attitude was one of disdain, with an overtone of "Don't touch them—just look."

According to Miss Head, she never recalled any of the clothes she might have designed for Paulette. "I only remember her tormenting my staff with that damn cigar box full of jewels." Edith Head was a likable woman who got along with almost everyone on the lot. But two she didn't get on with were Paulette Goddard and Claudette Colbert.

Naturally, Paulette had her own dressing room at Paramount. Not long afterward, a few of the teenage actors on the lot, including former child star Jackie Cooper, discovered that there was a special attraction to Paulette's dressing room.

Cooper has recalled, "One of us kids discovered the Paulette Goddard scenic view. Pretty soon we all knew about it. Somebody had noticed that there was a vantage point with a direct, unimpeded, and total view into her dressing room. Furthermore—and this was the juicy part—Miss Goddard liked to loll around her dressing room topless. . . . Miss Goddard was a lady of fantastic construction. I know that I would find many excuses to take myself to that particular vantage point and just hope that she was there and in her usual state of astounding undress."

Perhaps Miss Goddard was simply too tired from working to care about what she wore in the privacy of her dressing room. Shooting films at Paramount was certainly different from working for Charlie or for Selznick. Now she was involved in a factory operation: set up the camera, shoot, cut and print, get ready for the next shot.

Considering that her professional life was now so hectic, it was surprising that at this time she decided to launch a new project at home. She was determined to redecorate Charlie's house. Egged on by her friend Sylvia Ashley Fairbanks—"Can't you get him to do *something* with this house?"—Paulette and Sylvia began to wear down Charlie's resistance. Undoubtedly they succeeded in part because Chaplin was now immersed in preproduction for *The Great Dictator*. He had little energy to fight Paulette and her suggestions for redecorating. But there were verbal battles about the cost of the various items that Paulette was ordering on an almost daily basis—including $25,000 chandeliers, modern furniture, new carpets for the entire house and new wallpaper and curtains.

Eventually, Goddard succeeded in doing over the entire first floor of the mansion. She even redecorated two of the three bedrooms on the second floor; only Chaplin's bedroom was left intact. He would not, under any circumstances, allow her to touch anything in it.

Meanwhile, *The Women* had been previewed, and talk around town was that it would be a huge hit. It was booked to open nationwide in late summer, and word on *The Cat and the Canary* was "It'll be big." From the rushes, the studio executives saw that Hope and Goddard made a winning pair in this type of film, and word was sent to the writers' department to scout around for another suitable script.

Paulette's star was on the rise. The Chaplin movie, slated to begin production that September, would certainly further elevate her standing.

Paulette now made a major miscalculation in dealing with Chaplin. She was usually right on target in her timing, but not this time. He was under incredible pressure. There had even been threats on his life, and it was rumored that a bodyguard stayed with him day and night. (Reports that Chaplin's meals were prepared under the scrutiny of a special detective were somewhat exaggerated.)

U.A. did not want him to proceed with *The Great Dictator,* and he continued to have his own doubts about the project. While he was deep in work changing the script and dealing with preproduction hassles, Paulette arrived at the studio one day and breezed into his dressing room. Chaplin was shocked at the interruption, but Paulette assured him that it was very important. Accompanying her was a young man, very well dressed, "who looked poured into his clothes," Chaplin later remembered. Chaplin waved the two of them away. This was no time to interrupt him.

"No, Charlie, this is very important," she repeated, and, uninvited, sat down. She motioned the young man to join her. He sat down as well. Paulette said, "This is my agent." Chaplin's eyebrows arched. He had an inkling of what was about to happen. Paulette glanced at the young agent—the implication was that he should take over negotiations. He was very businesslike, and informed Chaplin that although Miss Goddard's salary was agreeable, "We haven't straightened out with you, Mr. Chaplin, her billing, which should be featured seventy-five percent on all posters, and must—" Chaplin let the young man get no further. He jumped up and shouted, "What the hell is this? Don't you tell me what billing she's going to get. Get out! The pair of you!"

Chaplin amassed an impressive cast of supporting players for *The Great Dictator.* He, of course, would play the dual role of the little Jewish barber and the great dictator, Hynkel of Tomania. He had signed comedy star Jack Oakie to play the dictator of Bacteria. At first, Oakie's character was named Benzino Gasolini. Oakie thought it was a perfect name, but as they began shooting Chaplin came to him one day and said, "I'm changing your name in the film. It's too broad, Muscles." ("Muscles" was Chaplin's nickname for Oakie.)

"But, Charlie, Benzino Gasolini is a terrific burlesque on the man's name." He of course referred to Italian dictator Benito Mussolini.

Blonde and seductive-looking, Paulette Goddard was sixteen and a Ziegfeld Girl in the famed producer's 1927 Broadway extravaganza, *Rio Rita*.
Phototeque

Paulette was a Goldwyn Girl in Hollywood and appeared with Eddie Cantor and other Goldwyn Girls in *The Kid from Spain* (1932). Paulette is seated on the left. *Phototeque*

Goddard with her mentor and husband-to-be, Charles Chaplin, in *Modern Times*, 1936. *Phototeque*

The dramatic Paulette in a scene from *Modern Times*. *Phototeque*

The Little Tramp and The Gamine walking off into the sunset. The classic finale from *Modern Times*. *Movie Star News*

The glamorous off-screen Paulette with
authors James Hilton and H. G. Wells.
Phototeque

George Gershwin. The genius
wanted to marry Paulette. (She
was Mrs. Chaplin at the time.)

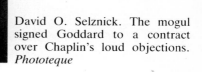

David O. Selznick. The mogul
signed Goddard to a contract
over Chaplin's loud objections.
Phototeque

Paulette (center) in the 1938 film, *Dramatic School*, flanked by Virginia Grey and seventeen-year-old starlet Lana Turner. *Phototeque*

The famous fight scene between Paulette and Rosalind Russell in George Cukor's film of *The Women*, 1939. *Phototeque*

With her soon-to-be ex-husband in *The Great Dictator*, 1940.
Goddard had just lost the role of Scarlett O'Hara to Vivien
Leigh.

With Chaplin in late 1940. The marriage was almost over. *Phototeque*

Diego Rivera. The painter and Paulette became good friends.

With Robert Preston in Cecil B. De-Mille's *Northwest Mounted Police*, 1940. The "Ciro's incident" had occurred the night before the picture's west coast preview. *Phototeque*

With Fred Astaire in *Second Chorus*, 1941. Goddard's dancing was fine. *Phototeque*

The "Second Chorus" principles—left to right: Charles Butterworth, Astaire, Burgess Meredith—the man who would become Paulette's third husband—and Artie Shaw. *Phototeque*

With Bob Hope in *Nothing But the Truth*, 1941. The duo made three hit films together. *Phototeque*

With James Stewart in *Pot o' Gold*, 1941. There was surprisingly little chemistry between the two stars. *Phototeque*

With Olivia de Havilland in director Mitchell Leisen's 1941 hit, *Hold Back the Dawn*. Goddard was so nervous that "her upper lip trembled." *Phototeque*

"No, Muscles," said Chaplin. "Mussolini hasn't joined the Axis yet, and nobody can tell what move he is going to make. For all we know, he may even join the Allies."

War had already broken out in Europe. The Nazis had invaded Poland, but for the time being Italy was remaining neutral. Chaplin was in a dilemma. He was about to make a comedy about a man who had just started a world war. But it was too late to turn back.

Chaplin solved the Gasolini problem by calling Oakie's character Napaloni. Chaplin had always wanted to make a film about Napoleon. Others in the cast of *The Great Dictator* were Henry Daniell, playing Garbitsch, a character based on the sinister Joseph Goebbels; and stout comedian Billy Gilbert as Herring, an obvious parody of Goering. Paulette was playing Hannah, an innocent young Jewish laundress in the ghetto. Again the character was a gamine, and again she was unglamorous, with tattered dress and uncoiffed hair. Quite a departure from the recent drop-dead glamour saturating *The Women* and even *The Cat and the Canary*.

Others in the *Dictator* cast were Chaplin buddies Carter DeHaven, portraying an ambassador; and Chester Conklin. (Chaplin was very loyal to old friends.) He had even hired Luis Buñuel, then ostracized by the film community, to help on the script. Reginald Gardiner was playing the key role of a pilot who saves the barber's life.

Gardiner has observed that there were striking differences in Chaplin's personality on the days he was playing the barber and on the days he was playing the dictator. "When he was in that uniform, he became severe, cold. When he was playing the little Jewish barber, he was his usual warm self."

Fortunately for Paulette, she was not in any scenes with the dictator. But she still had plenty of opportunity to view her volatile husband in action.

On this film, Chaplin could no longer work in his customary, leisurely way. The unions had taken over the industry, and now there were eight-hour days plus overtime if a producer went beyond the specified hours. Chaplin didn't mind paying his crew overtime, but he did mind the restrictions that he felt the new situation imposed. He hated the fact that he had to add people to his crew whom he obviously did not need, such as extra makeup artists, script girls, grips, et al.

Jack Oakie has recalled: "Although Charlie was extravagant with film and time, he sure watched his purse strings in every other way."

"Who are all these people?" Chaplin would ask, looking at the dozens of people crowded onto the set. "Who are all these people?" he asked Oakie over and over again.

"You have to have them, Charlie," Oakie answered.

Chaplin continued to balk. Alf Reeves, who ran the studio, and Syd Chaplin, who was Charlie's business adviser, kept explaining, "It's the law, Charlie. If we don't have them, they'll close down production." It further infuriated Chaplin that when he went out onto the sidewalk in front of the studio to shoot, it was considered location shooting and the studio had to provide lunch for the cast and crew.

"We don't need these people, we don't need these people," Chaplin kept muttering. "Why, on *Modern Times* the only crew was one cameraman, one propman. Who needs a script girl? The script was in my head."

As in the past, Chaplin never ventured far from the studio to do his exterior shooting. The setup one day was on Hollywood Boulevard, only a few blocks from a new Woolworth's department store. It was a scene with Paulette, and Chaplin told her, "Your costume isn't quite right. Get a cotton apron."

Chaplin undoubtedly assumed that someone on the crew would simply buy an apron at the nearby five-and-ten. Paulette asked Teddy Tetrick, the wardrobe man, to get an appropriate apron. Minutes later, the apron was on the set in time for the first setup of the morning. Chaplin was delighted with the apron; it was just the right touch for Paulette's costume.

After a week or so of shooting Paulette's scenes, Chaplin moved on to others. But then, a month later, after looking at rushes, Chaplin decided Paulette's scenes needed a few retakes. When Paulette appeared on the set for the new shots, Chaplin asked, "Where's the apron?"

"They don't have the apron in wardrobe," Paulette told him.

"What do you mean they don't have the apron? You don't know what you're talking about. It's that little old-looking cotton apron! You wore it in this scene," he reminded her.

"I know, Charlie. But the wardrobe department doesn't have that apron anymore."

"Get that wardrobe man over here!" Chaplin's ire was rising; it was apparent that he was trying to control his temper. "How can an apron disappear?"

Tetrick rushed out to the set. "Yes, sir?"

"I want Miss Goddard to wear the little cotton apron she had on in this scene."

"Oh, well, we don't have that apron, sir," Tetrick said meekly.

Chaplin was nonplussed. His voice lowered and the words came slowly. "You did have the apron."

"Yes, sir. We did have it. But I thought you were through using it so I sent it back."

"Sent it back?" Chaplin was shouting now. "What do you mean you sent it back? Where did you get it?"

"Western Costume, sir. It belongs to Western Costume."

"Western Costume!" Charlie bellowed even louder.

"Well, they were so good about sending it over by special messenger when we needed it, I thought it would be nice to send it right back just as soon as we were through using it."

"Western Costume!" Charlie yelled again. "Western Costume? You could have walked across the street and bought an apron for fifteen cents!" He gestured wildly at the nearby Woolworth's. "For fifteen cents the apron would have belonged to us, not to Western Costume!"

There was no alternative: they had to have the same apron, which ended up costing the Chaplin studio more than two hundred dollars in rental fees. Some thought Tetrick would be fired—but the young man was engaged to marry Sydney Chaplin's daughter Betty. His job was secure.

Paulette was used to these outbursts. Life with Chaplin was turbulent. Stories such as this were always cited to demonstrate the millionaire Chaplin's attitude about money. But it should be remembered that while he was not a spendthrift, he was hardly a miser. He risked his own—not investors'—money on his films. And he (like Disney and other geniuses) did not care how long it took or how expensive it was to achieve perfection.

Perhaps this period was made more difficult because Paulette was still redecorating their house. The Chaplins were wrangling over what Paulette was spending to make the mansion "a showplace," and there

89

were further disagreements when Chaplin directed his wife on the soundstages.

People who were there say that Chaplin brought Goddard "close to the breaking point." There is no doubt that, in retrospect, in her two films for him, Chaplin elicited fine performances from Paulette. But it was a taxing situation for both of them. One *Dictator* scene had Paulette scrubbing a floor. Chaplin made her do the scene for hours until he felt she'd got it right.

Charlie did not find Paulette a willing student on this picture. She felt that he embarrassed her in front of cast and crew. And, unlike work at Paramount, this was not a four- or six-week shooting schedule. *The Great Dictator* was to be in production for six months.

In the meanwhile, *The Cat and the Canary* opened to highly favorable reaction. The box-office take was excellent. *The Women,* as well, was a big hit all over the country. With *The Great Dictator* in the wings, Paulette was riding high.

Collier's, a popular, widely read and respected family magazine, ran an article, with beautiful pictures of Goddard, under the title "The Perils of Paulette." According to the article, by Kyle Crichton, Paulette was "the most famous non-actress in the world." Even though Paulette had lost the part of Scarlett, everything was "all right. The Selznicks and Chaplins are still good friends. The Selznicks still borrow baking soda; the Chaplins go over for a drink before dinner."

Anyone who believed this would also believe what the article had to say about Paulette's background. From the interview with the star, Mr. Crichton had reconstructed Paulette's past. "It seems that her mother fell in love with her second husband, Mr. Levy, and ran away from Mr. Goddard. Then came a battle for the custody of Paulette, the baby, and Mrs. Levy defied the order of the court in the matter of the custody and fled with her to Canada."

As innocuous as this piece of information seemed at the time, it would have unexpected ramifications for Paulette. One man who read the article was her father, Joseph Levy. He did not appreciate being referred to as her stepfather. And he was prepared to tell the world that his daughter could not get away with such a fabrication.

7

Shortly before Christmas, 1939, Doug Fairbanks, Sr., and his wife visited the set of *The Great Dictator*. Chaplin was delighted to see Doug—the men hadn't seen much of each other over the past couple of years. Fairbanks was out of filmmaking, had aged considerably and was spending most of his time traveling.

It was a severe blow to Chaplin when, a few days later, he learned that Fairbanks had died suddenly of a heart attack. Fairbanks was only fifty-six. (Chaplin was fifty.) The death of his beloved friend was a crushing blow to Charlie. Production on *The Great Dictator* was temporarily shut down. And, though Chaplin loathed funerals, he agreed to be a pallbearer at the rites for Fairbanks.

Christmas that year was very subdued at the Chaplin mansion. Charlie hinted that when shooting was completed on *Dictator* he might take the boys and Paulette on a cruise. Charlie, Jr., and Syd were now fourteen and thirteen, respectively. The youngsters were budding Lotharios and, occasionally kidding around, they would, according to Charlie, Jr.'s, recollections, "grab Paulette and kiss her just for practice."

"'Oh, that's a terrible kiss,' Paulette would laugh, wiping off our

91

clumsy attempts. And then, addressing herself to Dad, she would say, as always, 'Charlie, your sons are getting more like you every day.'"

After the holidays Chaplin resumed shooting on the film. While Paulette's role in *Dictator* was an important one, it wasn't a large part and permitted the actress ample time for other filmmaking activity.

At Paramount, attention was centered on the upcoming Cecil B. DeMille picture, *Northwest Mounted Police*. A search was on for an actress to play one of the key roles. This would be DeMille's first full-length feature in Technicolor, and as usual he had assembled an impressive cast. Gary Cooper and Preston Foster were playing the male leads, Madeleine Carroll the female lead. But the second female lead was the plum: a showy part of a tempestuous half-breed, Loupette Corbeau. In the story, the character has a smoldering affair with a young Mountie. That part was already cast; it would be played by DeMille favorite Robert Preston.

Many were in competition for the role of Loupette, including Marlene Dietrich (now almost forty), Simone Simon and Rita Hayworth, a twenty-one-year-old actress under contract at Columbia. Rita was making big strides in her career and her Latin look made her a natural for the part. But Rita didn't have the behind-the-scenes clout offered by Myron Selznick. Besides, Paulette was already on the Paramount lot and had made it her business to get to know the right people in the DeMille unit. Goddard's talent for public relations once again paid off. She sent DeMille frequent notes, along the lines of "Are you going to give me that part?"

DeMille, a stickler for technical authenticity in every aspect of script and production, was astonished when Paulette informed him: "By the way, C. B., Loupette, the character in the script, means little he-wolf. Shouldn't you change it to Louvette, little she-wolf?" This sent DeMille's staff into a veritable frenzy. Paulette was right and the change was made.

Although impressed with Goddard's knowledge and persistence, DeMille was still not sold on her for the part. Paulette went to work behind the scenes. She conspired with Wally Westmore, head of makeup at Paramount, with Natalie Visart, DeMille's costume designer, and with associate producer Bill Pine to transform her appearance into that of the character's.

One day DeMille's key personal secretary, Florence Cole, knocked on the door of her boss's office and announced, "Louvette is here to see you."

C. B. was not used to pranks, and certainly not from someone of Miss Coles' serious nature. He said, "Send Louvette in."

In DeMille's words: "Florence stepped back from the door, and a dark girl, with eyes that could smolder or melt, came in, made up as a half-breed and costumed as such a girl would dress on the wild Canadian frontier in the eighteen-eighties."

Paulette, carrying a bullwhip, slunk over to DeMille's desk and put her foot up on it. (Paulette had been informed of the director's penchant for small feet.)

DeMille recalled, "She gave me one insolent look and said, 'You teenk you wan beeg director, hah? Me, Louvette, show you!'

"That was enough; Paulette Goddard had the part."

Carrying this off had been no simple task. DeMille's office wasn't a light, airy, friendly place. Wood paneling, stained-glass windows and deep carpeting created a somewhat somber atmosphere. Antique weapons were mounted on the walls and the director's throne-like chair and desk were on a platform so he could stare down at you. The director often wore riding breeches and boots. His penetrating eyes did not sparkle with humor. But DeMille always admired actors who went to great lengths to convince him that they were right for a part. Unlike many other directors, who reveled in lengthy discussions with actors concerning motivation and characterization, DeMille preferred actors who simply performed on cue.

Before production started, there was time for Paulette to squeeze in yet another comedy-mystery with Bob Hope, *The Ghost Breakers*. Sydney Chaplin visited the *Ghost Breakers* set. The boy was asked who his favorite stars were. He mentioned several men.

"Don't you like any of the women stars?" a reporter asked.

"Well, I like her, my step-mama," he said, pointing to Paulette—further confirmation that the Chaplins were wed.

Somehow Paulette managed to find time to do a benefit for Finnish War Relief with Liz (Mrs. Jock) Whitney, and to spend time with her mother.

It was announced that Paramount was lending Paulette to RKO, where she would play the second female lead in Sam and Bella

Spewack's screenplay *Woman Overboard*. Irene Dunne would play the lead, and Leo McCarey was producing. The director: Garson Kanin. This loan-out never materialized. (Gail Patrick played the unsympathetic part in the Dunne-Cary Grant starrer, which was ultimately titled *My Favorite Wife*.)

Meanwhile, shooting on *Dictator* had resumed—with a vengeance. Chaplin later revealed that even before he and Paulette began filming *The Great Dictator,* both knew that their marriage was over. But others say that the marriage was hanging on and it was the tension and arguments during the filming that delivered the death blow.

Another blow occurred when Paulette's name unexpectedly—and unflatteringly—hit the headlines. Paulette's father, Joseph Levy, was irate; he told the world that his daughter had concocted a fanciful story about her past, and, to Paulette's surprise and dismay, he sued her—and *Collier's* magazine—for a whopping $150,000, claiming he had been libeled.

The press had a field day. Family troubles plaguing movie stars were surefire media material. Levy was living in upstate New York, and had been working in Syracuse as a salesman for one of the motion-picture companies when the *Collier's* issue appeared. He now claimed the article had damaged his reputation and caused him to lose his health and his job.

Collier's defense was simple: Miss Goddard herself had furnished the information in the article. The New York State Supreme Court sought Goddard for questioning, and Paulette soon found herself facing contempt action for failing to appear in court.

A bevy of lawyers on both coasts began working on her behalf to solve the matter. The suit was to drag on for several months.

After completing *Dictator, Ghost Breakers* and *Northwest Mounted Police,* Paulette was resting up in Arrowhead when a new storm broke. Her father was suing her directly and demanding $150 per week support. Paulette immediately called columnist Louella Parsons and told her: "I've never known my father. He left my mother when I was a very small child and never contributed to my support. Mother took care of me until I was fourteen, when I went out and started earning a living for both of us. I pay him $75 a week, which should be adequate."

Paulette did not explain why she was paying anything at all to a man she had never known, and she made it sound as if she had been paying him $75 a week for some time. The facts subsequently revealed that she had been doing so for less than a month. In order to settle the original suit, she had agreed to this condition. But after only three payments, Levy had sued again, claiming that since he had been earning $150 a week at his job, he saw no reason why he should not get $150 from his daughter. After all, she was earning thousands of dollars per week. Not to mention the fact that Paulette maintained her mother in a Beverly Hills home and gave her $250 a week spending money.

"Paulette has the sympathy of Hollywood," noted Louella.

In subsequent years, Paulette continued to deny that Levy was her father. In her charming, noncommittal way, she would often confuse the issue. Six years after the suit, a reporter asked, "Is your real name Paulette Goddard or Pauline Levy?" She replied, "Of course it's Goddard."

The reporter continued: "Didn't Mr. Levy win that suit?" Paulette said, "Wasn't that silly? All he got was thirty-five dollars a week, just thirty-five dollars a week. I thought that was so funny."

But the reporter persisted: "What was your mother's maiden name?" Paulette replied calmly, "Goddard."

When the reporter pointed out that her mother's maiden name was Hatch, Alta M. Hatch, Paulette said, "Oh, yes, of course. That was before she married my father, J. R. Goddard."

In the spring of 1940, in the midst of the Levy suit, Paulette fled to Mexico. *Look* magazine, and the Paramount publicity department, had come up with an idea to publicize *Ghost Breakers*. Paulette would go off on a vacation with her mother and prove that she could visit Mexico for one week with one suitcase and spend only one hundred dollars.

Look photographer Earl Theisen was assigned to accompany the women and record it all for a two-part article. Pan Am provided the travel in exchange for prominent mention in the piece, and Paulette and Alta were to be the guests of the fashionable La Reforma Hotel, which would also receive its share of publicity.

At first there were no problems. Paulette was photographed doing all the touristy things—visiting the floating gardens of Xochimilco, famed restaurants, cathedrals, monasteries, the tourist meccas of Taxco and Cuernavaca. And of course she was photographed attending a bullfight.

PAULETTE

But Paulette, it was said, had had her own motives for visiting Mexico City. She was intent on having her portrait painted by the leading Mexican artist of the day, Diego Rivera, the artist whose talent George Gershwin had made her aware of.

Goddard liked the idea of having her portrait painted. She had gotten used to sitting for portraits. Paramount had hired Salvadore Covarubia de Regil to do a surrealistic portrait of her for *The Ghost Breakers*. Like many beautiful women in Hollywood, Goddard enjoyed looking at herself—on screen and in photographs and paintings. She candidly observed on many occasions that any person who didn't find himself the most interesting person in his life "was simply not being truthful."

In Mexico, Paulette had no trouble convincing Diego Rivera to paint her. Indeed, the famed artist was delighted. Rivera, in his sixties, loved beautiful young women and, although noted for his naturalistic style and his murals, he often did portraits. He had painted a stunning portrait of Dolores del Rio, Mexico's internationally known movie star, in 1938.

Not only did Rivera paint Paulette, but the Hungarian artist Irene Borjus, with whom Rivera was sharing a studio (they were reputedly lovers), also painted the actress at this time.

The Rivera house, in the Mexico City suburb of Coyoacán, was on three levels and had a number of patios and, of course, lots of windows. It actually was the house of Frida Kahlo, Rivera's estranged wife, who was a noted painter herself.

Rivera had a fascinating background. After attaining some recognition in Mexico, he had been sent as a young man to study in Paris. There he became friends with painters such as Picasso and Modigliani. And in Paris he met Angeline Beloff, a Russian who became his first common-law wife. In the early twenties Rivera returned to Mexico to do murals and frescoes. Diego Rivera had been a member of the Communist Party from his days in prewar Paris until 1929, when the Party expelled him.

He had been commissioned to do murals in New York's new Rockefeller Center in 1933 (he'd done a series of murals in Detroit the previous year), and had angered many when it appeared that in one of the murals he had used the face of Lenin. The people in charge covered Rivera's Rockefeller Center murals and later destroyed them.

Diego Rivera and controversy seemed inseparable partners. In short order, Paulette Goddard unexpectedly found herself involved in a hazardous real-life adventure of the kind that most leading ladies played only on screen. The spring of 1940 was a tense period in Mexico City. Communist leader Leon Trotsky, exiled from Russia, was living in the city and attempts had been made on his life.

Though he had been instrumental in getting permission for Trotsky to come to Mexico, Rivera later openly argued with him, and he was now a suspect. The current government of Mexico did not look favorably on Rivera and others whom they considered part of the left-wing community of liberal artists and intellectuals. Rivera was put under house arrest.

At the time, Paulette was out of Mexico City visiting other places. When she returned, she discovered that Rivera's house was surrounded by police. But, unknown to her, Rivera had escaped by underground tunnel and was in hiding at a nearby inn.

It was almost like the scenario of a B movie. Rivera had somehow managed to get through to the American consul. (The artist had been dealing with U.S. officials for necessary visas, since he had been commissioned to do murals for the Golden Gate Exposition in San Francisco and was planning a trip to the States.)

The story goes that the American consul got in touch with Paulette and gave her a message from the artist. She was to go to his house to pick up "the twenty-five paintings she had bought." Of course she hadn't bought any paintings, but Paulette realized what the message meant: this was the artist's attempt to salvage some of his work, which was being impounded by the government. As an American citizen and a famous actress, Goddard might have easier access to Rivera's guarded house than would his other friends.

Paulette charmed her way through the police lines (something probably much easier to do than it had been to charm Cecil B. DeMille) and managed to take the paintings, under the pretense that she had purchased them and was picking up her purchases. From this point on, Paulette herself was under police surveillance.

Goddard and Rivera quickly left Mexico City by plane and landed in Dallas, Texas. From Dallas, they flew to Los Angeles. By this time, the press had been alerted to the "escape." When the plane landed in Los Angeles, Rivera told the press only that Paulette had "helped me escape from Mexico with my life."

Goddard smiled and nodded but wouldn't say a word. Paulette left the plane in Los Angeles, and Rivera continued on to San Francisco and his professional commitment.

Within weeks the story had taken on ridiculous proportions. It was printed that Paulette and other Rivera chums had clandestinely hired automobiles in Mexico City, driven by night, crossed the border into Texas and then gone on to Dallas, where Rivera boarded the plane for Los Angeles. This is a fabrication. The drive, thousands of miles over unpaved roads, would have taken a week. In fact, the two had left Mexico City and arrived in Los Angeles within twenty-four hours.

Rivera biographers subsequently downplayed Paulette's contribution, saying that Rivera had left from Mexico City's International Airport for San Francisco with much press coverage and fanfare. This is not true either. The couple did fly from Mexico City, but not with publicity. Rivera's chauffeur and one of his servants had been detained by the Mexican police, and there was no doubt that during a lull in the investigation the artist thought it best to take flight for San Francisco, where he would be employed.

In any event, in 1940 the whole adventure produced wonderful publicity for the Exposition, for Rivera and, not least of all, for Paulette. Headlines such as SCREEN STAR RESCUES ARTIST—and—GODDARD, THE ACTRESS, AIDS RIVERA'S FLIGHT—contributed a new dimension to the Goddard persona.

To Paulette's credit, this was not merely a lark or a publicity stunt. She and Rivera had become friends and would remain so through the next decade. (A fascinating footnote: While painting the murals in San Francisco, Rivera was joined by his wife, Frida Kahlo. He used Frida as the model for a main figure in one of his frescoes, but the figure had Paulette Goddard's face. Other sources state the mural depicted Paulette holding hands with Rivera, whose back is to Frida. And both Paulette and Rivera also embrace the Tree of Life. She was dressed in white and her gorgeous legs were shown to advantage. In his autobiography, Rivera said Goddard represented "American girlhood shown in friendly contact with a Mexican man.")

Shortly after Paulette's return to Hollywood, Walter Winchell claimed that the government was "quizzing" her regarding Rivera. But there was never any follow-up to this or evidence that any government official spoke to her. Perhaps it was the columnist's way of suggesting to the government—and the public—that he thought Paulette *should* be quizzed. Insiders knew that the right-wing Winchell sometimes reported what he wanted to happen instead of what had actually occurred.

Because of her relationship with Chaplin, Goddard had been of some minor interest to the F.B.I. After this international incident with the artist and political activist Rivera, the F.B.I. concerned itself with Goddard's own political views and activities.

Back in Hollywood, Paulette immediately went into another picture. The dancing lessons she had taken were going to be put to the test. Goddard would be Fred Astaire's partner in *Second Chorus*. It had been news when Paulette "talked" for the first time on screen; now it would be heralded that "Paramount has the first picture in which Paulette Goddard *dances!*" And the studio would devise the ad line: "Fred's Best Yet! 'Cause He's Got Paulette!"

This was to be a trendy "swing" musical featuring popular musician Artie Shaw. Astaire was a fan of Shaw's and was doing the picture primarily to be able to dance to Shaw's famous brand of swing.

Paulette's role wasn't demanding in the acting department; it was the lightweight sort of thing she had done so well with Bob Hope. But the dancing—that was another matter. The Astaire-Goddard production number together was titled, "I Ain't Hep to That Step but I'll Dig It," and it was intricate. One fanciful account said that it wasn't coincidental that Paulette made sure she was at the rehearsal rooms when Astaire was preparing his own routines. According to this tale, "Within three days Astaire was teaching her." Other sources, however, said that he worked with her—"like a dog"—from the beginning.

Writer-publicist Leo Guild was also on the scene, and states that Astaire labored through artistic torture "with a lovely girl, with a breathtaking figure, who couldn't dance and somehow resisted every attempt to break down her handicap."

Goddard later said, "I'll never try dancing on the screen again. I was determined that the dance would be good. Imagine me dancing with Astaire. And I guess it was all right. We did it just once, one Saturday morning for the cameras. Just one take. I'm glad it was all right, because I couldn't have done it again. I couldn't possibly ever have done it again." (Despite her apprehension, the dance number, viewed today, is not only totally professional; it is good.)

The other male lead in *Second Chorus* was a young stage-trained actor, Burgess Meredith. Meredith had the kind of background that awed Hollywoodites, moguls and stars alike. He was a Broadway star. His most successful play had been *Winterset,* in 1935, and that had brought him to Hollywood for the film version. Being a sought-after Broadway actor gave Meredith the freedom few others had in Hollywood. He didn't need to, and wouldn't, sign any long-term contracts. He had had a supporting role in the Gable-Shearer MGM film version of *Idiot's Delight* in 1939 (and had even dated Norma Shearer). Recently he had scored well with the critics in the film version of *Of Mice and Men.*

Like Chaplin, Meredith was short—about five feet seven inches. Accounts of the day described "Buzz"—or "Bugs"—Meredith as a man with ginger-colored hair and a pointed face that might "reasonably belong to a jockey." He was a person who wore crumpled clothes, and people said his nicknames suited his offhand appearance.

A publicist who knew Meredith well states that Meredith's reputation was as "quite a Casanova, a cocksman, both in his Broadway days and in Hollywood. The stories are legion." But at the time he met Paulette there was hardly an opportunity for Goddard to take Meredith's attentions seriously.

The F.B.I.'s interest in Goddard was piqued when her name began appearing in reports concerning others they thought suspect. The famed photographer Cecil Beaton was accused of being a Fifth Columnist, and J. Edgar Hoover was personally alerted that when Beaton was in Hollywood that summer, he did several sittings with Paulette. Any association, however nonpolitical, with someone like Beaton kept Paulette suspect in the minds of the F.B.I.

Goddard and Bob Hope had another hit in *The Ghost Breakers,* released that June. As was the practice of the day, she did a publicity tour for the film.

Regardless of Paulette's reputation for collecting famous men, a man didn't have to be a mogul, a movie star, a painter or a musician to capture Paulette's interest. In mid-1940, in Chicago for the opening of *Ghost Breakers,* the star met a handsome young college man. He was witty and sophisticated and a member of a well-known Illinois family.

100

PAULETTE

The young man, "Chuck" Percy, was twenty years old and belonged to one of the popular fraternities of the University of Chicago. Paulette was twenty-nine and taken with Percy. She invited him to be her escort for the three nights she was in Chicago. (She was staying at the Drake Hotel.)

Years later, Percy, by then a well-known United States senator, enjoyed recounting the weekend and telling friends how he remembered sitting in the Drake's Pump Room sipping champagne with the glamorous Goddard. "We even called Charlie Chaplin to say hello," recalled Senator Percy.

Paulette was at the time eagerly and nervously awaiting release of her two big pictures: *Northwest Mounted Police* and *The Great Dictator.* Chaplin's postproduction work on *Dictator* had been veiled in secrecy. *Life* magazine announced that it had obtained photos of the shooting of the film. Chaplin threatened a suit and the magazine backed down. Other news concerned threats against him: supposedly, "interested powers" were out to sabotage the film's release. Although Chaplin later revealed that most of these rumors were exaggerated, the stories helped to maintain eager anticipation of the picture.

When Chaplin was finally satisfied with *Dictator,* it was booked into two theaters in New York, the Astor and the Capitol. Its widely heralded première would be in mid-October.

Chaplin was truly worried about how the public would accept a comedy about Hitler. France had already fallen to the Axis powers. Italy had joined the war on the side of Germany, and it seemed that all of Europe was about to fall to the Nazis.

But in Hollywood it was the drama of whether Chaplin and Goddard would remain together that filled the columns. Louella Parsons was predicting that, no matter what their style of living, Paulette and Charlie *would* stay together: "There are many intimations that Paulette has passed out of Charlie's life—Paulette will have her interludes. And Charlie moments of indifference, but you can always be sure they will kiss and make up."

An alleged "interlude" that would hardly elicit feelings of indifference was on the immediate horizon for Paulette. It would rock Hollywood and become legend.

8

Virtually every personality who achieves stardom is plagued by some event—dogged by at least one oft-repeated scandalous tale—that builds, over the years, into mythical proportions. Paulette Goddard is no exception. Indeed, hers is one of the most colorful.

The setting was one of the most glamorous nightclubs in town: Ciro's, a playground familiar to movie fans all over the world. Major movie magazines in the late thirties and forties featured photo spreads of top stars, formally dressed, glittering with jewels, gathered to socialize and have fun at Ciro's. What New York's Studio 54 was to the Manhattan social scene in the early seventies, Ciro's was to Hollywood in 1940.

The club literally looked like—and created the feeling of—the fantasy nightclubs that existed only on the screen. It was a perfect setting in which tinseltown's gods and goddesses could see one another and be seen by others.

One entered the club through glass doors—a velvet rope kept the nonfamous and noninfluential off to one side. A celebrity, however, walked directly to the plush staircase that descended to the tables and the dance floor below. The stairway permitted people to make an entrance. One paused at the top of the stairway so the crowd below could look up and take it all in—then, a slow walk down the stairs to prolong the impact. These entrances were worthy of a similar scene from a lavish film.

Many an evening, the shimmering figures of women such as Lana Turner, Hedy Lamarr, Sonja Henie, Loretta Young, Madeleine Carroll, Constance Bennett, Marlene Dietrich—and, of course, Paulette Goddard—caused the jaded audience below to "oooh!" and "ahhh!" as the beauties made their way down to the crowd.

Paulette's flashing jewels always caused comment: "Chaplin gave her those bracelets!" "*Look* at those diamonds!"

The maître d' would lead the goddess and her escort to a choice table in a choice section of the room. A lady looked straight ahead, never glancing left or right, until seated. Then etiquette permitted a careful look around the room and a vivacious smile and wave of acknowledgment to friends (who had already gone through the same ritual).

It was exciting and fun to go to Ciro's. There was no way of sneaking into the place. If you were at Ciro's, people *saw* you at Ciro's. A lot of people saw Paulette and director Anatole Litvak at Ciro's that fateful night in 1940.

Litvak was a colorful figure in his own right. He had directed such notable films as *Mayerling,* with Charles Boyer and Danielle Darrieux; *Tovarich,* with Boyer and Claudette Colbert; and *The Woman I Love,* starring Miriam Hopkins. Hopkins was Litvak's wife at the time they made the movie. He had also directed a big Bette Davis hit, *The Sisters.* (Davis and Litvak subsequently had a romance and made another film together, *All This and Heaven Too.*) He was currently directing Joan Fontaine and Tyrone Power in a picture for Darryl Zanuck at 20th Century-Fox.

The Russian-born Litvak, who had studied at the Moscow Art Theatre, was a passionate, intense artist of the cinema and a connoisseur of women. Everybody in town knew that Litvak was at the time smitten with Paulette Goddard—indeed, he wanted to marry her.

There are many versions of the Goddard-Litvak encounter that night at Ciro's. Known facts are that they were at Ciro's; they had dinner; they had imbibed quite a bit of alcohol and they were in a fun-loving mood. From this point on, one has a smorgasbord of gossip to choose from.

One account was that supposedly a shoulder strap of Paulette's gown slipped—or broke—and the gown dropped quickly, exposing a bit of her breast. In a gentlemanly fashion, Litvak pulled up the edge of the tablecloth to shield Paulette while she repaired the strap. Paulette, in a spirit of fun, slid under the table and a few moments later Litvak slid under the table with her. Or so this story goes.

The management, of course, was instantly on the scene and is alleged to have surrounded the table with a screen. Then, continues this version of the story, Litvak and Paulette were quickly escorted out of the main dining room to the cloakroom, where the giggling Miss Goddard swooned onto a settee. Litvak went to a phone booth. Paulette, in a playful mood, squeezed into the booth with him. Later accounts implied that the actress and the director were intimate both on the settee and in the phone booth.

There are other versions of the story. One is that back in the main room Paulette was under the table while Litvak remained seated. Another version was that Litvak was under the table while Paulette remained seated.

Jean Negulesco, Rumanian-born film director, has remembered the Ciro's incident in his memoirs. He knew "Tola" Litvak well. "I was dating Alice Eyland—'Miss Chesterfield,' and was at a table next to his."

According to Negulesco's account: "Returning to the table from the dance floor Paulette dropped one of her earrings under the table. 'Tola'—quite drunk by now (as was Paulette), but still the perfect gentleman—disappeared under the table to find it. But how long does it take to look for an earring?" Negulesco relates, "The silly joke grew to be phony acting. 'Tola's' disappearance under the table lasted beyond the time limit of a prank. Paulette began to moan convincingly. Friends, waiters, and photographers became voyeurs. They laughed and whispered encouragement to 'Tola.' They felt they were witnessing a free and bold Hollywood scandal."

In Negulesco's words, "When finally fifteen minutes later 'Tola' appeared from under the table to the applause of the amused audience, he straightened his hair with just the right amount of embarrassment."

PAULETTE

Actress Joan Fontaine has recalled gossip of the day as follows: "The morning after their rendezvous the *Hollywood Reporter* and *Variety* were being passed from cast to crew and back again on every studio lot. Hollywood was abuzz.

"The gossip columns had printed that 'Tola' Litvak had disappeared for a suspicious length of time under the table at which Paulette sat serenely. 'Litvak' was altered into a crude pun, graphic enough to describe what the onlookers imagined was going on under the white table-cloth. Tola's version was that Paulette had simply dropped her evening bag, and, on his hands and knees, he'd had difficulty retrieving it in the dark. As with most gossip, the readers preferred to believe the lurid version."

Negulesco has claimed that "for poetic justice 'Tola' got a mouth infection at the height of the scandal . . ."

But through the years, the most widely circulated version of the story was that it was Paulette who slid under the table and Litvak didn't. Perhaps this version prevailed because men were the purveyors of the tale. In their fantasies this was the version they liked best.

In any event, this is the fanciful account that has gone into legend, further solidified by the fact that it was used as the basis for a scene in the nineteen-seventies film *Shampoo* in which an actress (portrayed by Julie Christie) slips under the table at a Hollywood restaurant to perform fellatio on the object of her desire, a sex-crazed hairdresser played by Warren Beatty.

Some people who were in the social swim back in 1940 today laugh at the Ciro's story, pointing out that the nightclub, frequented by top columnists, would have gone out of business quickly if the management had permitted such an incident to occur. Furthermore, there simply was not enough time, even if people slid under the table, to consummate any sexual acts.

Other diehards believe the tale to have some basis in fact, and point to stories of similar shenanigans that occurred in public places all the time. One publicist recalls a lunch he had arranged between Irv Kupcinet, Chicago columnist, and an Italian screen sex symbol of the late nineteen-fifties and early sixties.

"I was young then and so was she," recalls the publicist. "She spoke very little English, and her much older Italian producer husband spoke even less. She seemed bored as hell and preoccupied. I sat there wide-eyed wondering what was going on. We were in a posh Chicago restaurant and I realized that under the tablecloth the woman had her hand in her husband's lap throughout the entire lunch. It took me about ten minutes to realize that she was masturbating him! If that could happen, *anything* could happen."

Whether or not anything happened at Ciro's in that summer of 1940, all Hollywood thought something *had* happened, and that's what mattered.

As Paulette herself might have said about the whole story: "Isn't that silly?"—a phrase she often used when confronted with information she didn't wish to comment on.

At the time, it certainly seemed as if the gossip and innuendo would damage Paulette's burgeoning career. Jesse Lasky, Jr., one of the screenwriters of *Northwest Mounted Police,* has recalled: "It was scurrilously alleged that Paulette Goddard had participated in an unrehearsed love scene with a famous director at Ciro's. Waiters and guests were said to have formed a circle of delighted voyeurs around this spontaneous floor show." But Mr. Lasky quickly adds: "Hardly believable to anyone who knew Paulette, who, aside from being a lady of taste, would under no circumstances have fed her reputation to The Hollywood locusts." But Lasky also said: "Practically everyone in Hollywood knew, or said they knew, what happened at that nightclub."

A preview of *Northwest Mounted Police* was already scheduled for a theater in Westwood. Most of the audience would be industry people who read *The Hollywood Reporter*. The preview was taking place one night after the nightclub incident.

DeMille and his staff were at the theater to judge audience reaction, and it was a producer's nightmare. In the love scenes between Paulette (playing the sultry half-breed) and Robert Preston (playing the young Mountie), the dialogue, as in all DeMille movies, was corny to begin with. According to Lasky's recollections, "When Paulette dragged Preston into her arms with the threat 'I think I eat your heart, maybe!' a roar of salacious mirth rocked the house."

"Didn't you get enough last night?" shouted a man in the audience.

The love scene continued, a perfect opportunity for the hecklers in the audience. Each new line opened itself up for derision. When Robert

Preston pulled Paulette into his arms and said, "I'd come to you if you were on the other side of the moon," a loudmouth in the audience shouted: "Try Ciro's, it's closer!"

"Listen, you little wildcat," Preston said to Paulette, up on screen, "You're the only real thing that ever happened to me, and nobody—nothing—could ever make me let you go."

"Not even the headwaiter!" shouted another heckler.

The preview was an unmitigated disaster, but DeMille was undaunted. He knew that gossip about the incident was strictly local. He did some editing on the film and took it to Santa Barbara for another preview. The picture played to great audience reaction there.

Northwest Mounted Police was set to have its première in Regina, Saskatchewan, Canada, in October. Then it would subsequently open across the United States. But shortly after the Ciro's gossip broke, both Paramount and United Artists began receiving phone calls threatening to boycott Paulette Goddard's films.

Meanwhile, the beleaguered Chaplin was under a lot of fire from various political groups because of what they considered his liberal leanings. It was thought that the right-wingers were using gossip about Paulette as a further weapon against Chaplin and his upcoming film.

But motion-picture distributors knew that the gossip couldn't possibly reach print or influence the masses. The public, as always, was eagerly awaiting "the little fellow's" new film. United Artists, initially hesitant about making *The Great Dictator,* was now pressuring Chaplin to release the film quickly, nationwide and in England. In these difficult days of the early months of World War II, people wanted to be able to laugh at—make fun of—Adolf Hitler.

Chaplin wanted Paulette to accompany him to New York for the press preview and the opening of *The Great Dictator.* But Paulette needed a breather and left for Mexico instead. There was much speculation on whether she would join Chaplin in New York. She did, and it seemed more than a coincidence that Anatole Litvak flew to New York at the same time.

Present at the *Great Dictator* press preview at the Astor Theatre, a few days before the picture's official opening that October, was Chaplin's old pal Harry Hopkins, who was now an adviser to President Roosevelt. Hopkins depressed Chaplin by telling him, after the screening, that while *Dictator* was a great picture and a worthwhile endeavor, in his opinion it didn't stand a chance of success. Chaplin was, of course, more than nervous. *The Great Dictator* represented two years of work and over two million dollars of his own money.

However, the première, several days later, was a huge success. After the film was over and the ovation from the first-nighters quieted down, Chaplin came on stage and thanked them. He introduced his wife and called her up to the stage with him. "My wife and I hope you enjoyed the picture," he said modestly.

This was the second recent reference by Chaplin, in public, to Paulette's being Mrs. Chaplin. Some felt these references were Chaplin's last attempts to patch up his differences with Paulette. But insiders knew there was no chance of a reconciliation.

Others said he'd introduced Paulette as his wife to neutralize the gossip about Anatole Litvak's interest in Goddard. If that was so, it didn't work. The very next day columnists Dorothy Kilgallen and Dixie Tighe were noting that "Litvak has been casting sheep-eyes at Paulette," and that he "was there last night kissing her hand."

There were others, more cynical, who pointed out that Chaplin was now acknowledging Paulette as his wife only because he was afraid of a backlash at the box office from various women's groups who were demanding proof of their marital status. It was true that United Artists was concerned about the box-office outlook for the film. The New York critics had been mixed. But much to Chaplin's relief and delight, the public responded with overwhelming enthusiasm. *The Great Dictator* would go on to be the biggest moneymaker of all Chaplin's pictures to date.

Usually, Hollywood marriages split up in the wake of failure. The Chaplin-Goddard marriage split up in the wake of success. Charlie stayed in the East for other openings of the film. He took an apartment in the elegant River House, overlooking the East River, in Manhattan. It was across the street from where Garbo lived. Soon Chaplin was squiring local beauties around town, including Betsy Cushing Roosevelt, estranged wife of the President's son Jimmy Roosevelt.

Paulette returned to the West Coast. At first she moved back into Chaplin's mansion, and again the pundits were confused. *Were* they still together? H. G. Wells was visiting California and Charlie asked Paulette to serve as hostess, since Chaplin had offered Wells his house.

PAULETTE

Hedda Hopper related an amusing story about spending the weekend with Paulette and Wells. Paulette and Hedda had been invited up to Myron Selznick's lodge in Arrowhead, and Paulette suggested they take H. G. along. Miss Hopper remembered: "The Charles Chaplin Rolls-Royce, complete with Japanese chauffeur, Paulette and H. G., arrived at my house to pick me up and off we started."

Paulette had already telephoned Hedda and informed her that en route they'd stop in Pasadena at the Huntington Hotel to have dinner. Paulette had phoned the author Upton Sinclair, who was going to join them to meet Wells.

According to Hopper, "We dined. Sinclair joined us. Wells loathed him. As we finished coffee, in came Johnny McClain, handsome newspaperman. I looked at Paulette. She winked. Then she left in McClain's car."

Hopper was left to continue the rest of the trip up the mountain with Wells, "who was notorious for his clutching hands and random lovemaking." Although it's hard to believe (Hopper at this time was well into middle age, and Wells had obviously been led to believe his companion would be the beautiful Paulette), Wells was still, according to Hopper, "undaunted."

"Sure enough, we had barely started upgrade when it started." Wells and Hopper were riding in the limousine with a fur throw over their laps. Hopper grabbed the fur throw, wrapped it around her legs, and, she said, "tucked myself in tight."

Wells was not deterred—Hedda was adamant. "Mr. Wells," she told him, "you're a brilliant writer but I'm not interested in your exploring talents." Wells seethed. Whether to excite Hopper, or to embarrass her, he began to detail his lovemaking abilities. He told her how many women he had known, and how many illegitimate children he had fathered. According to Hopper, "When we arrived at the cabin, he was still furious. No host was in sight, no visible guests. We were assigned our quarters and I found myself sharing a room with Paulette, who arrived three hours later."

Myron Selznick was not expecting John McClain. He hadn't been invited and Paulette hadn't told Selznick she was bringing him. But they found a room for him, and he stayed the weekend. However, it was obvious that McClain and Paulette had had a tiff of some sort and now weren't speaking.

PAULETTE

Through the years, Hedda was both amused and impressed by Paulette's ability not only to live the high life but never to spend a penny of her own money while doing it. The weekend at Arrowhead was no exception. When it came time to depart, Hedda asked, "Paulette, what are you tipping the servants?"

Paulette looked at Hedda in mock surprise. "Are you kidding? What a babe in the woods you are, Hedda. Watch me."

Myron was heading down the hallway. "Darling!" Paulette called out. "I forgot my pocketbook. Let me have some money for tips?"

Selznick took out a roll of bills and Paulette gingerly took a twenty. "Thanks, sweetie."

When the butler came to take their bags to the car, Paulette gave him the twenty. "This is for you to share with the others. It's from Miss Hopper and me."

Hopper of course assumed Paulette would be driving back with her and Wells. After all, the young woman hadn't exchanged more than a few words with McClain the entire weekend. But when they left Selznick's lodge and Hopper climbed into the limousine with Wells, Paulette, to Hedda's surprise, waved a jaunty goodbye. She was riding back to town with McClain.

As the new decade began, Paulette Goddard was—professionally speaking—riding the crest. Her pictures in current release were all hits. *The Ghost Breakers* had even outgrossed *The Cat and the Canary*, and theater owners across the country were badgering Paramount for more Hope-Goddard pictures. The studio scheduled another light comedy for them, *Nothing but the Truth*.

Paramount realized it had a valuable property in Paulette, and was willing to renegotiate her already rich contract. One of the clauses Myron Selznick was insisting on was Paulette's right to make one outside picture per year.

Meanwhile, Paulette had been loaned out to United Artists for a comedy musical, *Pot O' Gold*. U.A. had also borrowed James Stewart from Metro. James Roosevelt was producing the picture, George Marshall directing. Currently popular bandleader Horace Heidt and his orchestra were featured. (The film's title came from Heidt's hit radio show, "Pot O' Gold.")

110

Much was made over the fact that Goddard would do a rumba and "sing for the first time on screen!" in this opus. It was budgeted at a reported $800,000.

Visitors to the set were surprised that Goddard and James Stewart didn't appear particularly chummy. In fact, they were described as "cool and distant." It was noted that between takes Paulette seemed more interested in working on her needlepoint, which, the world had been told, was designed for her by Diego Rivera. Stewart, on the other hand, while waiting for a new camera setup, often sat silently staring at his feet.

During production, producer Roosevelt was called to duty in the Marine Corps at the U.S. Naval base at San Diego. The press noted that rushes on the film were flown to him daily.

While Paulette was working on *Pot O' Gold,* she had her eye on a big project at Paramount. With a story by Billy Wilder and Charles Brackett, the film had been assigned to director Mitchell Leisen.

One of the other young rising actresses on the Paramount lot was Susan Hayward. Hayward felt especially thwarted at the studio, because every part she wanted seemed to go to Paulette Goddard. Hayward, too, heard of the upcoming Leisen film. She went to the powers in charge and asked to test for the role. She knew Goddard was scheduled for the Hope picture. But production chief Buddy Da Sylva informed Susan, "We've already rescheduled the Hope picture just so Goddard could be free to do the movie with Leisen."

In addition to the Leisen picture, the studio announced Paulette would co-star with Ray Milland in *The Lady Eve,* a new comedy being prepared by writer-director Preston Sturges.

It was amidst all this activity in her professional life that Paulette now made a decisive move in her personal life. Charlie Chaplin recalled: "My butler telephoned that when she returned to the Beverly Hills house, she did not stay but packed up her things and left."

Paulette moved out of the Chaplin mansion in early December, 1940. She moved into Myron Selznick's beach house.

The years with Chaplin were over.

PART

9

Hitler had overrun Europe. As the year 1941 began, only England held out against the madman satirized in *The Great Dictator*. People in England, Canada and the United States flocked to see the film.

Hollywood, however, was at least six thousand miles from any field of action. Although the British in Hollywood—actors, writers, producers—were either returning to England to fight or staying in Hollywood to make propaganda films, the war was as far removed as the moon for others in the movie world.

At Paramount there was far more interest in who was going to play the lead opposite Gary Cooper in *For Whom the Bell Tolls,* Hemingway's classic about the Spanish Civil War. Paulette was in the running; she was the darling of the lot, for the moment.

The Leisen picture, *Hold Back the Dawn,* began filming on February 18, 1941. A great deal of controversy surrounded the project. Paramount producer Arthur Hornblow, Jr., had bought a film treatment, obviously autobiographical, from writer Ketti Frings. It was about refugees on the Mexican border trying to get into the United States. Ketti, née Katharine Hartley, a former writer for *Screenland* and *Photoplay* magazines, had married Kurt Frings, a German refugee and former boxing champion.

PAULETTE

After Mrs. Frings sold the treatment to Paramount, but before it was filmed, she wrote a novel, *Hold Back the Dawn*. In her novel version of the same story, the woman was a writer, the man a prizefighter. In the Brackett-Wilder script, however, the male character was changed to a gigolo and the woman to a schoolteacher. Kurt Frings was furious about this. But Paramount already owned the property and Frings could do nothing.

In addition, the script had political overtones that the Mexican government objected to. Even after these problems had been solved, Wilder and Brackett had difficulty with the leading man, Charles Boyer, who would not film certain scenes they had written.

Consequently, the writers built up the female parts. Olivia de Havilland had been borrowed from Warners to play the schoolteacher—and Paulette had landed the plum role of Anita, the gigolo's former dancing partner in Paris. It was a great role for Paulette; she was not required actually to dance, only to play a flashy former showgirl who had married a rich, stupid American in order to obtain her citizenship.

The film boasted a wonderful supporting cast, including Rosemary De Camp, Walter Abel and Victor Francen. Leisen himself played the role of the movie director who listens to refugee Charles Boyer's story, which then unfolds on screen.

Leisen signed dialogue coach Phyllis Laughton to work on the picture. According to Eleanor Broder, who also worked on the film: "Phyllis was on the picture to help Paulette Goddard along; Paulette couldn't make a move without her. I don't know how much they worked together ahead of time in Paulette's dressing room. Then Phyllis would get all of the cast together and they would do the scene together. Phyllis was officially only the dialogue director, but she gave so much more than any other dialogue director ever did. She went over the characters and their motivations and what should be going through their minds when they played a certain scene."

Obviously, Goddard was accustomed to working under the Chaplin method. She *had* to go over the scene many times before the cameras rolled.

According to Olivia de Havilland, "Paulette was so very nervous I felt sorry for her. I was nervous too, but nothing like this. When we did our scene together, Polly's upper lip was trembling so badly. I was afraid it would show on the film."

But "Polly," as always, got through it. She was also shooting the Hope picture *Nothing but the Truth* at the same time. It was another silly comedy but Hope was riding high. His hit radio program had helped to propel him to the top in record time, and he too had renegotiated his Paramount contract several times.

Paulette was making big money; she was now receiving $85,000 a film. But money, she said, was not the driving force in her career. "I have to work, to be busy, to learn something new. It isn't that I have any goals. I haven't. But I've lots of energy and I'm lucky that I can put it to work in something I enjoy."

Her energy was being utilized. DeMille wanted her again. He would begin shooting *Reap the Wild Wind* that summer.

Meanwhile, *Pot O' Gold* was released and again Paulette's presence on screen was reviewed candidly. *Variety* stated: "Miss Goddard flashes an ingenue smile, rolls her eyes and sings at the microphone. She is also variously photographed registering vexation, determination and romance."

Since Goddard was set for *Reap the Wild Wind,* there was no time for *The Lady Eve.* Preston Sturges happily cast Barbara Stanwyck in the lead opposite Henry Fonda for that film. Sturges' forte was fast-moving bright comedy dialogue—not Paulette's long suit.

Jesse Lasky, Jr., who worked on the script for *Reap the Wild Wind,* described that production as Paramount's answer to *Gone With the Wind.* Paulette was playing the Scarlett O'Hara-like heroine (with the ridiculous name of Loxi). Loxi, like Scarlett, had a Mammy (portrayed by Louise Beavers), and an aunt (played by Hedda Hopper) who was virtually a carbon copy of Scarlett's Aunt Pittypat.

Paulette's rival on the lot, Susan Hayward, was given the second female lead. But the real star of the film, everyone agreed, was the mechanical octopus that leading men Ray Milland and John Wayne had to battle underwater.

DeMille pictures were physical, and apparently the director enjoyed putting his leading ladies through various perils. In *Reap,* for example, Paulette's character is at various times spanked by Milland, thrown overboard and compelled to endure typhoons and other "natural" hazards. But there was glamour to the part as well. And everybody knew that a DeMille film was bound to be a huge hit, furthering the careers of everyone associated with it.

At this point, with DeMille's *Northwest Mounted Police* and Chaplin's *Great Dictator,* two of the top moneymakers of the year, Paulette's status was assured. Escapist fare was still the order of the day for 1941 audiences, and the completed *Reap the Wild Wind* would fit right in. With Paramount's vast publicity resources working for Paulette, the actress's popularity was soaring. In 1941, she appeared on more magazine covers and in more newspaper and magazine layouts than ever before.

"Understand her or not—you just can't ignore her," observed one typical piece. "She's the most daring, most exciting woman in Hollywood."

There were sittings with the top photographers in Hollywood. George Hurrell recalled: "I always looked forward to my sittings with Paulette Goddard, because she was as fresh as a schoolgirl, both in looks and attitude. She was fond of big hats which framed her 'sweetheart' face. She never played the great star, even if she was dressed in furs and jewels for a fashion layout. She took the business of making pictures in stride. She could take direction expertly and gave exactly what was wanted. I always shot the dramatic stuff first, with soft music, then turned on a hot swing number or boogie-woogie, and her mood changed instantly. I did impersonations, stood on my head, and acted the complete fool, and she loved it. She would laugh, her eyes would sparkle, and I'd press the bulb in my hand."

John Engstead, another well-known photographer of the period, was then working on the Paramount lot. He remembered Paulette as "a sharp number in anybody's book." Engstead told a story involving Paulette and a commercial tie-in, a common practice of the day. "As an incentive, the players were usually promised one of whatever product they endorsed," recalled Engstead, "but when it came time to collect the loot, the stars often never received it. Either it was never sent or some sticky fingers along the way annexed it."

But Paulette was too shrewd for the promoters. According to Engstead, during one of these commercial tie-in photo sessions, Paulette was asked to pose with a large console radio. "Paulette did her pose and she said nicely that she would take her radio then and there. 'You can't have this one,' the advertising man said. 'We have to shoot it with other actresses.' 'No,' said Paulette, 'I'm taking it now. Open the doors, boys.' Waiting outside was a truck she had hired to haul it home. And out it went."

Paulette appeared on radio often during these years. Bob Hope had asked her to guest-star on his first broadcast of the fall season. *Nothing but the Truth* was being previewed, and Hope and the publicity boys had come up with an idea: on the air he and Paulette could do material from the film.

Hope had already talked the advertising men into another gimmick. To promote the picture, he had written his mock autobiography, *Nothing but the Truth,* and his sponsor, Pepsodent, would offer the book to listeners for ten cents a copy plus a Pepsodent box top.

Hold Back the Dawn was in theaters before *Nothing but the Truth,* and the drama was a resounding hit critically as well as commercially. In fact, it was considered one of the prestigious Hollywood films of the year, dealing with pertinent and provocative issues. In addition, director Leisen was adept at presenting female stars at their best, and Paulette looked particularly slim, chic and beautiful in this production.

That fall, Paulette and Boyer repeated their roles on C. B. DeMille's "Lux Radio Theatre." Susan Hayward played the Olivia de Havilland role on this broadcast. Paulette was also set to do *The Gorgeous Hussy* on the "Cavalcade of America" program.

In the thirties and through the forties, radio drama was a very important facet of the entertainment industry. Stars could earn as much as five thousand dollars a broadcast. Shows such as "Lux Radio Theatre," "Screen Guild Theater" and "Hollywood Hotel" often dramatized current movies. Others, such as "Silver Theater," used original dramas.

True Boardman, a writer who got his start in radio drama, does not have fond memories of Paulette Goddard. He gives some insight into radio drama of this era, explaining that it was no hurried, slapdash endeavor. "We rehearsed three or four hours on Thursday night, the same on Friday night—and then from ten in the morning to 3 p.m. showtime on Sunday. I say 'we'—meaning the cast, orchestra and production staff."

One of the virtues of radio drama during these years, according to Boardman, "was the opportunity it gave all of us to work, if only for a brief few days at a time, with the really top stars of the day. With only one or two exceptions, it was a fulfilling experience—and I personally

119

treasure my memories of writing for Loretta Young, Jimmy Stewart, Roz Russell, Clark Gable, Jimmy Cagney, Pat O'Brien—"

Boardman explains, "It was a time when—if one read screen magazines—'stars' were an exotic breed of people apart, living, many of them, lurid lives. The truth is they were hardworking, thoughtful professionals—as dedicated and as concerned as we were with turning out a good show."

However, one of Boardman's memories involves Paulette in an unflattering light. "On a certain Sunday the scheduled show was to star Paulette Goddard, who had been rehearsing since Thursday. Only, Miss Goddard's maid called Glenhall [producer Glenhall Taylor] at ten on Sunday morning to state that 'Miss Goddard was indisposed—and couldn't do the show.' At 10:05 Glen was on the phone trying to line up a substitute. By 10:15 he had one. Miriam Hopkins said, sure—she'd be right down. She was in Studio A of CBS by noon—did one read-through and a dress—and went on before the live audience at three—and never missed a cue. What's more, she was a hell of a lot better in the part than the 'indisposed' Goddard ever could have been."

According to Hedda Hopper, C. B. DeMille and Paulette did not get along as well on *Reap the Wild Wind* as they had on *Northwest Mounted Police*.

"There were some days when they went at it hammer and tong," said Hedda. "But she learned to take it, and came out a full-fledged star, with even Cecil—who is the toughest taskmaster in our business—singing her praises."

DeMille was famous for this loyalty to old friends, and often employed former pals, children of friends and out-of-luck actors in his films. An actress who had once starred for DeMille in 1921 was given a job as an extra in *Reap the Wild Wind*. She was Mildred Harris, the first Mrs. Charlie Chaplin. It was a sad end to a once-promising career. Paulette Goddard was determined that no such fate would befall her.

Immediately upon finishing *Wind*, Paramount cast Paulette in *The Lady Has Plans*. She replaced Madeleine Carroll in the comedy-drama spy thriller co-starring Ray Milland. (It's amusing that Paulette's character in the picture is described by another with words that definitely applied to Paulette herself: "There's a smart, levelheaded gal who knows her business.")

Not too long ago, when Chaplin was procrastinating about scripts for her, Paulette had complained about not working enough; now she had the opposite situation. She was perhaps working *too* much, but this kind of back-to-back picturemaking was standard stuff of the day.

Her social life, too, continued at a hectic pace. She was seeing Burgess Meredith. His checkered career in Hollywood films hardly reflected his reputation as a fine actor, but without a powerful studio behind him his film career had not yet taken off. Besides, even if he had signed with an MGM or Paramount, he was not the physical type Hollywood was adept at merchandising. He did not in any way have the traditional leading-man "look." He was an actor, not a star.

But, unlike a lot of Hollywood actors, he had intellect and taste, characteristics he shared with Paulette. And Goddard liked Meredith's social group, which consisted mostly of artistic, intellectual Easterners. However, Goddard was not interested in dating one man exclusively. She enjoyed her freedom and dated others. Since her split from Chaplin her name had been linked with many men, including Artie Shaw and director Mervyn LeRoy.

Some, including writers John Steinbeck and William Saroyan, were dazzled by Paulette and happy to be in her company. For those curious about why men of intellect were drawn to Paulette Goddard, Saroyan observed: "What she has is an inner twinkle, and it goes around in a strictly non-sorrowing frame; all of it is attractively tough, challenging, mischievous, coquettish, wicked and absolutely innocent. It's probably less sex appeal than fun appeal, which in some cases are the same thing, and in all cases should be."

During this period, Paulette also dated Bruce Cabot, a handsome he-man type quite the opposite of "Buzz" Meredith.

The war, which had seemed so far off to those in Hollywood, suddenly hit home. Shortly after the Japanese attack on Pearl Harbor, on December 7, 1941, Hollywood, along with the rest of the country, was thrust into the reality of war. Burgess Meredith was quickly drafted, as were many other men in the industry.

In the spring of 1942, both *The Lady Has Plans* and *Reap the Wild Wind* were released, and the DeMille picture was of course a blockbuster. Paulette attended the Los Angeles première with Jinx Falkenburg (whom Chaplin had reportedly dated the previous year). Paulette was obviously not a woman who feared close comparison with another stunning brunette—she and Jinx were a spectacular pair.

In deference to wartime austerity, many of Hollywood's star ladies were downplaying their glitzy images, but Paulette would have none of that. Goddard and Falkenburg attended the *Wind* première dressed to kill. Paulette wore ermine and diamonds, and Falkenburg white fox.

Paramount quickly cast Goddard in another movie, *The Forest Rangers,* with Susan Hayward. George Marshall directed and Fred MacMurray was top-billed. Paulette played a society girl, Hayward a lumber-mill owner, both in love with forest ranger MacMurray. It was a hodgepodge film, with some slapstick comedy and a song that went on to become a hit: "I've Got Spurs That Jingle-Jangle-Jingle."

The highlight of the film was a blazing forest fire, during which city girl Goddard proves her mettle and takes charge when outdoor girl Hayward panics. In reality, however, the situation was just the reverse: Paulette was frightened of any potentially dangerous scenes, and was likely to burst into tears when she was confronted with one. It was the feisty Hayward who grabbed Goddard's hand and literally pulled her through the fire sequence.

After location shooting in Santa Cruz, California, Paulette returned to Hollywood, where she again appeared for DeMille on "Lux Radio Theatre," re-creating her role in *Northwest Mounted Police.* Gary Cooper and Preston Foster co-starred.

It was a time when Goddard's name and picture were virtually everywhere. During the war, she was one of the most cooperative of Paramount's stars in publicity activities. She agreed to give a "prize kiss" to the person in the Hollywood area who collected the most aluminum for a national drive to aid the war effort. It was announced the kiss would be no ordinary kiss but an exact duplicate of one Goddard had given Ray Milland in a recent picture.

H. B. Clifford, owner of a small restaurant, was the happy winner, and Paulette, photographers on hand, dutifully awarded her prize kiss to Mr. Clifford. Mrs. Clifford's ringside observation—"He never kissed me like that!"—was duly noted by reporters.

Paulette's expertise at pointing the spotlight of public attention on herself was always evident. She showed up for dinner one evening at a fashionable Santa Monica hotel attired in shorts and a blouse. Others in the dining room gasped. Goddard's ensemble wasn't informal, however; her "evening shorts" and blouse were beautifully tailored of crêpe and embroidered with sequins. A matching scarf was tied around her waist. The outfit, as well as Paulette, was a knockout—a dramatic fashion statement that would in later years have made page one of *Women's Wear Daily* and started a trend.

At the time, however, American women weren't ready for such daring. Paulette merely garnered standard movie-star publicity, although she claimed she hadn't done it for publicity. She had, she said, worn the outfit "for comfort."

Meanwhile, Burgess Meredith had been saved from an ignominious fate—cleaning latrines in an Air Force camp in Santa Ana, California. Stage star Katharine Cornell had convinced the government that Buzz could serve a greater purpose by starring with her in *Candida* (directed by her husband, Guthrie McClintic). The proceeds would go to the Army-Navy Relief Fund. Meredith was given leave to star with Cornell in New York.

Goddard went to New York to see him, but at the same time her name was also linked with Presidential confidant Harry Hopkins. Hopkins even took Paulette to Hyde Park, New York, to meet the President and Mrs. Roosevelt.

Although Paulette had always been adept at social situations, she was in considerable awe of F.D.R. And, to make matters worse, she had had to compromise on her wardrobe. Her trunk, containing all her clothes and shoes, was sidetracked in Chicago. In New York, "in the confusion of trying to find something to wear, I was fifteen minutes late for lunch—and I'm never late! To put me at my ease, the President said when I walked in: 'You're late, Goddard. Sit down!'

"Just like that. I was scared stiff—and wearing ballet slippers. And I couldn't walk out—only Zorina could make an exit in ballet slippers! I sat down fast, clenched my fists in my lap and stared straight ahead. The first course came and I didn't touch it. I had a good reason.

"'Are you on one of those diets?' asked the President. 'You don't look as though you needed it.'

"I just smiled and swallowed a wisecrack and shook my head—my reason for not eating had nothing to do with a diet. Along came the soup, and I passed again. The President noticed that, too, and asked if I wasn't hungry.

"So I told him: 'I'm not on a diet. I'm half-starved—but my hands are shaking so hard I'm afraid to pick up a fork!'

"Well, the President roared! He took it from there—told a couple of stories about times he was scared, and I was back to normal!"

The government, as it had during World War I, was enlisting the help of film stars to raise money by selling War Bonds. Paulette agreed to go on a bond tour, and it is interesting to note that the territory she was given was eastern Pennsylvania and Maryland, an area where Quakers, Amish and Mennonites resided. These were people who were anti-violence, anti-war and anti-glamour. It would be a hard sell, but the people in charge reasoned that if anyone could soften this group and sell War Bonds to them, it would be the charming Paulette.

The tour was a success, and afterward Goddard found time to revisit Mexico. She obtained her Mexican divorce from Chaplin in June, 1942, and there were instant rumors that she would marry Harry Hopkins. But Hopkins shortly announced his engagement to Louise Macy. Paulette's only comment: "Isn't it wonderful? Louise is such a nice girl."

Since there was a good eighteen months between the time Paulette and Charlie split until she gained a divorce, there was little interest in the details other than that the divorce meant they *had* been married. Little interest, that is, except from the F.B.I.

According to government files, the Immigration and Naturalization Service obtained an authentic copy of the Goddard-Chaplin divorce decree. But according to a member of the Immigration and Naturalization Service office in El Paso, "Confidential information was received from a person who was familiar with the divorce proceedings in this case to the effect that he had gained the impression from the lawyer involved that the parties had never actually been married but had secured the divorce to clear up an apparent common-law status."

Furthermore, the Immigration and Naturalization Service stated that the divorce decree showed the marriage took place the first week of June, 1936, in Canton, China. If true, this adds confusion to the case, since Paulette and Charlie docked in San Francisco on June 3, 1936. So the marriage must have taken place much earlier.

In any event, although no marriage certificate was ever produced, they said they were married. And now they were divorced.

PAULETTE

* * *

Though Paulette and Burgess Meredith kept their relationship quiet, it was a serious one. They took trips together down to Palm Springs. Jinx Falkenburg accompanied them on one jaunt to the Springs.

Meredith was being transferred to England by the Air Force to make training films. (While he was in London, he also appeared on stage.) Paulette was in Hollywood shooting a new film with Ray Milland, *The Crystal Ball*. (Ginger Rogers and Charles Boyer had been the studio's original choices.) Paulette later said that she regretted making this film and not going to England instead. But at the time she was more interested in her career, and, as with every film, she thought this would be an important one. She subsequently discovered it was just another programmer.

But her next film *was* an important one. The attention of the entire country—indeed the world—had been caught by the story of the courageous American nurses who had been on Bataan and Corregidor in two of the earliest and bloodiest battles of the war in the Pacific.

Corregidor had fallen in May of 1942. Ten nurses, however, escaped. Paramount producer-director Mark Sandrich, who had previously been known for musicals, was also caught up in the story. He told the Paramount brass, "We've got to make a picture about those nurses."

One of the nurses who had escaped was Lieutenant Eunice Hatchitt and Sandrich hired her as technical adviser. Sandrich got Allan Scott, the screenwriter, to fly to Washington with him to speak to the other nurses who had escaped and to get permission from the government to make the picture. The producer also hired Colonel Thomas Doyle, a veteran of the Philippine campaign, as another technical adviser, to make sure that the picture was authentic in every detail.

Sandrich signed Claudette Colbert for one of the leads, then announced that Paramount's two leading pinups, Paulette and Veronica Lake, would play the other key roles. Others in the cast included Barbara Britton, George Reeves (later to attain fame as TV's Superman), Walter Abel and newcomer Sonny Tufts.

Veronica Lake was *the* hot young property on the lot. Her star had even momentarily eclipsed Goddard's. Lake was fresh from three hits: *I Wanted Wings, This Gun for Hire* and *I Married a Witch*. The entire female population of the United States (or so it seemed) was emulating Veronica's long blonde peekaboo hairdo. But now she was wear-

125

ing her hair pulled back, at the request of the U.S. government. It seemed that some lady factory workers who had been emulating Veronica's hairdo had gotten their long tresses caught in the gears of machinery.

"Besides," said Miss Lake, "I *wanted* to pull my hair back, to prove I could act and that I wasn't just a sex symbol."

Many in the industry assumed that Lake would be a problem. "I think most people assumed I'd act like a little bitch on the set and fight the others all the way," she later recalled. There was no doubt that she had already acquired a reputation for cockiness. But as things turned out, Veronica was not the problem. It was Paulette and Claudette who did not "get along."

According to Veronica, one of the incidents that fueled the fire was an interview Paulette had given during production. When Claudette read the subsequent piece, she was furious. The reporter had asked Paulette whom she liked better, Claudette or Veronica. Goddard had answered: "Veronica, I think. After all, we are closer in age."

In fact, this was questionable. Although Colbert was almost twenty years older than Veronica, Paulette's somewhat indeterminate age might have been closer to Claudette's than Veronica's. In any event, others suggest that it was not comments regarding age that caused the feud. It was "working conditions."

Sandrich certainly had his hands full on this production. Stars like Lake and Goddard were personalities rather than actresses, and needed a great deal of time and discussion concerning how they should play their roles. In order to draw performances from them, Sandrich had to give them constant guidance. They were used to doing as many takes as necessary to get the proper reading.

On the other hand, Colbert was a consummate professional, totally skilled in technique. She could deliver what the director wanted in one or two takes.

In addition, Sandrich had problems with the script. Paulette's character had to be given more dimension; the character was *too* flip, too flirtatious. The writer and producer agreed the character couldn't just be a nurse "dropping black nightgowns as she trails across Bataan." No girl, no matter how callow, could have lived through Bataan and not done "*some* growing up," said Paulette.

Despite the rewrites and clash of temperaments, the picture was turning out extremely well. Colbert's characterization was, as always, right on target, and the studio was confident the picture would be a winner.

Around this time Paramount used Goddard and Lake, along with Dorothy Lamour, in a specialty number for the all-star revue *Star Spangled Rhythm*. The three women did a song-and-dance routine, "The Sweater, the Sarong and the Peek-a-Boo Bang." While Lamour was truly the Sarong, and Veronica was indisputably the Peek-a-Boo Bang, the writers had had to stretch a bit to find a tag for Paulette. It was Lana Turner who was the screen's Sweater Girl. But Paulette was one of the genuine pinups of World War II.

Through 1943, Goddard joined other Hollywood stars working at the Hollywood Canteen, which had been founded by John Garfield and Bette Davis. Garfield was an old pal of Meredith's. The two had met back in the early thirties when they were both members of Eva Le Gallienne's Civic Repertory Theater Company in New York. Buzz and Garfield had made a film at Warners together, *Castle on the Hudson*. Now Paulette, too, became one of "Julie" Garfield's friends.

Paulette continued her busy film schedule, shooting *Standing Room Only*, with Fred MacMurray, a story about the wartime housing shortage. Goddard also had time to star for DeMille in the Lux radio version of *Reap the Wild Wind*, with Ray Milland and John Carradine.

Paulette made a trip to Texas for a Red Cross tennis benefit. She and Jinx Falkenburg had been invited by their friend Tex Feldman. Jinx has recalled, "He sent a special plane to Hollywood for us and we flew to Texas, where, as Paulette says, 'Men are men and *do* carry thousand-dollar bills.' The usual tennis garb which we all wore, was, of course, white. Paulette, on the other hand, appeared on the court in black shorts and white gardenias. Maybe that had something to do with the fact that we raised ten thousand dollars for the Red Cross during the tournament. Paulette was going on to Mexico and left with a promise that we would join her."

So Proudly We Hail opened at the Radio City Music Hall in June and was an instant success commercially and, for the most part, critically as well. Although hardly an upbeat story, it was an inspirational film. The entire cast received excellent reviews and Sandrich was lauded for bringing the story to the screen. It was a fictionalized account, of course, but it realistically depicted the hardships the American fighting men and women were enduring and the courage they displayed.

The most memorable scene of the film is when Veronica Lake sacrifices her life to save the others by walking into a nest of Japanese with a hand grenade hidden in her bra. Veronica's role was showy, but Paulette's part was bigger and had more scope. Her character evolves from the sophisticated, know-it-all, wisecracking nurse to a woman who encounters true love. Kansas, the farm boy played by Sonny Tufts, was a perfect complement to the worldly Paulette. When the characters part, knowing full well that they will never see each other again, it is a poignant moment. Paulette displayed unexpected depth in the role. The New York *World-Telegram* critic said, "The surprise of the group is Miss Goddard, until now not much more than a fluttery pretty-pretty, but this time an actress of vigor and zest for life."

It was the actress's vigor and zest for life that led her to return frequently south of the border. Her friends said that during this period Paulette had "a winter palace and a summer palace" in Mexico. Diego Rivera had painted other portraits of her. There were rumors that she was having an affair with the President of Mexico.

Jinx Falkenburg has recalled, "Paulette, who knew everybody in Mexico, including all the govermental dignitaries, saw to it that we met everyone she knew. Three cars of us followed Paulette around wherever she led us . . . Mexico City, Taxco, Cuernavaca. We even followed her to Miguel Alemán's office, where I first met him. He became President later but he was then Secretary of the Interior. We went to the races and the bullfights and to parties but for one brief period I felt like Paulette's little sister. I had small fears about just how good a friend I was of Paulette until she did a typically Goddard thing. It was decided that she should give a big party for a lot of important people and—she asked *me* to co-hostess the party. And she meant exactly what she said. We did the *whole* thing together and all my fears were gone."

There are so many tales of Goddard's acquisitive actions that an anecdote told by Jinx Falkenburg is an amusing counterpoint. It seems that sometime in 1943 Jinx was taking a trip to Mexico and, in her words, Paulette "asked me to take a little emerald ring band with me for Max Cámacho, the brother of President Ávilla Camacho, who wanted to buy Paulette a ring. He wanted to give her a little friendship token but didn't

128

know her ring size." Jinx was to use the band to show Paulette's ring size and then bring it back.

But things did not go according to plan. "I did show the ring to Camacho, as she had requested. But, instead of Paulette getting a new ring, he kept hers. It was quite a shock to me. I was terrified to tell Paulette when I got back to the Coast. She invited me to stay with her in her house on Lindacrest so I guess she really wasn't too angry."

During these years Paulette brought back many valuable paintings and Mexican objects of art to her Beverly Hills residence. And not only men gave her gifts. If Frida Kahlo Rivera had at one time been jealous of Paulette, Goddard apparently won her over and the two women became friends. Kahlo later gave Paulette one of her still lifes, "The Flower Basket."

"I am told Paulette has cars down there to match the color of her gowns," said her pal Hedda Hopper. Mexico and Goddard were definitely simpatico. It was during these years that Paulette's reputation as a beauty with brains was further solidified. She had set her mother up in a business buying old houses in Beverly Hills, refurbishing them and then either renting them out or selling them at a substantial gain.

When Paulette was asked why she was involved in selling property, her reply was candid: "For profit. I can't resist forty percent over what I paid." And when Chaplin was queried about Paulette's penchant for making money, he quipped: "She has more money than I have."

Because of the housing shortage during these years, Jinx Falkenburg had found it difficult to find suitable accommodations in Hollywood, and Paulette invited her to move in. But the ever-practical Paulette added, "Bring your maid along." There were always at least two servants in Goddard's domiciles: cooking and cleaning were definitely not on her agenda.

While Paulette and Jinx were roommates, Falkenburg learned first-hand that Goddard took her work seriously. One night Jinx had received some upsetting news from her then-boyfriend (later husband) Tex McCrary. Tex was dating others. "I ran all the way off to the other end of the house to Paulette's room," recalled Jinx. "Maybe she could tell me what I was reading wasn't true. I knocked on her door.

"'Paulette, I have to talk to you.'

"'Not tonight. I'm busy.'"

Paulette wasn't kidding. "When Paulette is working on a picture . . . *nothing* can disturb her after nine o'clock at night," declared Jinx. On that particular evening she didn't give up easily: "You *have* to talk to me," Jinx implored. "I have a terrible problem."

"You'll just have to postpone your problem until tomorrow, Jinx."

Burgess Meredith was soon back in Paulette's circle. After serving time making films for the Office of War Information in London, he had been transferred back to the States and was now part of the team at "Fort Roach." The old Hal Roach studio in Culver City was being used by the Air Force for making training films. Incidentally, at Fort Roach, Meredith made a film with Lieutenant Ronald Reagan.

Although Goddard's relationship with Burgess was still not public knowledge, they were quite close. She called him "Sugar," and his nickname for her was "Miss Busy-Mitts." In May, 1943, Paulette accompanied Meredith, John Garfield and other Hollywood stars to Chicago, where they participated in the "I Am an American Day" pageant at Soldiers Field. Meredith had often been active in politics. Back in New York in the late thirties he had even been vice-president and acting president of Actors Equity.

The "I Am an American Day" pageants were sponsored each year by the Hearst newspapers (at least two of which were called American: the Chicago *Herald-American* and the New York *Journal-American*). Other stars announced for the pageant included Bing Crosby, Buddy Ebsen, Constance Collier and Dinah Shore.

Few people in Hollywood realized how close Paulette and Meredith had become. Goddard even employed her business acumen to Meredith's benefit. She persuaded him to let the government plant crops on land he owned in upstate New York; he later made a profit on the crops. Reports were that on the set of *Standing Room Only,* Paulette, ever the businesswoman, spent more time on the phone to New York discussing farm business than on learning her lines.

Although everybody thought Paulette was out of Charlie Chaplin's life, this was far from true. The year 1943 was a very bad one for Chaplin. The previous year he had angered his critics by again getting involved in politics. He had twice publicly called for a second front in the war in Europe; he wanted the British and American forces to invade Europe from the west, to take the pressure off the Eastern Front in Russia, where the Nazis were dealing heavy blows against the Soviets. (One must remember that for a few years, in the early forties, Russia, Britain and the U.S. had joined forces to fight Germany, Japan and Italy.)

Then, as now, the public and the press lambasted movie actors for telling military men how to do their job. Chaplin was definitely skating on thin ice, and, in addition, scandal was once again erupting in his personal life.

After Paulette had left Charlie, he was lonely and despondent and his pal Tim Durant had introduced him to another young Hollywood hopeful. She was Joan Barry, who also used the name Joan Berry (she had been born Mary Louise Gribble). Barry was a stagestruck girl from Brooklyn, whom Durant had met through billionaire oil man J. Paul Getty.

Chaplin put Joan under contract at $75 a week, and their affair continued for many months. But then, when it cooled, he cut her salary to $25 and Barry began causing scenes. She threatened Chaplin's life and was arrested; then her mother, Gertrude E. Berry, filed a paternity suit against Charlie on behalf of her daughter, who, she claimed, was "with child."

The F.B.I. now began intensive investigation of the Chaplin-Barry affair, hoping they could nail Charlie under the White Slave Traffic Act. The Bureau was trying to pin something specific on Chaplin. F.B.I. files state that the investigation was "initiated on information that he caused victim to travel from Los Angeles to New York City in October 1942, in order that she engage in sexual intercourse with him and his friends."

After further investigation, the F.B.I. concluded that "through Chaplin's intimate friend and pimp, one Tim Durant, two abortions were committed on Barry; that she broke her contract with Chaplin Studios in May 1942, but thereafter Chaplin continued to be intimate with her and supported her."

But in June 1943, all the public knew was that Chaplin, then fifty-four, was again involved with a young girl. It was scandalous. And just a few days after the lawsuit broke in the papers, Chaplin married another young girl, eighteen-year-old Oona O'Neill, the beautiful daughter of famed playwright Eugene O'Neill. It was almost as if Chaplin were daring public opinion to condemn him.

Naturally, any investigation of Chaplin also included Paulette. When the F.B.I. again investigated Chaplin's past, a Bureau document noted that Los Angeles attorneys were hunting for the records of Chaplin's divorce from Paulette Goddard: "It is recalled that she was his third wife, they allegedly having been married at sea somewhere around Canton, China, six years prior to their allegedly having been divorced on June 4, 1942, in Juárez, Mexico. These attorneys had also looked over the records at Cuernavaca and Chautla, Mexico, and nowhere did they find any record of the divorce."

The F.B.I. was, for the most part, run by men with very moralistic attitudes. It upset them that they had not been able to find absolute proof of the Chaplin-Goddard marriage, and now it appeared they could not find absolute proof of the Chaplin-Goddard divorce.

As previously noted, Goddard was not a sympathetic character in the F.B.I.'s perception. In addition to her dealings with Chaplin, the actress was still under investigation in her own right. The Bureau had already tagged her, Frances Farmer and Dalton Trumbo, at Paramount, as "contributors to Communist Party causes."

Whether or not Goddard was aware of these allegations at the time is unknown, but chances are she was not. She—and others who knew her and her acquisitive nature—would have found the allegation that she had Communist leanings absurd. In any event, the Bureau was highly suspicious of Goddard. Her name kept popping up in F.B.I. memos concerning her former husband.

In late 1943, Chaplin learned that his butler, Edward C. Chaney, had been questioned by the F.B.I. When Chaplin phoned a friend—a judge—to ask if he could learn why the F.B.I. was investigating him, the Bureau discovered it. And they also discovered that Paulette and Chaplin were still involved with each other.

R. C. Davis, in a memorandum addressed to his superior, summarized the report of J. C. Ellsworth, of the Los Angeles Field Division of the F.B.I.: "Mr. Ellsworth . . . stated that during the past weekend Chaplin had been getting some advice from his friend Paulette Goddard. She said that Chaplin wasn't getting the proper publicity and that it would be a good idea for him to be first of all to buy a $1,000,000 War

Bond, strictly for publicity. She also recommended that Chaplin get hold of Leon Henderson, whom she described as a good guy not now in Government service, and he might be able to see that Chaplin did get some proper publicity. Paulette Goddard also suggested that inasmuch as Chaplin had learned that the F.B.I. was making inquiries concerning him, he should go directly to the Director and find out what those 'bastards' are doing investigating him."

It seems that Chaplin did not follow Paulette's rather good advice on either count. He did not buy the War Bond, and it seems he did not try to call J. Edgar Hoover directly. However, there was no mystery about why they were investigating him; they were doubtless trying to build a case against him for possible deportation.

Even more frightening to Chaplin, of course, was the possibility that the government might impound his assets. It was not generally known, but as early as 1943 Chaplin was sending money out of the country. He had transferred $200,000 to a Canadian bank, and the U.S. government obviously viewed this as the beginning of Chaplin's move to leave the country with his assets intact.

At the very peak of the Chaplin-Barry scandal, Paulette took flight. Her pal Hedda Hopper observed, "It was smart of Paulette Goddard to go into hiding and escape answering questions over the Chaplin case."

When she returned to Hollywood, Paulette kept mum on anything to do with Chaplin. Pursuing her career, she rounded out 1943 by filming *I Love a Soldier,* the story of a girl left behind to work as a welder in a factory. Sandrich and Scott had prepared this vehicle for Paulette after working with her on *So Proudly We Hail,* and since she and Sonny Tufts had scored such a big success in that film, Tufts, the hot new wartime "hunk," was cast as Paulette's leading man.

Goddard continued to do radio, appearing with W. C. Fields on the "Chase and Sanborn Hour." Then she and her co-stars from *So Proudly We Hail,* Colbert, Lake and Tufts, re-created the story for the airwaves. This Lux radio broadcast generated a lot of gossip in Hollywood because Paulette had been determined to outshine her two rivals in glamour. Although they were portraying nurses in the thick of battle, for the broadcast Paulette wore a form-fitting black satin dress, with one of her diamond necklaces as a shoulder strap.

Paulette often used her glamorous wardrobe and jewelry collection to dazzle the boys in uniform at the Hollywood Canteen. Although she had intended to go back to Mexico for the Christmas holidays that year, she did in fact spend Christmas day with the servicemen at the canteen. Other stars on hand were Bette Davis, Spencer Tracy, Olivia de Havilland, William Bendix, John Garfield and Paulette's pal Jinx Falkenburg.

Paulette, Buzz and their friends spent New Year's Eve at Goddard's beach house. A friend recalls, "We made prune whip in the kitchen or ate Chinese dinners on the beach."

As the year 1944 began, Paulette's star in Hollywood was at its zenith. *Standing Room Only* was released and became a big hit. Although the film was a programmer, Goddard was for the first time top-billed. And it was billing over successful, established star Fred Mac-Murray.

But the real news occurred when Paulette received an honor that no other Hollywood glamour/pinup girl had achieved. She was nominated for an Oscar. *So Proudly We Hail* had received only three Academy Award nominations: best screenplay, best cinematography and best supporting actress—Paulette. That Goddard had received an Oscar nod was a real surprise. Colbert was considered the actress in the cast.

There was considerable controversy over categorizing Goddard as a supporting actress. She was star-billed (Colbert, Goddard and Lake was how the credits read), and Paulette's role was equal to her co-stars. Apparently the studio had figured Goddard wouldn't stand a chance in the best-actress category, so they campaigned for a supporting-actress nod.

Other supporting-actress nominees that year were very strong, and included Gladys Cooper and Anne Revere (both for *Song of Bernadette*) and Lucile Watson (*Watch on the Rhine*). They all lost to Katina Paxinou (*For Whom the Bell Tolls*), but Paulette's nomination had, for the moment, established her as an actress, not just a star.

Ironically, now that Meredith was in the States, Paulette was leaving. She had been persuaded to make a tour for the U.S.O. One of Paulette's friends assumed that perhaps a meeting between Paulette and famed war correspondent Ernie Pyle, a close friend of Meredith's, had led to the tour. But there are, of course, other versions.

134

PAULETTE

One story goes that the previous year, while Paulette was on a short trip to New York, she ran into some old acquaintances from Washington at the El Morocco nightclub. They joined her party. Paulette was a bit high from champagne. One of the bigwigs asked, "How would you like to go to China and entertain the troops?" Paulette answered, "Sure!" She probably forgot all about it until the U.S.O. got in touch with her to say that the entertainment unit she was assigned to was set to leave for the Orient.

Once the U.S.O. tour was a reality, Goddard approached it with her usual enthusiasm. It would be a great adventure. But when she went to New York to get her shots, she became so ill she had to remain in New York and could not travel to Washington, D.C., for President Roosevelt's birthday ball. Jinx Falkenburg attended the gala and rushed back to New York to give Paulette all the details.

Jinx has recalled, "Paulette was staying at Constance Collier's house on West Fifty-seventh Street and, since Constance was away and there was room, she suggested I stay there too.

"By the time I arrived Paulette was feeling no better. She was in bed with her shot reaction and in no mood to talk to anybody. As a matter of fact, I wasn't feeling too well myself."

Jinx's discomfort grew worse and she was running a fever. "Paulette, I think I feel a little sick, too," she told her friend.

"Well, go lie down in the other room," Goddard answered.

"But I have so many things to tell you . . ."

"You just go and lie down and tell me all about it tomorrow."

Jinx, by this time, "had a terrible pain in my side and I was moaning and groaning."

"Jinx, you're making me nervous," exclaimed Paulette. "You *do* look awful. We'd better call a doctor."

Falkenburg remembered, "The doctor arrived and pronounced that I was the proud possessor of acute appendicitis. By this time I was completely out of my head and the doctor called an ambulance. They laid me out on a stretcher and Paulette decided I looked cold or something, so she threw her ermine coat over me. Then her wild eye caught a glimpse of a basket of flowers on the piano, which she grabbed and thrust into my hand.

"'Oh, I wish your mother were here, Jinx. I feel as if I'm sending you off to the butcher's.'"

The humor of the situation was not lost on Falkenburg. "It was quite a sight, this girl laid out on a stretcher in an ermine coat and a basket of flowers, in between two orderlies and followed by Paulette Goddard."

Jinx, of course, recovered, and not long afterward Paulette embarked on her U.S.O. tour. The itinerary included China, Burma and other parts of the Far East (her first trip there since 1936).

In Paulette's troupe were comedian Keenan Wynn, actor William Gargan and accordionist Andy Arcari. It was always difficult for the U.S.O. to know how to utilize the talents of glamour girls like Paulette who weren't singers or dancers. A presentation had to be built around them. For Paulette, it was decided that she and Gargan would do a mind-reading sketch. Gargan would put her into a trance and, blindfolded, she would become Madame Svengali Goddard.

During the show, Paulette would always pick one G.I. out of the audience and bring him up on stage to kiss him. Traveling between the various camps, she wore an army uniform, but during the shows she wore sexy dresses. After all, that's what the boys wanted to see.

One running gag involved Paulette walking on stage in a sexy white gown and long gloves. The boys in the audience would naturally roar their approval, and after the catcalls and whistles died down Gargan would quip, "What's the matter, haven't you guys ever seen a pair of gloves before?"

Richard Watts, Jr., the New York *Herald Tribune*'s entertainment editor and critic, was at the time a war correspondent and was in Chungking, China. He filed a story about Goddard's tour: "The most famous of the quartet of traveling minstrels was the beauteous Goddard of the films, although most of the work was done by William Gargan . . . by Keenan Wynn, one of the best of the younger American comedians, and by Andy Arcari, a brilliant virtuoso of the piano accordion. They offered a show that dipped liberally and with fine ashamedness into the old corn barrel, and a good time was had by all."

Watts noted that while Goddard did not disappoint her audience in looks and charm, some complained of her acting ability. And the critic noted, "This struck me as being the height of ingratitude. It has been my longtime belief that screen histrionics were more a matter of good looks and inflammatory personalities than of deep emotional powers. I felt that Miss Goddard's handsomeness went far to justify me [in this opinion], as did her speaking of lines."

PAULETTE

During the tour, the radio code name for Paulette was "Miss Precious Cargo." It was a long tour—two months—throughout the Burma-India-China theater of war. Goddard was exhausted by the time she returned to Hollywood in early May. According to her account, Meredith met her at the plane and she was in such a state of fatigue, and had been pawed at by so many soldiers and told how beautiful she was and been propositioned so much, that it was a welcome relief to return to normal.

Goddard's friend Anita Loos recalled that Goddard told her, "I staggered off the plane in California and found Burgess waiting there. The first thing he said was, 'Gee, you look awful!'" Miss Loos said that Burgess' honesty negated all the "double entendre which had nauseated her for weeks. And when Burgess added, 'Let's get married,' it seemed to put a limit on sex once and for all." Loos quotes Paulette: "I let him lead me straight off to the license bureau."

Of course this somewhat fanciful explanation does not take into account that Meredith and Paulette had been involved in their relationship for several years. Furthermore, the marriage wasn't that quick. It didn't occur until two weeks after Paulette's return, and there was ample time to plan the marriage ceremony and small reception that were held at the home of Paulette's friends and former neighbors Irene and David Selznick.

Hollywood had expected Paulette, when she married again, to wed someone even wealthier than her previous two husbands. And yet here she was marrying an actor who, while not poverty-stricken, was not remotely in a league financially with Chaplin—or even Paulette herself. In addition, Meredith was currently a captain in the Air Force earning about $250 a month.

The conclusion was obvious: this was a love match. Like Goddard, Meredith was twice divorced and had no children. His second wife had been Margaret Perry, daughter of Broadway producer Antoinette Perry, from whom he was divorced in 1938.

Goddard told Louella Parsons: "Both of us have had unhappy marital experiences in the past. This is the third marriage for both of us. But I think you will realize how deeply we feel when I tell you that this is the first religious ceremony for either of us."

On Sunday, May 24, 1944, an army chaplain, Stanley Brown, performed the ceremony, joining Paulette Goddard and Oliver Burgess

Meredith in holy matrimony, in the presence of a very select group of guests. According to Paulette, "There were only seven people present."

As soon as the news that the marriage was official reached print, both Paulette's friends and enemies asked her what she thought the chances were of the marriage lasting—and wouldn't there be problems since she was the big income earner?

She retorted, "He's a fine actor and when the war is over he will do big things. We'll both have our work and we're going to try our best to make a go of our marriage."

There would be no honeymoon. "We'd rather be here in our own home than anywhere else," she stated. "Burgess has been away for so long—and so have I—that where could we be happier?"

After their marriage, Paulette and Meredith held regular Saturday night dinners at their beach house. One of their frequent guests was Clark Gable, who was in the service then and carrying the torch for his great love, Carole Lombard. (Lombard—Gable's third wife—died in a plane crash during the war.)

To reciprocate Paulette and Burgess' hospitality, Gable invited the Merediths to his ranch in the Valley for a dinner. At Paulette's, the evenings had been informal and casual. But someone who attended the dinner at Gable's recalls, "The fare was pressed duck. There were six of us for dinner and eight people in the kitchen cooking for us."

Meredith, who had heretofore been considered a rebel and hence not "worthy" of the standard Hollywood buildup, suddenly began receiving flattering major attention from top columnists. Louella Parsons called him "a grand person—a wit and a gentleman."

Paulette's movie with Sonny Tufts, *I Love a Soldier,* was released that June. Barry Fitzgerald headed the supporting cast and was featured in many of the ads to capitalize on the popularity he was achieving with *Going My Way.* To give some sex appeal to Goddard's role, the ads for the movie called Paulette "a welder by day—wilder by night."

Goddard's personal life was paralleling the film. She did love a soldier, Captain Buzz Meredith, and she did return to work. However, now there was a new goal. She was already a movie star, but she wouldn't have been human if the Oscar nomination hadn't whetted her appetite for further artistic recognition as *an actress.* With Meredith's encouragement, it seemed that this could be attained.

The next few years would see a meteoric rise in her career—and then a sudden, devastating plummet.

10

At Paramount in 1944, as at every other studio, the story editors were looking for properties similar to the current best-selling novel *Forever Amber*. Someone at Paramount remembered a novel, *Kitty,* by Rosamund Marshall, and from it producer Karl Tunberg and writer Darrell Ware fashioned a screenplay. The obvious choice of director was Mitchell Leisen. It was the kind of film that Leisen, who had started his career as an art director in the silent days under C. B. DeMille, would do to perfection—an elaborate historical costume drama.

For *Kitty,* Leisen assembled an incredible cast: Ray Milland, Patric Knowles, Reginald Owen, Cecil Kellaway and Constance Collier. Paulette would be playing the title role, the most demanding assignment of her career to date. Filming began shortly after her marriage to Meredith, and there was no doubt that behind the scenes he played an integral role in helping his wife to cope with the new artistic demands placed on her.

Goddard told a friend, "We have so much in common. We like to laugh, to study together, and Burgess takes great pride in my career as an actress."

In *Kitty,* Paulette portrayed a cockney girl in eighteenth-century En-

139

gland, who, because of her beauty, is selected by famous artist Thomas Gainsborough (Cecil Kellaway) to pose for a portrait. Through the artist, Kitty meets Sir Hugh Marcy (Ray Milland), who, although a nobleman, has lost all his money. He sees in Kitty a way to recoup his fortune. With the aid of another indigent member of the nobility (Constance Collier), Marcy teaches the girl manners and passes her off as someone of the higher classes.

Naturally, the film required a happy ending. In the story Kitty is first married off to a tradesman, but he dies and she marries into the nobility. Her second husband, joyous over the news of her being with child (not knowing it is the child of her first husband), also conveniently dies. And at the film's fade-out, Kitty is now free to marry the reformed Marcy, whom she has loved all along.

Kitty was not a one-dimensional character. The role called for two accents—indeed two personas, like Shaw's character Eliza Doolittle in *Pygmalion*. Before shooting on *Kitty* began, Leisen hired dialogue coach Phyllis Laughton to work with Paulette for several weeks. The director also hit upon the idea of putting Paulette together with someone who could effect a genuine cockney accent. And, in Leisen's words, "Finally we thought of Ida Lupino's mother, Connie Emerald. We moved Connie into Paulette's apartment and they spoke nothing but cockney day and night. I spoke cockney with Paulette on the set; Ray did too. Whenever Paulette talked to anybody, it was in cockney."

For the cockney accent, Paulette used a high-pitched voice. For her accent as the Duchess, Constance Collier had her lower her voice at least a full octave.

Constance, although she personally liked Paulette very much, confided to others on the set that being her coach was often exasperating. "I really don't know," Collier would complain. "It's as if she just doesn't hear what I'm saying." Although Paulette may have had trouble with the nuances of Kitty's character, in overall interpretation she certainly related to the part and worked well with the director.

Leisen and Paulette were great friends personally as well as professionally. In fact, Paulette and Buzz had moved into a sumptuous apartment complex in Hollywood that was owned—and the apartments had been personally decorated—by Mitch Leisen.

Unlike other directors on the Paramount lot, who might lose patience

140

with Paulette, Leisen knew exactly how she worked; she simply had to keep repeating a scene until she got the timing correct, however long that might take. Even when she did get it right, according to Leisen, she wouldn't necessarily know it—but Leisen would. And then they would have a print. However, the production people were often nervous during Paulette's films because of the number of takes her scenes required.

Phyllis Laughton has said, "As a human being, Paulette is very spontaneous, but it was always very hard to get her to be spontaneous on the screen. She held everything in because of the strict discipline she learned from Chaplin."

Kitty was Ray Milland's fourth film with Goddard. And although in his memoirs he barely mentions Paulette, in other instances he confided that he liked working with her despite the fact that she was not a brilliant actress and had no sense of timing and that he thought everything about her acting was "mechanical and contrived." But Milland asserted that no one knew this better than Paulette herself. "She was completely honest about it." And Milland has implied that most other stars like Paulette were not honest about what they could—or couldn't—deliver. Milland concluded that in *Kitty* Paulette "worked her ass off trying to give it all she had, and in the end her performance was quite all right."

Her performance was better than "all right." And she was surrounded by such talented and skilled professionals as Collier, Kellaway, Reginald Owen, Eric Blore, Mary Gordon, Sara Allgood and Mae Clarke. Moreover, Leisen had taken enormous care with production values, personally choosing the paintings and overseeing every detail of costume and set design.

When it was completed, *Kitty* was something special. After shooting was over, Paulette and Meredith made a trip to New York. There they met Jean Renoir, French filmmaker and son of the famed painter, who was a refugee in the States making films for the government. He and Meredith had already made a war documentary, *A Salute to France*, with Claude Dauphin.

Renoir was enchanted by Paulette Goddard. He had been a fan of hers since *Modern Times*. In fact, the portrayal of one of the characters in his 1936 film *The Lower Depths* had been inspired by Paulette's performance in *Modern Times*.

The Merediths became good friends with Renoir and his wife, Dido.

Renoir has described Paulette as "a beautiful woman with a lively mind. One can never be bored in her company."

Naturally, the famed filmmaker wanted to know how Chaplin could have ever left her, and she instantly explained that Chaplin hadn't left her, she had left him. She told Renoir it was because Charlie had had no sense of humor—he had saved all his humor for his films. Besides, she explained, it was very hard to live with a genius. According to Renoir, Paulette told him that when she had lived with Chaplin, his house was devoid of paintings and the only objects of art were a collection of English porcelain figurines.

After a while, when Paulette had become friendly with Dido Renoir—took her under her wing—she asked her, "Have you any jewels?" Dido answered, "No," and Paulette gently rebuked her: "Every woman needs jewels. They're small, easy to carry—easy to hide, in case the woman has a falling out with the man whom she regards as a keystone in her life."

Around this time, the press was critical of Paulette and other stars, including Ann Sheridan, who had cut short their U.S.O. tours. In Paulette's defense, however, it should be noted that she was on tour for fifty-four of the sixty scheduled days. And she returned with only the clothes she had on; she had given her dresses and shoes to the Wacs and the nurses. The criticism died down when Paulette returned to Hollywood to resume work.

In late October, Goddard re-created her film role in *Standing Room Only* with Fred MacMurray, on "Lux Radio Theatre." But there would be no new films for a while. Paulette, thirty-three, the girl who had *almost* everything, was expecting a first child. She withdrew from *The Well-Groomed Bride,* her next film assignment, in which Ray Milland and Sonny Tufts were to be her leading men. The part went to Olivia de Havilland.

Everyone who knew Paulette recalls her as a woman of robust health with a constantly positive attitude. However, shortly after the announcement of the expected baby, Paulette suffered a miscarriage. She was hospitalized. Friends recall this is the only time they can remember her being hospitalized, and the only time they saw her despondent.

Meredith wooed her out of her despondency. There were plans for them to work together. Paulette at this time was very much awed by Meredith's talent. She told friends, "It's amazing. If you want him to, Burgess can act anything. If you want an Oriental, he suddenly becomes Oriental! He looks like one, he talks like one, walks like one. He can do it all instantly."

There was no doubt that Meredith's training and natural ability were highly impressive. Furthermore, he was once again a movie star. He had just completed *The Story of G.I. Joe* for RKO, in which he played Ernie Pyle. Meredith looked very much like Pyle, who had been killed in the Pacific. During the war, when Pyle was back at his home in Albuquerque, New Mexico, between assignments, Meredith had visited him there. *The Story of G.I. Joe* was directed by William Wellman and co-starred young Robert Mitchum.

Hollywood again recognized the talent of Burgess Meredith and, for the moment, he had clout in the industry. Meredith and Paulette now began discussing doing work on the stage together. First, however, there were other projects. The Merediths appeared on radio in an original drama, *The Crew of the Model T,* and then they planned their first film project together.

Ever since he had met her, Jean Renoir had wanted to do a film with Goddard. A person who knew Paulette well says that while she is one of the most intelligent of women, and she projects that intelligence when she's sitting across from you at dinner, Paulette has never projected it on the screen.

Obviously, Renoir knew the in-person Goddard. He felt that he could be the one to translate her magic to the screen. With Renoir as director, and Meredith interested in producing his own films, a project blossomed. Buzz wanted to adapt Octave Mirbeau's French classic *Celestine's Diary* for the screen. It had already been a stage success in Paris, and was now titled *The Diary of a Chambermaid.*

Meredith has recalled how the package materialized. "There was a man, Ben Bogeaus, and he was a free-swinging independent producer; he liked me and liked my ideas, and he asked me to produce. I brought two general ideas to him which he bought. One was *Diary of a Chambermaid,* which I also wrote."

Benedict Bogeaus and the Merediths formed a producing company, the Camden Corporation. It was reported that Paulette was its largest stockholder.

Again, an impressive cast was assembled to surround Paulette. Meredith would play a small but key character role, and the other leads would be played by Hurd Hatfield, Francis Lederer, Reginald Owen and the superb character actresses Judith Anderson, Florence Bates and Irene Ryan.

The Diary of a Chambermaid was definitely not a Hollywood-type story or project that would be produced by a major studio. Paramount had nothing for Paulette at the moment. Even *Kitty*, though scored and edited and ready for release, was on the shelf owing to Paramount's backlog of product. Besides, Paulette's contract gave her the right to make one outside film a year.

However, before starting *Diary*, Paulette's home studio did use her in a bit, playing herself, in the all-star *Duffy's Tavern*, the hit radio program brought to the screen. Paulette would receive third billing, after Bing Crosby and Betty Hutton, and before such other Paramount powerhouses as Alan Ladd, Dorothy Lamour and Veronica Lake. Paulette's cameo cast her as the woman Sonny Tufts and Brian Donlevy fight over.

With *Diary of a Chambermaid*, the attempt was made to fuse The Star with The Actress and, for the most part, it succeeded. In retrospect, this is the only Goddard starring vehicle that has achieved cult status. And critics have been impressed by Renoir's ability in *Diary* to marry the dramatic and the comic.

The story concerns an ambitious chambermaid in France in 1885. The underlying theme of the script is that lust for possessions corrupts.

Paulette was back to being a blonde for this role, and was photographed magnificently by cameraman Lucien Androit. As in earlier films, there were lines in the script that some thought reflected Paulette's own attitude. "I'm going to fight hard and I'm going to grab the very first man I meet to get where I'm going—just so long as he has *money*," says Celestine. Later, when an old man offers her "romance," she accepts: "I'll use men—rich men—to get places." When the master of the house wants to give Celestine gifts, she tells him she wants "a remembrance"—like the snuffbox with rubies and diamonds in the vault

144

below. Other lines in the picture, such as "Girls like lots of presents, you know," could be directly from Paulette's life.

While Paulette's fans might accept all of this, there were other aspects in the movie that were probably difficult for American audiences to swallow. For example, Meredith's character, an ugly, elflike old man whom Celestine sets her cap for, "eats anything, dead or alive." He eats beetles as well as rose petals.

Supposedly, during shooting the film, Meredith, although spared the beetles, ate real rose petals. It was said that Goddard wondered if they might be harmful to Buzz. He also had to work with a squirrel who bit him. (The character kills the squirrel in the film.)

Although Paulette may not have realized it at the time, it was obvious to Meredith and Renoir that they were creating an artistic film, a *film noir*.

Paulette enjoyed working with Renoir. She called the filmmaker "an amazing man. He likes actors, and situations, and insists on telling a story. This is so unlike most directors who like only directors"—she paused—"one director—you know who I mean." The reference to her former husband was unmistakable.

When shooting on *Diary* was finally completed, everybody was enthusiastic over the film's prospects—everybody except the distributor. Paulette later conceded that RKO had rejected the film: "They said it violated all the accepted standards of picturemaking. I framed their letter and took it as a challenge. I recognized their business sense. My reaction is not a criticism of the studio. It just is not my conception of what picturemaking ought to be." A distribution deal for the picture was struck with United Artists.

Paulette and Buzz were off to New York. During their marriage, they split their time between their homes on the East Coast and the West Coast. In New York, they were favorites of both the movie and the theater worlds: a husband and wife who moved easily within various societies—intellectual, artistic, theatrical.

The couple appeared on radio shows and gave interviews. Paulette eagerly drummed up interest in *The Diary of a Chambermaid*. She told *Life* magazine's Oliver Jensen that the movie was about a girl "who has all sorts of interesting arrangements—you know what Jean Renoir said

145

about me? He said this movie would be a documentary of me if I'd lived in France in 1885 and if I had been a chambermaid."

While they were in the East, the Merediths also attended political rallies. Buzz had kept Paulette interested in politics. Earlier in the year, the couple had arranged a dinner to honor Vladmir Dedier, one of the leaders of Yugoslavia's National Liberation Army. There was an American Committee for Yugoslav Relief (Mrs. Roosevelt was honorary chairman), and Meredith served as chairman of a clothing campaign launched by the committee.

Chaplin had hosted a luncheon in his home for Dedier. The Goddard-Meredith dinner for the political figure was attended by dozens of Hollywood's top writers, directors and executives. It was a time when America was saluting the Yugoslav guerrillas who fought valiantly against Nazi occupation of their country.

In New York, Paulette seemed to be mixing politics and art. She made statements such as: "Here we have a wonderful medium [films], which formerly we merely exploited. Now with the world in a state of chaos, with Europe starving and we in America fat and comfortable, it is time we adopted a realistic and progressive view toward pictures.

"Because I believe in this I bought, or perhaps I should say my company bought, Aldous Huxley's *Brave New World*. This is a book about the world two thousand years hence, and I have asked Mr. Huxley and his brother, Julian, to come out and do the script."

But Paulette's critics pointed out that perhaps she wasn't as concerned with art and message pictures as she was with making money. As a salaried performer at Paramount, 80 percent of her income went for taxes. As an independent producer, her income was only subject to the 25 percent capital gains tax. Therefore, even if her own films were not nearly as successful as her Paramount features, she would still make more money from them.

Ironically, with *The Diary of a Chambermaid* now set for February, 1946, release, Paramount was ready to release *Kitty* and it would open the following month. Paulette was, of course, the centerpiece in ads for both films.

Visually, both ad campaigns were tastefully done. But the ad copy for Paramount's *Kitty* was distinctly Hollywood. "She made a career out of love . . ." ran the ad line. And, to make the film appealing to the masses and not sell it as highbrow, the Paramount campaign used some silly poetry: "Kitty and the Duke were a handsome pair . . . Soon they were married with a son and heir . . . But Kitty had her eye on his bank account, and she got what she wanted, thanks to Paramount." Another couplet declared: "From rags to ermine, Kitty made no stop . . . On a ladder of husbands she climbed to the top."

Needless to say, the ads for *Chambermaid* were more artistic and restrained. But they did include a double-entendre tag line: "I tried to be good—always."

Before either film opened, Buzz and Paulette were off on an adventure. Although they made many trips to New York together during the forties (either by the Super Chief-20th Century luxury train or by transcontinental plane routes, which had several refueling stops), they made one very memorable trip in early 1946.

Howard Hughes had invited the Merediths to join him in a group that included William Powell and his wife, Diana, Cary Grant and Betty Hensel, restaurateur Dave Chasen and others. It was to be a fabulous private junket—and a genuine happening. Hughes was personally going to pilot the first nonstop transcontinental flight from Los Angeles to New York.

This was the kind of experience that Paulette loved—a journey that would be exciting and certainly unpredictable. Of course she and Burgess accepted.

Actress Constance Moore had been invited but didn't want to go. However, when she drove her husband, Johnny Maschio, to the airport, the others convinced her to join them on the trip. The flight East was smooth and fast, and in New York the party continued. Hughes had booked suites for everyone in the Sherry Netherland Hotel. Each couple had a car and chauffeur at their disposal for the three days they were in the city.

On the flight back to Los Angeles, however, the glittering group of carefree adventurers were unexpectedly bumped back into reality. The gliding silver bird seemed suddenly to be lurching through the air as it hit a patch of inclement weather, shortly before they were to land in L.A. Hughes, at the controls, called for a drink.

"Christ," said Paulette. "Howard doesn't drink!"

There was a slight panic among the passengers. If Hughes was calling for a drink, the situation must be even worse than it appeared. Supposedly, Dave Chasen broke open a bottle of eighty-five-year-old vintage vodka and brought a tumbler of it into the cockpit, then stood aghast when Hughes splashed the priceless vodka on the plane's windshield. The pilot had only needed the alcohol to de-ice the window, or so the story goes.

They landed safely, of course, and Hughes had accomplished his mission: to publicize nonstop transcontinental travel.

Buzz was planning a return to the New York stage. Paulette returned to filmmaking.

In the studio-system heyday, stars and directors, with few exceptions, followed a similar routine: they would make both "small" and "big" pictures. A lavish historical production à la *Kitty* would be followed by a contemporary drama or comedy. Mitch Leisen was making a comedy, *Suddenly It's Spring*. Claudette Colbert had been set for the role, but eventually Paulette landed it. The script was co-authored by Claude Binyon, who was a good friend of Fred MacMurray's. Binyon was also producing the film, and although MacMurray had already left the lot, Paramount hired him back for this one picture.

Eleanor Broder, who worked on *Suddenly It's Spring* with Leisen, has recalled Binyon as a very shy man. She said that Binyon was intimidated by Paulette, and when he came to the set he would anxiously ask, "Where is she?" It seems he tried to avoid Goddard because the actress, "in her peppy way," would say things like "Oh, come on, Claude, can't you write me some better dialogue?"

This was just Paulette's way. She was not demanding, as others might be, but Binyon could not cope with her brand of coquetry. And he hadn't the experience working with Goddard that Leisen and other members of Leisen's staff had.

Fred MacMurray was expert at comedy timing, but Paulette wasn't. Those on the film remember that she would play a scene either too fast or too slow, and it would take many attempts before she got it right. In some instances, she never did get it right, and it was up to the film's editor to cut the scene so it would work.

While she was shooting *Suddenly It's Spring,* her two costume pictures opened. *Diary* opened first, and although the film and Paulette received good reviews ("Miss Goddard is equal to all the requirements of her assignment," said the New York *Herald Tribune*), the public did not respond enthusiastically.

Burgess Meredith has recalled: "At times I feel that *Diary of a Chambermaid* was an underrated film in this country. I thought it was a much better film than anybody had any idea of, but for some reason they didn't grasp the notion; then it became a classic, a minor classic, later. It was always appreciated in France, very much so. It was one of my favorites."

Unbeknownst to Paulette and Buzz, *The Diary of a Chambermaid* appeared on a list of pictures (eighteen in all) the F.B.I. thought should be screened closely to see "if there is a possibility of propaganda of a subversive nature." The F.B.I. agents hadn't seen any of the eighteen. They were basing their assumptions solely on the point that these films had been "produced, directed and written by persons whose connections with the Communist movement have been established by reliable and dependable records."

Among others, the film projects under surveillance included *Scarlet Street, Tomorrow Is Forever,* John Huston's script of *Three Strangers* and even a Western, *Abilene Town.*

Kitty, while not arousing the attention of the F.B.I., did get the attention of the public. It was an immediate, huge hit. One critic noted, "Paulette Goddard has worked up blazing temperament to go with her ravishing beauty in the title role."

Life magazine picked *Kitty* as its Movie of the Week, and called it "One of the lushest pictures to come out of Hollywood since pre-War days." They gave fine notices to *Kitty*'s "excellent character actors and settings and costumes of almost inconceivable luxury and elegance." They said leading man Milland added "another accomplished performance" to his career. As for Paulette, they noted she "struggles hard with a cockney accent but seems to grow more beautiful each time she wears another of her twenty-six costumes."

The picture went on to gross nearly four million dollars, and was one of the industry's top ten grossing films of the year.

While *Kitty* was racking up its grosses, Paulette began renegotiating her contract with Paramount for even better terms. She was in a strong position. *Kitty* was a box-office hit, *Diary* was a *succès d'estime*. And, most important, DeMille had chosen Paulette for the female lead in his new epic now in preparation. Goddard would star opposite Gary Cooper in this film, another historical costume picture.

Around this time a Paramount executive said, "Paulette is the only artist in Hollywood who doesn't need an agent. . . . If Paulette went into an agent's office she would come out with his pants."

A new contract was finalized. Paulette had several weeks free before the DeMille assignment. She planned a trip to Europe to discuss a picture with Alexander Korda.

Behind the scenes, a volcano was rumbling and about to erupt. World War II was over, but the Cold War was just ahead. The political views of many in Hollywood would soon be world headlines. It is interesting to note that while Paulette Goddard was palling around with such obvious capitalists as Howard Hughes, and had been a guest at the home of President and Mrs. Roosevelt, her activities were *still* under the surveillance of the F.B.I.

After the war there were several political groups formed by people in the industry that turned out to be front organizations. All these groups were under investigation by the government. There were many actors, writers and others in the industry who, because of their social consciousness and political convictions, had joined organizations some of which, they soon discovered to their horror, were indeed—as the F.B.I. charged—front groups for the Communists. Even Screen Actors Guild board member Ronald Reagan learned that one organization he was involved with at this time was not what it appeared to be and he quickly dropped out.

Other people in the industry, like Paulette, while never officially joining any political groups, often lent their names to what they thought were merely charitable activities or unaligned political causes. One such group Paulette had lent her name to was planning a "Win the Peace Conference." Many people, in and out of show business, were also involved in sponsoring this conference. Among them were several senators and congressmen, including Estes Kefauver, Adam Clayton Powell and Helen Gahagan Douglas. There were also rabbis, bishops and other clergymen listed as sponsors.

From the show-business world, in addition to Paulette, Oscar Ham-

With Ray Milland and John Wayne in Cecil B. DeMille's 1942 blockbuster, *Reap the Wild Wind*. Goddard's role was a blatant facsimile of Scarlett. *Phototeque*

With Dorothy Lamour and Veronica Lake in the famous "Sweater, Sarong and Peek-a-Boo Bang" number from *Star Spangled Rhythm*, 1942. *Phototeque*

With George Reeves in *So Proudly We Hail,* 1943. Goddard's portrayal of the wisecracking, seductive nurse won her an Oscar nomination.

At a radio station with *So Proudly We Hail* co-stars Veronica Lake and Claudette Colbert. Note Paulette's shoulder strap; it's one of her diamond necklaces. *Phototeque*

At the *I Am an American Day* pageant in Chicago in May 1943. Goddard led the throng in pledging allegiance to the flag. Bing Crosby was master of ceremonies. *Movie Star News*

Popular World War II pinup shot of Paulette.

Goddard at the height of
her glamour girl appeal.
Movie Star News

Rags-to-riches: Goddard as the title character in Mitchell Leisen's *Kitty*. Released in 1946, it was Paulette's most successful picture. *Phototeque*

With husband Burgess Meredith (in heavy character makeup) in Jean Renoir's *Diary of a Chambermaid*, 1946. The film was produced by Paulette and Meredith. *Phototeque*

DeMille directing Paulette in *Unconquered*. The director refused to cast her in any more of his films. *Movie Star News*

With Gary Cooper in *Unconquered*, a big hit of the 1947 season. The cameraman complained that both stars had been difficult to photograph as "young" leads (Goddard was thirty-six; Cooper, forty-six). *Phototeque*

The dice symbolized Goddard's character's gambling fever in *Hazard*, 1948, a box office dud. *Phototeque*

Taking a bubble bath in *Anna Lucasta*, 1949. The film was not a hit. *Phototeque*

Clark Gable, the forty-eight-year-old actor, and Paulette were a romantic duo for a while, but he married one of Paulette's friends. *Phototeque*

With John Lund in *Bride of Vengeance*, 1949. A critical and financial disaster, it was Paulette's last film for Paramount. *Phototeque*

Erich Maria Remarque (left) and John Gavin in a scene from the 1958 film based on Remarque's novel, *A Time to Love and a Time to Die*. The literary lion became Paulette's fourth husband that year. *Phototeque*

Goddard at fifty-five, during the filming of *A Time of Indifference*, 1966. *Phototeque*

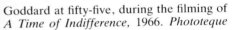

merstein II, Norman Corwin and Paul Robeson were on the group's letterhead. Others involved from the entertainment world included Sidney Buchman, Uta Hagen, "Yip" Harburg, Albert Maltz, Margo, Donald Ogden Stewart, Herman Shumlin and Robert Rossen.

After the war there were many who felt that it was clear the world was dividing into two camps: the Eastern bloc (Russia) and the Western bloc (the United States and her allies). It seemed the United States and Britain had only accepted Russia as an ally during the war out of necessity. All the idealistic statements made during the war—unity, world cooperation, etc.—were now forgotten.

In greatly simplified terms, the "Win the Peace" group espoused having no blocs but advocated re-establishing the Big Three unity as essential to durable peace. Their slogan was "Unity won the war, Unity must win the peace."

Naturally, the F.B.I. viewed this as a subversive tactic. In their minds all the activities of these groups were aimed at "softening American policy toward Russia." Bureau documents noted that "the Conference sponsors lost no time in condemning the recent speech made by Winston Churchill, who called for a Western bloc."

Not only was the Bureau concerned with Communist infiltration of the film business, they were also convinced that the Communists were infiltrating the radio industry. Paulette had been mentioned in their report on *The Crew of the Model T*, the radio program she had done with Buzz the previous year. In fact, the F.B.I. had obtained a copy of the script even before its broadcast and had done investigations into the backgrounds of all the people in the cast, including Paulette, Meredith, Ray Collins, James Gleason, Rex Ingram, Norman Lloyd, producer John Houseman and director Paul Stewart. The authors, Abraham Polonsky and Leon Meadow, were, of course, under special scrutiny.

The Bureau's point of view was that all such activities, whether on radio or—like the Win the Peace Conference—geared for press coverage, were attempts to undermine America. However, it would be a year before the public became aware of the "Communist threat in Hollywood." Meanwhile, for the industry, it was business as usual and Paulette Goddard was off to England.

11

□□□□□

"Carmen! Let's do *Carmen!"* It was one of several stories that Korda and Goddard were considering. Another was an episodic tale that would have Paulette playing four different women in different generations. This was a film concept that was currently popular among British film-makers and had been used successfully in other pictures. For Paulette's proposed venture, she would play four different gypsy women through the centuries.

Several Oscar Wilde stories were under consideration as well. Costume pictures and Paulette seemed to be a commercial combination. Although on this trip plans on a property weren't completed, Korda and Goddard did decide on the date she would begin production. Studio space was very difficult to obtain in postwar England, and scheduling had to be done well in advance. The picture—whatever it was—would be shot in April and May of the following year.

Paulette returned to Hollywood within a month. "It's unbelievable that you can travel so quickly," she marveled, "that it's no problem to go to England for story conferences."

Buzz, too, was making a film. Universal had signed him to play James Madison in *The Magnificent Doll,* which would star Ginger

152

Rogers as Dolly Madison and David Niven as Aaron Burr, her love interest.

The Merediths still had their production company and they talked of making short-subject travelogues. It would be a way to combine business with pleasure. Paulette told friends, "The shorts might be called 'The Perils of Paulette,' except that I can't be in all of them—commitments." She was even willing to give up the lead. "We talked about it with Jinx Falkenburg and Tex McCrary [Jinx's husband]. Maybe Jinx would be the heroine and I could make two a year as a comedienne."

Both Meredith and Goddard had a sense of humor that was never captured in their films. Just as Paulette liked to bait certain friends, like David Selznick, part of the Goddard-Meredith relationship was teasing each other.

Buzz and Paulette had bought a lot at Trancas Beach, just north of Malibu. Merle Oberon had a sumptuous beach house on the lot next door. Oberon was now divorced from Alexander Korda and married to cameraman Lucien Ballard, and since her husband was not in the same social set as most of her friends, the couple lived mainly at the beach.

Merle and Paulette, who had known each other for some time, had much in common. They were both friends of Joe Schenck; Merle had, in fact, had an affair with Schenck back in 1934. And Oberon shared Goddard's passion for Mexico and Mexican art treasures.

Before leaving for England, Paulette had jokingly told Buzz that she expected the house they were planning at the beach to be up by the time she returned. Now that she was back, Oberon invited the Merediths for a weekend at the beach. It was evening when they arrived at Merle's, and, unknown to Paulette, Merle and Buzz had concocted a practical joke.

"Did you tell Sugar what happened to your lot?" Merle asked in a stage whisper.

Meredith played along. "Why did you mention that, Merlie? I didn't want to spoil her first evening back."

"What happened?" Paulette demanded.

"No, no, it'll only upset you."

"For God's sake, tell me!"

Meredith relented. "You wanted me to start building, so I hired a contractor to level off the property. I'm sorry, but they bulldozed most of the lot into the ocean."

Paulette shrieked, "They did *what?*"

"It looks like the top of Vesuvius," Merle chimed in.

"We'll eventually be able to build," Meredith explained. "Of course not a real house—maybe a Quonset or something that won't rot from seepage."

The joke had gone too far. Paulette was furious and was shouting things like "It's just the sort of thing you'd do!" She wanted to go out and look at the property immediately but it was pitch dark. In the morning, of course, Paulette discovered the property was intact and realized she'd been taken. It was another example of Meredith's superlative acting ability and his offbeat sense of humor.

There weren't too many jokes, however, during the filming of the new DeMille epic. The director's sense of humor was practically nonexistent at the best of times. And this was a tense time for DeMille. On this production, he was out to make a statement regarding his personal concept of freedom.

Since January, 1945, DeMille had been off the radio. He had refused to pay a one-dollar assessment that the radio union A.F.R.A. (American Federation of Radio Artists) had imposed on all its members. The one dollar was going to a political fund, and DeMille was opposed to any union having the right to assess its members.

After leaving the union, he formed the DeMille Foundation for Political Freedom. In his words: "Our purpose was to work for political freedom and the right to work. . . . It should not seem surprising that for my next picture my thoughts turned to the birth of freedom."

DeMille had chosen a story about slavery in Colonial America from a novel, *The Judas Tree,* by journalist Neil Swanson. The director set his researchers and writers to working on a script that was eventually titled *Unconquered.*

According to screenwriter Jesse Lasky, Jr., "To the boss, *Unconquered* had become more than a film. It was a cause embracing his struggle with A.F.R.A., which had assumed the dimensions of a battle for free men's survival in a world threatened by Red subversion."

Everyone in Hollywood knew that by upholding his principles DeMille had given up a great deal of the only thing that Hollywood respected: money. He had had to relinquish his $100,000-a-year job as host of the "Lux Radio Theatre."

The director's enormous intensity was now focused on *Unconquered,* which had been in preproduction for almost a year and had an enormous budget of $5 million. There was a strike at Paramount during the work on *Unconquered,* but the strike soon petered out and the production moved forward.

When she was in London, Paulette had engaged a teacher to help her with her English accent for the film. Goddard was playing a bond slave from England who is shipped to the American colonies in the seventeen-seventies. Paulette observed, "This accent will be different from *Kitty.* Cockney is easy for me, but this is straight."

Ray Rennahan, the man who had filmed *Gone With the Wind,* was director of photography. Indeed all the technical people involved in *Unconquered* were tops in their field. As with all DeMille productions, the cast had been carefully handpicked. Gary Cooper was still one of the top ten box-office draws in films, and Paulette was finally his leading lady (almost a decade after Chaplin had talked of teaming them).

Supporting the leads were Howard da Silva, Cecil Kellaway, Ward Bond, Henry Wilcoxon, C. Aubrey Smith, Virginia Grey, Porter Hall, Mike Mazurki, Alan Napier, Raymond Hatton. Boris Karloff and Marc Lawrence had key roles as American Indians. DeMille's daughter Katherine also had an important supporting role.

Since DeMille's pictures were populated by hundreds of extras and stuntmen, his sets were always noisy. "The Chief" (or "The Boss," as he was alternately known) directed from behind an amplified megaphone. He would often shout at the cast and crew, "Quiet! What I want is quiet! Quiet behind the camera, intelligence in front of it. I know I can't have both at the same time, but let's see if I can get one or the other."

Insiders on the lot also knew that The Boss was going through a difficult time emotionally. He was often despondent because his longtime friend, former lover and aide, Jeannie Macpherson, was dying of cancer.

After Paulette began her scenes, cinematographer Rennahan was soon conferring with DeMille over the rushes. There were circles under Paulette's eyes. The director spoke with Goddard about her late nights and suggested that for the next few months she get to bed early. After all, she had to look young and sexy. DeMille leading ladies were expected to.

DeMille leading ladies were also expected to go through the rigors of every conceivable pitfall that melodrama could provide. Many people who worked with DeMille, and many critics, have accused him of having sadomasochistic tendencies when it came to scenes involving his leading ladies. They were often whipped, spanked, shackled, thrown into water and physically mistreated by evil villains. "C.B. was way ahead of his time in that regard," mused writer Ben Hecht.

Others contend that this had nothing to do with C.B.'s personal tastes—it was merely part of the formula he had developed. He knew what the audience wanted. For example, his audiences had come to expect the leading lady to take at least one on-screen bath. For *Unconquered*, the writers had devised a scene where Paulette bathes in a rain barrel. Her cleavage was covered by soapsuds, and although De-Mille's researchers had pointed out to The Chief that in 1775 there were no soapsuds à la Lever Brothers, the censors insisted and DeMille had to acquiesce on this historical anachronism.

Another part of the formula was for the leading lady to be constantly rescued by the dashing, handsome leading man. In this regard, cinematographer Rennahan encountered another problem. Gary Cooper, at forty-six, was photographing as forty-six. Therefore the film editor had to pick the best take based not on acting performance but on making the leading man look young. All in all, the production was not going smoothly.

While Paulette was shooting *Unconquered,* during the Fourth of July hiatus, she and Buzz joined David Selznick for a holiday weekend cruise on his yacht. Selznick and Irene were now separated, and David's new love (and future wife) was his contract star Jennifer Jones. Other guests on the cruise included CBS founder and president William S. Paley. Selznick had invited beautiful blonde actress Evelyn Keyes, ostensibly as Paley's date, but Keyes had asked if she could bring along her current love, director John Huston. "Of course," Selznick replied.

Orson Welles, Howard Hughes and Alexander Korda were others who joined the party on sea or on land during the weekend. Meredith, too, was set to make a film for Korda in England. John Huston was an old friend of Buzz and Paulette's; he had visited the Merediths at their upstate New York farm during the war.

Evelyn Keyes has told an amusing incident about this weekend. "We anchored off Avalon, and Paulette popped in to take a swim first thing in the morning, daintily slipping into the water in a blue bathing suit, hair piled high on her head, a diamond necklace—the real McCoy— nestled around her neck. She made delicate paddling movements with her hands and feet, with as little effort as possible, never putting her head in the water."

Keyes has described herself as "a Paulette Goddard fan. I adored her sparkle, her infectious laughter and *joie de vivre,* her ability to gather such men as Charlie Chaplin, Aldous Huxley and John Steinbeck in her web and make them happy while they were there."

Keyes emulated Goddard to such an extent that "it annoyed John. He told me in no uncertain terms to stop it, that one Paulette Goddard in the world was enough."

Back on the Paramount lot, Goddard and Cooper were chummy during *Unconquered.* She called him "my hero." DeMille and Goddard were not getting along well, however. He felt she no longer had the spontaneity she had displayed in 1940 and 1942. He now found her acting too studied. He thought she was posturing in front of the camera instead of simply playing the scene as written. And then came the fatal blowup. Paulette refused to appear in part of the crucial sequence where Fort Pitt is being attacked by the Indians and firebombs are being hurled at her.

As were many in the industry, DeMille was of the breed that said, "Films are my reason for breathing." He expected a similar attitude from those who worked for him—no risk was too great if it would result in "a *better* movie." His current leading lady, however, was not a maniacally devoted believer in risking life and limb for her profession *or* her director. (Perhaps Paulette and Hitchcock would have been a good team. His retort, when pressed for results by an overanxious producer or actor, was "It's only a movie.")

On the set all present had just witnessed an incredible scene. An elaborate battle sequence was in progress. As with all battle scenes, there were many takes because scores of people were involved and something always went wrong. By the twentieth take the production staff was getting very nervous. If they went into "golden time"—overtime—costs would double and triple.

During the next take, a flaming arrow hit the head of a drum carried by one of the drummer-boy extras. DeMille was all set to holler "Cut!" when he realized the boy hadn't stopped beating the drum, even though the drumsticks themselves were on fire. The scene continued to its conclusion. It was magnificent. Finally DeMille yelled, "Cut!" Fortunately the boy had been wearing gloves, and he now instantly immersed his gloved hands in a bucket of water.

Cast, crew and doctor on the set rushed over to him. His burns were not serious. The crowd parted as the great director approached the brave lad. It was DeMille's custom to award silver half-dollar pieces to those he felt had "earned them." He handed the coin to the boy, and said: "For courage, far above and beyond the call of duty."

Photographers were summoned and recorded the award. And DeMille declared, "America won't have to worry as long as there are boys like this growing up."

When DeMille was ready for Paulette, she was shown where he wanted her to stand. Her stand-in was already in the spot.

"Is *that* where you want me to stand?" asked Paulette.

"Yes, right there."

"Exactly where do you mean?"

"Right over *there*." He was pointing and he was getting angry.

"Me?"

"You."

Paulette refused. She knew the scene involved firebombs being hurled onto the set, and she would not do a scene where she felt she was in danger.

DeMille berated her in front of cast and crew. He called her a coward, told her she wasn't being fair to the production or her fellow artists.

Nothing, however, could convince Goddard. She burst into tears when DeMille continued his tactics. Paulette called for her agent—*he* could deal with working out the details. DeMille was fuming. Paulette later recalled, "He kept yelling, 'Get her out of here—before I kill her.'" And, she said, "I took the hint and headed for New York. My stand-in became my double and they shot her in the scene. And here's a postscript on that story—my double wore a wig, and in the picture it caught on fire. All I had was my own hair!"

It is true that Paulette left the set and DeMille was forced to use a double in the scene, which meant that it had to be a long-shot and was therefore less effective. It is also true that the double suffered minor burns—and so did thirty extras that day. In any event, the film was over but DeMille was furious. He would never trust Goddard again. She had lost an important ally at the studio.

Even Paulette has admitted, "Mr. DeMille wouldn't speak to me for years and years."

That fall, Paulette joined Buzz in New York, where he had gone to star on Broadway in a revival of J. M. Synge's *The Playboy of the Western World*, with Mildred Natwick. It seemed to be the season for Hollywood stars on Broadway: Ingrid Bergman was appearing in *Joan of Lorraine*; Fredric March and his wife, Florence Eldridge, were doing Ruth Gordon's *Years Ago* and Louis Calhern and Dorothy Gish were in *The Magnificent Yankee*.

The Merediths' pal John Huston and his new wife, Evelyn Keyes, were in town. Evelyn and Paulette had become close friends. John was directing a production of *No Exit*, and Buzz was busy rehearsing, so the women spent their time in New York shopping. On weekends, when their husbands were free from theater commitments, the foursome would go to the Meredith house in the country.

Paulette and Buzz had done radio and films together. Now they embarked on the next step: they would act on stage together. Another play on Broadway that season was *A Flag Is Born*, with Paul Muni and a newcomer, Marlon Brando. It was a drama about the formation of the new state of Israel, and this was the vehicle that Meredith, Paulette and their friend John Garfield proposed to appear in at the Studebaker Theater in Chicago. It was to be a limited run, opening December 26, 1946, and closing on January 18, 1947. Paulette, however, didn't take the plunge; she postponed her theater début with Buzz for a future date.

That winter, *Suddenly It's Spring* was released and proved to be a surprise hit. The studio had expected it to make money but it turned out to be one of their top grossers. It seemed Alexander Korda had made a wise choice in signing Paulette. But before leaving for Europe, where she and Buzz would each make a film for Korda (Buzz's was *Mine Own Executioner*), Paulette did a cameo, along with all Paramount's stars, in another of the studio's all-star productions, *Variety Girl*. To capitalize on her glamour, a short scene was written wherein Goddard takes a bubble bath.

Then she had to make *Hazard,* a comedy-adventure in which Paulette would be playing a compulsive gambler. On paper, *Hazard* was the kind of picture Paramount was adept at turning out: a comedy about a lady chased across the country by a private eye, with the pair eventually falling in love. But the script was weak, and even under the tutelage of veteran director George Marshall, the finished product wasn't very good. Furthermore, Paulette's leading man, MacDonald Carey, although a fine actor, did not have the box-office following of Cooper, Milland or MacMurray. Paulette's name would have to carry the film. But for the moment she was still riding high.

John Huston was going to Mexico to scout locations for a new film, *The Treasure of the Sierra Madre.* Evelyn wanted to go along and asked Paulette to join them. Keyes has noted: "Paulette was practically a native. Rumor had it she had had a fling with one of their presidents, but what did I know? She sported a mammoth gold filigreed watch that indicated *somebody* Mexican had been interested."

One of Paulette's acquaintances in Mexico City was the owner of the Plaza de Toros, and Paulette introduced Keyes to the bullfights. The women visited with the famous matador Manolete before one of his fights. They had brought bouquets of flowers, and, according to Keyes, "Paulette threw her bouquet to him when he made his triumphant walk around the ring. She made me save mine for the other matador. I knew what she was up to; she wanted him to dedicate the next bull to her. He didn't. And when we saw him later in a restaurant, he passed our table without looking in our direction. Even Paulette couldn't win them all."

Occasionally, harsh reality intruded on these fantasy excursions. Goddard, Huston and Keyes took a side trip from Mexico City to Acapulco. When their small plane landed on a primitive dirt strip, one of their tires had a blowout. The plane spun around several times and almost skidded into the ocean. The three passengers came close to serious injury.

Despite the danger of travel, Goddard never developed any fears in that department. She left for Europe with the requisite dozens of pieces of luggage that a movie star was expected to travel with. She brought along her Swedish maid and hairdresser, Hedvig Mjordu.

The script Korda had finally chosen for Goddard was an adaptation of

Oscar Wilde's *An Ideal Husband,* in which Paulette would be portraying Mrs. Cheveley to Michael Wilding's Lord Goring. Perhaps Korda chose a Wilde play because the playwright was enjoying a postwar popularity revival at that time. Cornelia Otis Skinner had done a successful production of *Lady Windermere's Fan* on Broadway in the 1946 season, and 20th Century-Fox was preparing a film version. But more likely he chose the property because it was an easy answer to the problem of finding Paulette a role that would allow her to wear period costumes and fabulous jewelry and take advantage of her talents as a light comedienne. And, he no doubt reasoned, there's nothing like a proven script.

Reports indicate that Korda's ex-wife, Merle Oberon, wanted the part and had several friends suggest this to the producer. Korda was also directing the picture and spared no expense in its production. British star Diana Wynyard headed a superb supporting cast: Glynis Johns, C. Aubrey Smith, Hugh Williams and Paulette's old pal Constance Collier.

But before the production had barely begun, there was a problem. By insisting on her own hairdresser, Paulette had inspired a two-day strike of the makeup artists and hairdressers at the London Films Studios. There was a walkout that had affected over a thousand studio employees. Korda, naturally, wanted Paulette to be happy and so he went through high-level channels to obtain the necessary permissions from the Labour Ministry for work permits for Paulette's hairdresser.

Also, to bring Paulette into the proper mood to portray the elegant Mrs. Cheveley, Korda rented magnificent jewels for her to wear in her scenes. When he was criticized for this seemingly unnecessary expense, Korda shrugged and said, "It makes her feel better." (One person who definitely didn't feel better was Merle Oberon, who seethed when she learned that one of the necklaces was an exact copy of one that Korda had given her.)

Cecil Beaton designed Goddard's wardrobe for the film. Everything pertaining to an Alexander Korda production was first-class, and Korda's reputation as a man who had an appetite for the finest things in life—houses, clothes, women—was also internationally known. This soon led to rumors that Paulette and Korda were having an affair. Korda's nephew Michael has reiterated these rumors in his account of his famous family.

But at this point Paulette and Buzz were still very much a pair. In fact, they were planning a major theatrical adventure. Upon completing their respective films, Paulette and Meredith went to Dublin, where, in August, they opened a production of *Winterset,* with Buzz re-creating his famous role and Paulette in the small but memorable part of the young girl.

Paulette has recalled, "I'll never forget that first performance. On a movie set you are surrounded by people and cameras, and there is a feeling of proximity and warm companionship. When a scene begins, the lights flash on, and as the cameras roll there is utter silence.

"My entrance in *Winterset* was made in complete darkness, and I had to cross the full width of the stage; and as soon as the curtain went up the audience began talking. They had come to see the 'fil-lum' stars, and immediately began to discuss us in whispers. You know—'Gee, where's the di'monds?'

"That was the longest walk I've ever taken, and I've never felt so alone in my life.

"But the feeling soon wore off, and everything was fine, until they began throwing pennies at us—large, oversize British pennies. That, we found, was because there was a line which the audience regarded as sacrilegious. We took out the line and, after that, no more pennies."

Paulette was interviewed by the local press. One journalist asked her a question that any Irishwoman would want the answer to: "Tell me, Miss Goddard, how is it you've been married several times and have no children?" In her sweet and sexy way, Paulette countered, "Well, honey, it hasn't been for lack of trying!"

Patrick Brock, an aspiring actor at the time, has remembered seeing Paulette and Buzz in Dublin. "She was quite young then, in her mid-thirties, and strikingly beautiful, with long dark hair, vivid blue eyes and a gorgeous smiling vivacity." According to Mr. Brock, her reviews in the play had been "indifferent." However, he recalled that "the impact she made on Dublin was considerable."

Despite lukewarm reviews, the fil-lum stars drew incredible audiences. They broke the house record that had been set by Sir Henry Irving back in 1893.

The Merediths returned to the States, where *Unconquered* had opened. Although reviews were caustic, it didn't matter. The DeMille following was legion, and the film was racking up huge grosses.

Undoubtedly the ad campaign—stressing sex and sadism—helped. The ads showed pictures of Paulette in Cooper's arms with the line "I own this woman." Other ad lines included: "See the Slave Auction"—"See the Whipping at the Stake—soft white flesh helpless against the stinging lash."

Unconquered became one of Paramount's top moneymakers of the time. It was a good time for films—*The Best Years of Our Lives, Duel in the Sun, The Jolson Story* and *Forever Amber* made even more money than *Unconquered*.

But the bottom was about to drop out at the box office. And the public's perception of what Hollywood stars were all about would soon change.

In September, 1947, the House Un-American Activities Committee, which had been in existence for almost ten years, now turned its full attention to Hollywood. Experts seemed to agree that H.U.A.C. did this for two reasons: first, the Communist Party had opened a branch in Hollywood back in 1936 and there had been a legitimate attempt to infiltrate the industry; second, H.U.A.C. now wanted publicity for its crusade and there was no publicity like the glamour of Hollywood.

The Committee had had its eye on Hollywood since 1940 but it was only now, under the direction of New Jersey Congressman J. Parnell Thomas, that H.U.A.C. began subpoenaing Hollywood's famous. Many were "happy" to appear before the Committee and help rid the industry of what they thought were Communist infiltrators. Soon those subpoenaed had been divided into two groups, "friendly witnesses" and "unfriendly witnesses." Some had been interviewed in Hollywood. Others were scheduled to appear at hearings in Washington, D.C., the next month. It seemed that Hollywood was about to go on trial. Although nineteen people were subpoenaed, it was ten writers and directors whom the Committee, and hence the press, concentrated on, and these became known as the "Hollywood Ten."

A group of industry members, to demonstrate their revulsion at what they considered witch-hunt tactics and infringements on Constitutional rights, formed the Committee for the First Amendment. The group was headed by John Huston, writer Philip Dunne, director William Wyler and actor Alexander Knox.

At first, almost any freethinking individual in Hollywood was eager

163

to add his or her name to the list, and in short order there were five hundred names on a petition, including such celebrities as Paulette Goddard and Burgess Meredith, Humphrey Bogart and Lauren Bacall, Katharine Hepburn, Gregory Peck, Danny Kaye, Burt Lancaster, Edward G. Robinson, John Garfield, Charles Boyer and Billy Wilder. Other citizens, not movie stars, had also added their names to the list, among them Thomas Mann, Albert Einstein and Helen Keller.

John Huston later said that after the formation of the group they were urged by attorneys (including Bartley Crum) who were representing some of those subpoenaed to "take positive action." "So a representative group of us decided to go to Washington and attend the hearings," Huston recalled. "We weren't sure what we would be able to do, but at least we could demonstrate our support."

Some celebrities, who in retrospect are not remembered as having particular political convictions, felt strongly at the time about the government infringing on the Constitutional rights of the individual.

Judy Garland said: "Before every free conscience in America is subpoenaed, please speak up! Say your piece. Write your congressman a letter! Airmail special! Let the Congress know what you think of its Un-American Committee. Tell them how much you resent the way Mr. Thomas is kicking the living daylights out of the Bill of Rights!"

Cornel Wilde quoted columnist T. L. Stokes: "'The inquisition becomes the concern of everybody who believes in freedom of expression in writing and the arts. Moreover, the fright technique has been chosen for this job. It does all seem confused and quite strange to be happening here.'"

Lucille Ball had this to say: "All of us agree that the Constitution of the United States must be defended! But the way to do this is not by shutting up the man you disagree with; you must fight for his right to speak and be heard. All civil liberties go hand in hand, and when one goes the others are weakened, just as the collapse of one pillar in a house would endanger the whole structure."

Bennett Cerf voiced his fear: "If Hollywood can be bullied into producing only the kind of stories that fall in with this Committee's opinions and prejudices, it seems obvious to me that the publishers of books, magazines and newspapers will most certainly be next on the agenda."

Frank Sinatra: "Once they get the movies throttled, how long will it be before the Committee goes to work on freedom of the air? How long will it be before we're told what we can and cannot say into a radio microphone? If you make a pitch on a nationwide network for a square deal for the underdog, will they call you a Commie?"

Robert Young noted: "The Thomas-Rankin Committee is not a new idea. It goes back for centuries. There was a similar committee on Un-Italian activities which subpoenaed Galileo, and a committee on Un-French activities which subpoenaed Joan of Arc. And a committee on Un-New England activities, three hundred years ago, which burned old women in a witch hunt at Salem."

Paulette, too, spoke out: "There is not a court in America which will admit questions that put words or opinions into the mouths of witnesses, or that indicate exactly what answer is wanted. Yet members of the Un-American Committee have repeatedly done this in the examination of witnesses. Time after time, they have asked questions which began 'Is this what you mean to say?' Or—'Does this sum up your feelings?' Or—'In other words, you would say that . . . ?'

"In spite of this handy technique of putting words into the mouths of witnesses—to this day no one has been able to point to any character, any scene, or any line from any picture which can be understood to advocate the overthrow of our government."

In the heady days of that fall, the Committee for the First Amendment held a rally in Hollywood, and announced plans to continue fighting for the rights of individuals. Paulette, Fredric March, Edward G. Robinson and war-hero-turned-actor Audie Murphy were among those who appeared on a coast-to-coast radio broadcast to protest H.U.A.C. tactics.

Some of the luminaries on the Committee for the First Amendment flew to Washington, D.C., in a plane lent to them by Howard Hughes. Although there had been much sympathy for the well-intentioned group, when they got to Washington they discovered that they had all been "very naïve." It seemed clear that those on trial—the Hollywood Ten—were not interested in defending the same principles as those well-intentioned people on the Committee for the First Amendment.

The group returned to Hollywood. Soon the controversy heated up and the Committee for the First Amendment was suddenly labeled another Communist-front organization. As the furor continued, Paulette was among many who were accused of having Communist leanings.

Her retort was classic: "If anyone accuses me of being a Communist, I'll hit them with my diamond bracelets."

Although Paulette had been under investigation for years, the F.B.I. had no evidence against her and H.U.A.C. had no reason to subpoena her. But the congressional investigations would go on for years, and behind the scenes there was much speculation and fear about who would be branded next.

Certainly one of the government's prime targets was Paulette's ex-husband Charlie Chaplin. There had even been debate on the floor of Congress that year concerning Chaplin's political beliefs. While nothing could be proved against him, many in the country believed him to be a Communist, despite his denials and the fact that he was one of the world's leading capitalists.

With Oona, Chaplin had already had two children, and although he was still making pictures it appeared that his interest had turned from filmmaking to his new family. Within the next few years, however, both Chaplin and Paulette would have to deal with the government's—and the industry's—concern and interference with their political views.

Meanwhile, Paulette and Buzz completed *A Miracle Can Happen,* their second independent picture for Benedict Bogeaus. The film was an episodic piece loosely hung together by the tale of a reporter (Meredith) whose wife (Paulette) keeps after him to investigate human-interest stories. Different segments were directed by King Vidor and Leslie Fenton. The story idea was credited to Arch Oboler, the screenplay to Laurence Stallings. The cast included other top names: James Stewart, Fred MacMurray, Dorothy Lamour and some great character actors—Hugh Herbert, Victor Moore and William Demarest.

With *The Diary of a Chambermaid,* the Merediths had gone for artistic success. With this, they were obviously going for a commercial hit. Filming did not go smoothly. There were reports that Buzz was grumbling at the length of time it had taken to shoot certain scenes with Paulette.

Columnist Sidney Skolsky was on the set the day Goddard and Meredith were filming a scene that called for them to be in bed together. When Meredith became annoyed at the number of takes, Paulette informed him: "At five hundred a minute, you can afford to relax and enjoy it, Sugar."

The Merediths returned East and entered into another business venture together. They opened an antique shop, which they called High Tor Associates. It was located on Route 202 near Haverstraw, New York.

A gala opening was held and the Merediths invited their New York friends Jinx and Tex; Helen Hayes and her husband, playwright and wit Charles MacArthur; Carmel Myers; Cartier's Jules Glaezner; and playwright Maxwell Anderson, the author of Buzz's stage successes *Winterset* and *High Tor*.

The Merediths had hired a young man named Ed Feltus to run the shop. And, to promote their upcoming film, the Merediths had dubbed a corner of the bargain loft in the shop the "A Miracle Can Happen" corner.

Columnist Earl Wilson was on hand. Everybody at the party participated in a recorded broadcast for the McCrarys' radio show, "Hi Jinx!"

When one of Buzz's friends remarked on this being yet another Goddard-Meredith business venture, Buzz quipped: "I started the antique business because I thought as long as we're going to lose money, let's lose it on old things." Paulette's comment, which might also have applied to their film ventures, was "Art for art's sake is all right, but solvency is not to be sneered at."

Buzz may have had no regard for a profit on "artistic" ventures, but Paulette's profit-oriented thinking was well known among the group. When the party at High Tor was breaking up, Charles MacArthur couldn't find his coat.

"Oh, I know what's happened to it," he said. "Paulette's sold it."

The merry-go-round continued as the Merediths were off for Europe. United Artists had retitled *A Miracle Can Happen* and now called it *On Our Merry Way,* a title that seemed to reflect the Goddard-Meredith lifestyle.

Paulette was vacationing in St. Moritz at the time of the 1948 Winter Olympics. When photographers crowded around America's young skating champion Dick Button, who had just won the Gold Medal in the men's figure-skating division, Button suddenly found himself being hugged by a beautiful brunette in an ermine coat. Flashbulbs popped as Paulette Goddard congratulated her compatriot with, in Button's words, "a big furry hug and kiss."

Early 1948 was a good time to be away from Hollywood. It was a time when political lines were clearly and rather heatedly drawn. Some rabid anti-Communists formed action groups to rid the film capital of those they felt were "undesirable." One group of women called themselves Citizens United for American Principles. They published a pamphlet titled *Red Stars in Hollywood: Their Helpers, Fellow Travelers, and Co-Conspirators*.

They proudly announced that they did not care whether an individual was proved to be a Communist. "As far as we're concerned any man or woman who is a fellow traveler, or belongs to a Red front organization, or has supported Communism with financial or moral support, à la Charlie Chaplin, or has come out in open support of the ten branded men . . . or associates with known Communists, openly or in secret, is just as guilty of treason and just as much an enemy of America."

With those criteria, it was surprising that the group found only a hundred people to put on their list. Paulette and Buzz were listed along with Chaplin. They were in stellar company. Also listed were Katharine Hepburn, Gene Kelly, Ruth Gordon, Frank Sinatra, Henry Fonda, Myrna Loy, Walter Huston, Groucho Marx. In fact, most of the stars who had joined the Committee for the First Amendment—but not all. Many top names who'd signed that document were not listed in *Red Stars*. Had they bowed to pressure from groups like this one to renounce their previous convictions? Had their powerful studios intervened? Had certain names been left off to give the impression that others truly had been investigated and found wanting?

No. This group, like others that sprang up at the time, merely targeted those people they chose to label. It was a period when almost everybody in Hollywood was running scared and few dared to speak out against such obvious and brutal tactics. To the credit of the American moviegoing public, none of the smears and slander campaigns ever amounted to a box-office boycott, as these groups proposed.

Anyway, in Paulette's case, it was not politics but artistic content that was about to bring her career down to earth, and with a thud. *An Ideal Husband* was released in the United States by 20th Century-Fox. The picture received disastrous reviews, and, more important, was a total dud at the box office. Shortly afterward, *Hazard* was released, to the same fate. And *On Our Merry Way* soon followed. The last was Paulette's final attempt at independent production with Buzz. The cou-

168

ple were drifting apart. Buzz was pursuing film offers in Europe and continuing his stage career.

In 1948, because of the enormous success of *Unconquered*, Paramount decided to rerelease DeMille's *Reap the Wild Wind*. (Prior to the days of TV, the studios would reissue or remake classics about every five to seven years.) However, as often happened, some stars had risen while others had fallen, so billing was changed in rerelease. Although Ray Milland had won an Oscar in 1945, he was now relegated to third billing, after John Wayne and Susan Hayward. Goddard was billed fourth—a further indication that her star days at Paramount were numbered.

It must have given Hayward some satisfaction finally to overtake her old rival. Susan had just been nominated for an Oscar for her role in *Smash-up* and her career was at last about to take off.

For the time being, Paulette's ego was assuaged since she'd been picked for an important new costume drama to be directed by Mitchell Leisen. His career had suffered a recent blow. He had directed Betty Hutton in *Dream Girl,* a property that had been a huge hit on Broadway. Betty Field had starred in the Elmer Rice play, and Hutton, a genuinely popular star, played the role in the film version. But the picture turned out poorly, was a flop, and Leisen was blamed. However, *Golden Earrings,* directed by Leisen, was also in release and it was a hit, so for the moment the jury was out on Leisen's future at the studio.

The unlikely property chosen to reteam Leisen and Goddard was *The Mask of Lucretia,* in which Paulette would play the infamous Lucretia Borgia. Leisen read the script and flatly said, "No. I'll go on suspension first." However, his business manager and agents convinced him to do the picture—"just get the script rewritten."

Certain aspects of the story did intrigue Leisen. For one thing, it would be the kind of historical re-creation he liked to do. The costumes and sets representing Florence in the Renaissance were from a period that Leisen's artistic sensibilities could do justice to.

Paulette, at thirty-seven, was still a beautiful woman in person, but as far as the camera was concerned her face was not photographing as it used to. There had been scenes in *Unconquered*, despite cinematographer Ray Rennahan's expertise, where Goddard had looked a bit long in the tooth. In less expensive films like *Hazard* and *On Our Merry*

Way, where not as much time was devoted to lighting, Paulette was also beginning to show her age.

One is reminded of Bette Davis' complaint to her cameraman when she was displeased with the rushes on her latest picture. "Why can't you photograph me the way I looked in *Jezebel?*" she asked. The cameraman diplomatically replied, "But, Bette, I was ten years younger then."

When one wants to look younger on film, the rule is to soften makeup, not thicken it. At this time, however, Paulette Goddard wanted a totally new look, including dramatically different eyebrows. The makeup department did not think this was a good idea. For the first time, Paulette was not the friendly, beguiling, bubbly lady who cheerfully went along with the experts.

Hedda Hopper reported that Paulette had tossed the first tantrum of her career while filming *The Mask of Lucretia,* and, regarding her new makeup, Hedda noted that "she got her way, all right, but I'm wondering how much damage she's done to herself with that absurd, unbecoming face? If she's as smart as I think she really is, she'll never use it again."

The project seemed jinxed from the start. Ray Milland had refused to be the leading man; according to him, this was the one and only time he took a suspension, the script was that bad. He was told there would be a rewrite, but, to his consternation, the rewrite was the same script. Furthermore, the story was a duplicate of a current Tyrone Power picture, *Prince of Foxes.*

John Lund had been scheduled to play Cesare Borgia (Lucretia's brother). Now he inherited the lead (Paulette's love interest), and MacDonald Carey was cast as Cesare.

Shortly into filming it was apparent that Leisen was not functioning well; indeed, it was dialogue coach Phyllis Laughton, now Phyllis Laughton Seaton (she had married director George Seaton), who, in effect, unofficially took over the direction of the film. The script was so unplayable that they rewrote dialogue as they went along.

It seemed that the role of Lucretia was far beyond Paulette's range. One of the rewrites of the script had been done by a playwright who had inserted dialogue that was in blank verse. Another obstacle for Paulette.

Leisen had given up on Goddard's performance and concentrated on how she looked. Cinematographer Daniel Fapp took extreme care with her lighting. Leisen personally supervised her costumes and head-dresses. There were few closeups, so Leisen could maintain the illusion of Paulette's "youth."

But everyone's efforts to make the picture work failed. And when it was finished, the film was momentarily shelved.

Meanwhile, Goddard's agent had lined up an important and pres-tigious independent deal. Philip Yordan was producing his hit play *Anna Lucasta* for the screen. Yordan had written the screenplay with Arthur Laurents. Irving Rapper was signed to direct. Columbia Pictures would produce and distribute the picture. The producers' initial choice for Anna was Susan Hayward, but Paulette was available, and landing the role was a coup. *Lucasta* had run for a whopping nine hundred perfor-mances on Broadway and many top actresses were vying for the part. It was the kind of bravura star vehicle that could mean an Oscar.

According to reports, Goddard received $175,000 plus a percentage of the profits, but that seems highly unlikely. It was Columbia's practice to announce these huge salaries to give the "poverty row" studio pres-tige, when in effect Columbia usually hired actors for about half the announced salary. In any event, it would be an AA package for Colum-bia, with a supporting cast including Broderick Crawford, John Ireland, Oscar Homolka, William Bishop, Will Geer and Mary Wickes.

The story was reminiscent of *Anna Christie,* the tale of a daughter and her incest-minded father. In *Lucasta,* the girl escapes to the big city but is later lured back when her drunken father wants to use her in a scheme to marry her off to a wealthy neighbor. In the stage version of *Anna Lucasta,* the girl, of course, had been a whore. But for the cleaned-up film version, Paulette's character, when forced to earn a liv-ing in the big city, had become a waitress.

With *Lucasta* completed, Paulette had two films awaiting release. Off screen, it was obvious that the marriage between her and Buzz was over. Goddard was leading a more social life than ever. She saw a lot of Evelyn Keyes, who had taken an apartment just below hers in the Shoreham apartment complex. Keyes and Huston were still married but, like Paulette and Buzz, had now decided on separate living arrange-ments.

Evelyn was allergic to animals, and Huston was a great animal lover.

171

In his menagerie he had a white German shepherd named Paulette. But Goddard wasn't being singled out; another of Huston's dogs, a fox terrier, was named Jennie, in honor of Jennifer Jones.

Keyes was still in awe of Paulette, and later suggested, "Perhaps what I should have copied was her acquisitive talent. Not only did she have plenty of diamonds and emeralds picked up from some man or other, she had also gathered in a fine collection of paintings, of the Modigliani and Renoir genre. Generosity for her did not always operate the other way around," noted Keyes. "One Christmas I gave her some perfume; she responded by sending over a half-eaten turkey."

Paulette's friendship with Evelyn, and the fact that the two were now living in the same apartment complex, was probably the basis, years later, for absurd rumors that Paulette and Evelyn had lived together with Peter Lawford in a beach house. Keyes and Goddard never lived together. Lawford had dated Keyes, not Goddard. But Hollywood delighted in rumors of real or imagined *ménage`a trois*.

Paulette enjoyed the party scene. It was at this time that Bogart lamented that Hollywood nightlife was getting stodgy. He noted that there were only "a few broads left who know how to drink and have a good time—Lana, Shelley and Paulette."

Others say Paulette was not much of a drinker. There is one story, however, that her friends delighted in. She had driven back to her apartment in Hollywood from a party in the San Fernando Valley, and the next morning, to her horror, discovered she had left the keys to the car and her emerald bracelet lying on the front seat!

There is no doubt that, as always, Goddard knew how to have a good time and was excellent company. She was a scintillating conversationalist and could roll with the punches, so to speak. This was undoubtedly why she held—temporarily, at least—the attention of one of Hollywood's leading luminaries.

Since his return from the war, Clark Gable had dated many women. In fact, he wandered from woman to woman, "still living with Carole's ghost." Gable was drinking heavily and had even been involved in a drunk-driving accident that had been covered up by his studio, MGM.

During these years the actor, now forty-eight, was available to many women. He was used to being pursued. He preferred women with personality and sophistication who, it was said, weren't terribly sexually demanding. And he preferred mature women rather than young starlets.

172

For a while, old friends Goddard and Gable were a viable team. However, people who knew Gable also knew that the star was notoriously cheap. Even Lombard had had difficulty trying to wean him from his frugal ways.

During the early months of 1949, as Gable and Goddard continued to see each other, it seemed Paulette had the inside track on landing him. Some of her friends reasoned, "She'll get a diamond or at the very least a Rolls-Royce out of him." A few said the Rolls was her goal. The affair continued and all eyes were focused on the pair when they attended Desi Arnaz's opening night at the Mocambo that spring.

While personally things seemed to be going smoothly for Paulette, professionally the story was quite different. Paramount had done the best they could with *The Mask of Lucretia*. They had retitled it *Bride of Vengeance* and had built the ad campaign around Paulette and sex: "Not since the ever famous *Kitty* has Paramount brought you Paulette Goddard in a picture as spectacular as this adventure-filled story of the strangest bridal night in history."

The film opened in New York and closed within a week. "Miss Goddard plays Lucretia as a grande dame right out of a wardrobe room, with the suavity and voluptuousness of a model in a display of lingerie," wrote *The New York Times*.

At least *Anna Lucasta* was waiting in the wings. Meanwhile, Paulette accepted a starring role in an independent quickie, *Beloved,* to be shot in Mexico. Gilbert Roland and Pedro Armendariz would be her leading men.

When she left for Mexico, photographers and newsmen were alerted that Gable was driving her to the airport in his chauffeured Rolls. The Hollywood press corps was there as Goddard was about to board her American Airlines flight. She turned to Clark and asked, "Don't you think you ought to kiss me?"

Gable refused. Goddard bounced back quickly. "Well, that's that," she said with humorous resignation. "So long, Sugar!" She laughed and waved to the photographers.

The reporters pressed Gable about their supposed love affair.

"Just say we're a couple of longtime friends" were the King's final words.

It was fortunate for Goddard that she was headed south of the border and not back to Hollywood or New York. In both places, the kind of humiliating scene that had just reportedly taken place would be a topic of savage gossip for weeks.

Paulette had brought her maid and Spanish-speaking secretary along, although by this time Goddard spoke Spanish well enough to get by. As always, she was combining travel with business. She not only shot the movie but she also, in Cuernavaca that June, received her divorce decree from Burgess Meredith.

12

Anna Lucasta was released in the summer of 1949 and was a major disappointment. What had been dynamite on stage was diffused and flat cinema melodrama. It certainly did nothing to revitalize Paulette's sagging career. Variety was harsh, stating that Goddard did not have the "physical accoutrements" needed for the "lush requirements of the part." Most other critics were equally unflattering. The total emphasis placed on Paulette in all advertising and publicity left no doubt that she was the drawing card expected to pull the customers in. She didn't.

As far as the public was concerned, all was well between Paulette and Paramount. But insiders knew the handwriting was on the wall when it was announced that the studio and the star had come to a mutual agreement to renegotiate her contract again.

When reporters located Paulette in Mexico, they described her as "enthusiastic in discussing the status of her career." Goddard said, "It's set up so that any mistakes will be on my own head. Even Paramount, where I have a contract for a picture a year for ten years, has to give me sixty days' notice and then send me the script."

Confident words. But translated by people who knew how to read industry trade papers, this meant she would *only* be paid her $5,000-per-week salary when she was making a film, Otherwise her ten-year contract called for a yearly stipend much smaller than she had been receiving.

She lived it up in Mexico while making *Beloved,* staying at a beautiful country club, with golf course and swimming pool, that was only minutes away from the studio. She socialized with Mexico City's film and artistic élite, including her old friend Diego Rivera.

Evelyn Keyes, splitting from Huston, was longing for solace. She later said, "Who would I talk to if I wanted to talk? Paulette? Her marriage to Burgess had come apart, they had taken her out of a picture at Fox, Gable hadn't given her the Rolls-Royce. No, she had *tsouris* of her own to think about."

Nonetheless, Keyes went to visit Paulette. Goddard's resilience was inspiring. While they were in Mexico, the two women continued their rounds of partying and other diversions. Paulette took time out for another of her interests—bullfighting. She had acquired a protégé, a slim and handsome young matador named Ramón Ortega, whom she was sponsoring in his professional début in the Plaza de Toros. She even helped the matador pick out his cape and publicized his début. (Señor Ortega photographed almost young enough to be Goddard's teenage son.)

Paulette returned to Hollywood to appear on an episode of the Theater Guild radio program, *The Passing of the Third Floor Back,* with Sir Cedric Hardwicke.

As the year ended, Goddard was as shocked as anyone when she learned that Clark Gable had gotten married. In fact, Paulette was more shocked than most, because Gable's bride was her old friend Sylvia Ashley Fairbanks. (Gable's pals at MGM had tried to talk him out of marrying the blonde, who reminded him of Lombard. And indeed they were right: the marriage was over in less than eighteen months.)

Early in the new year, Hollywood, especially the Paramount lot, was abuzz with news of C. B. DeMille's latest epic. He had bought the rights to John Ringling North's story, *The Greatest Show on Earth,* when David Selznick had dropped the option. DeMille was determined to make this his greatest picture—a formidable task, since he had followed *Unconquered* with an even bigger hit, *Samson and Delilah.*

DeMille had toured with the circus to absorb the vital atmosphere first-hand, and now casting the picture was the talk of Hollywood. Kirk Douglas and Burt Lancaster had been considered, and rejected, by DeMille. Hedy Lamarr, DeMille's Delilah, and Marlene Dietrich (now almost fifty) were mentioned for possible leads. Betty Hutton was hell-bent on landing the role of the aerialist and was pursuing DeMille.

According to all reports, Paulette wanted very badly to be in this picture. Such a career move was essential to restoring Goddard's prestige in the industry. Few commodities were as out of date—and out of demand—as yesterday's glamour girl. Goddard had seen it happen to many along the way and it was not a position to be envied. The moguls, agents, gossip columnists and sycophants were even more treacherous when the going got rough.

Goddard was in New York at the same time the circus was, and saw DeMille. In fact, she later said, "Who do you think took me to the opening of the circus at Madison Square Garden this year? C. B. De-Mille."

This was not quite true. She was at the circus and joined DeMille in his box. She subsequently sent him a note: "Dear C.B.: I'm sorry I missed saying goodbye to you after my thrilling evening with you at the circus. I do hope and pray that I get 'The Part' in your coming film. I will be a good, good girl. In the meantime I shall be working hard in summer stock. Yours, Paulette. P.S. You can get me from Paramount. I have pretty feet, too. Love P.G."

Summer stock! Hollywood didn't even approve of its stars appearing on Broadway; it was considered a comedown, a medium in which one's earning power was considerably less than in films. But to perform live on anything *less* than the Broadway stage was, to someone like De-Mille, virtually inconceivable. Was it possible that Paulette was appealing to his sympathies? Was this an indirect plea to The Chief to save her from a future that, in Hollywood's view, was worse than death? If so, the plea fell on deaf ears.

DeMille sent Paulette a note and said, "Yes, your feet are beautiful. What bothers me is that those same lovely feet might be tempted to walk off the set a second time." Privately, C.B. told people at Paramount that Paulette didn't stand a chance. "No one ever walked off a DeMille set and came back."

Paulette's pals Tex and Jinx nonetheless predicted that the star on the highest wire when DeMille filmed the epic would be none other than Paulette Goddard. "It won't be me, it'll have to be my double," quipped Paulette, trying to make light of her last encounter with the chief.

Goddard had joined many other stars politicking for a lead in *The Greatest Show on Earth.* There were two key female roles: the aerialist and the elephant girl. Both parts were physically demanding and dangerous, since DeMille could not use doubles if the scenes were to be at all authentic.

Although she was having difficulty recharming DeMille, one man who appreciated Paulette was John Ringling North. North was a consummate showman. At dinner one night, he heard Paulette say, "I'm not temperamental—I just know what I want, and if I don't have it, I try to get it." He suggested an edited version. "Why not say, 'I never know what I want, but I always get it.' It sounds more like you, anyway."

"I love it like that! Perfect!" Paulette exclaimed, and subsequently used the line in interviews.

Paulette and Buzz were now both giving witty commentary on why their marriage hadn't worked. Meredith told friends Paulette had only married him to get some sort of tax deduction. Paulette countered, "Actors are for Dr. Menninger. The ideal man is one who has eight million dollars and no complexes. To such a man could I give security."

It appeared the ideal man was still far off. During the year, Goddard dated writer Cy Howard and nutritionist-author-commentator Gaylord Hauser.

Paulette's Mexican-made film *Beloved* was retitled *The Torch.* It was quickly released and forgotten. ("Her whole manner is cheap and coarse and throws the character of a lady of breeding completely off-key," said *The New York Times.*)

Paulette appeared again on radio, with Pat O'Brien, dramatizing *The Trial of Mary Dugan,* then headed East for her summer stock commitments. For her stock début, Paulette had chosen Shaw's *Caesar and Cleopatra,* saying she had read it five years ago when she heard Vivien Leigh was making the film. The play was scheduled to open at Olney, Maryland, outside of Baltimore, and then move for three weeks to summer stock theaters in Massachussets.

Paulette had already gone from making major films at a major studio to doing programmers for independent distribution. Now she was doing summer stock.

In all fairness, however, it should be pointed out that it was not un-
common for stars to embark on highly lucrative "in person" careers.
Kay Francis, for example, had made the transition. It was simply common sense to try out one's acting ability in the hinterlands, where a
performer could learn whether she was any good without falling on her
face in front of important Broadway critics who would telegraph the
disaster to the world.

Paulette had no illusions about her abilities. Lilli Palmer had recently
done *Caesar and Cleopatra* on the London stage, and when asked if she
would play Cleopatra as Palmer had, Paulette gave an enigmatic smile
and said, "Of course not, Sugar. Lilli is a professional. In the movies, I
am a professional—but in a play, I'm an amateur. As Cleopatra, I'll
just be—*myself!*"

According to Paulette, producer Richard Aldrich had asked her to
replace Lilli Palmer in the London production when the actress was
taken ill. "But I refused. I didn't believe they would welcome an American in the role; it would just be putting my head in the lion's mouth."
Needless to say, Paulette could not have prepared adequately to be an
immediate replacement.

But their discussions had led to the idea for the summer stock tour.
As Paulette said, "A well-rehearsed company doing four weeks, in
Olney, Dennis, Falmouth and Beverly. This will be my vacation."

Aldrich noted, "Since she agreed to do this, she has done nothing else
but study and work. She has given up parties. She is concentrating on
becoming a fine actress."

"I've wanted to do this—to act on the stage, to be in this play—for a
long time," said Paulette. "I want to learn." She added, "Screen acting
is better training for this than many people think. It's true that in pictures we need learn only the dialogue for one day's shooting, but this,
nevertheless, develops the memory.

"The film actor also learns to react instantly and instinctively to cues,
like a trained dog. We have to swing into a mood the instant the camera
begins to turn, and we can drop it the moment the director shouts 'Cut!'
These quick reflexes are very valuable on the stage."

Goddard's statements to the contrary, the fact is that everyone knows
there is a tremendous difference between film and stage acting. An enormous amount of concentrated energy is required for stage work; a performance must be built and sustained in a two-hour running time, during

which a characterization is created with a beginning, a middle and an end. While a stage-trained actor might find it difficult to tone down a performance for the camera, a film-trained actor often finds it nigh on to impossible to deliver a performance for the stage. In the case of an actress like Paulette Goddard, her screen performances were the direct result of intense effort on the part of her directors, dialogue coaches and others—and the final result was in the hands of a film editor who could cut out all the mistakes. For Paulette, and others like her, to deliver a live theater performance is analogous to an everyday jogger suddenly being expected to run the New York Marathon in record time.

The director of *Caesar and Cleopatra,* Arthur Sircom, noted that Paulette wanted "every phrase, every word, every gesture, to be perfect." When he suggested a bit of business, "she'd want to do it five times, to get it exactly right.

"She had two hangovers from screen acting. At first, she kept worrying about the exact location of her face, which side to present to the audience, and so forth. That, of course, is an important thing in acting for the camera, but she was soon convinced that it is superfluous in the theater."

Often, when Sircom stopped a rehearsal, Paulette protested. "I want to keep doing this over and over! I want to learn, and that's the way I'm going to learn, by doing it over and over!"

Before people could ask the obvious questions, Paulette provided the answers. "Certainly I didn't do this for money, or for self-aggrandizement. I am on vacation now between pictures. I have a ten-year contract with Paramount Pictures—that sounds like a life sentence, doesn't it?— but the contract says I can do what I like between pictures. If I wanted, of course, I could have made an outside picture. Or I could have loafed. I like to work, but I can have fun loafing, too."

There was a major difference between Paulette Goddard and most of her star contemporaries: Paulette's social life was not dependent on her professional success. When she loafed, she loafed in style. In Mexico, on the Continent or in New York, where she took a fabulous apartment, Paulette's life-style was always first-class. Her close friends were people like Anita Loos and society photographer Jerome Zerbe, and her socializing was always newsworthy.

Paulette's acquaintances at this time included such eminent people as the King and Queen of Yugoslavia; Adele Astaire Douglass (Fred's sister, who was a leading figure of international society); designer Valentina (a close friend of Garbo's); French couturier Jacques Fath; and other distinctly non-Hollywood types.

Back in Hollywood, Betty Hutton had landed the role of the aerialist in *The Greatest Show on Earth*. But the elephant girl part was still not cast. In the running were Lucille Ball, Gloria Grahame and Dorothy Lamour. Columnists were still mentioning Paulette as a possibility, and she sent DeMille a telegram: HOPE ALL THOSE RUMORS ABOUT MY GOING INTO THE GREATEST SHOW ON EARTH ARE TRUE. AM RETURNING MONDAY TO SIGN THE CONTRACT.

This time DeMille did not answer. When Lucille Ball, on the verge of being signed, discovered she was pregnant, reports are C.B. suggested she "do something about it." She didn't.

Gloria Grahame got the part. C.B. cast Dorothy Lamour in a smaller, but still showy, role and Lamour received star billing along with the others. It was an example of how Paramount could be loyal to those who had been loyal to them. (An ironic note: the Gloria Grahame character in the picture calls the men in her life "Sugar"—the term Paulette was famous for in her private life.)

Paulette's success in summer stock had at least opened a new door, or so it seemed. She announced, "From now on I'm going to play the straw hats every season." She added, "In the meantime, perhaps, the right play for me to do in the winter theater will turn up."

There were even announcements that Paulette was negotiating to do *Anna Lucasta* on stage in Paris. But through the next year Paulette worked neither on stage nor in films, although there was talk, with producer Gene Markey, about a comedy to be shot in Europe.

In the following year, Paulette led the life of a glamorous nomad—the nonworking star, who, like all nonworking stars, had to fill up her days and keep her name before the public.

Paulette had no films to publicize. Nothing really to say. But friends like Jinx helped keep her name in the columns with puff pieces such as this one on Goddard's attitude about clothes: "I know better than anyone when I look *right*. When I buy a new dress I wear it around the apartment for a long time, before I let anybody else see me in it. When a dress finally feels right on me—it *works* right on the spectators."

And her views on travel: "My theory of travel? I travel light—and I travel alone! And I will not take a transatlantic phone call! Romance gets rusty on long-distance. The only thing I like to hear a man say on a telephone is—'I'll be there in five minutes!'"

In the spring, Goddard was the star attraction at the New York Art Students League Diamond Jubilee Ball. Over two thousand attended the fête, held at the Waldorf-Astoria. The theme for the evening was "Come as Your Most Persistent Dream," and Paulette was the Dream Girl. She was costumed spectacularly as a harem beauty, complete with glittering headdress and bare midriff. (The diamond headdress was on loan from Van Cleef & Arpels.)

Paulette was maintaining her movie queen persona. She was carried into the ball atop an elaborate Oriental sedan chair, borne by four bare-chested, muscular men costumed as Turks.

In her private life, Paulette was between men. Charlie Chaplin, Jr., who was in New York working on Broadway, was surprised and pleased one day when he got a call from her. She told him she had been dating a rear admiral. "And," she added, "he's very dull. Why don't you take me out, Charlie?"

Chaplin, Jr., said, "I'd love to, Paulette, but you know how actors are, always broke."

Paulette laughed. "Oh, don't worry about that. You know your ex has a little money stashed away. Especially having been married to your father." "Ex" was Paulette and the Chaplins' term in referring to their former relationship. The Chaplin boys called Goddard "my ex"—ex-stepmother.

According to Chaplin, Jr., Paulette would joke about the undisclosed settlement she had gotten from his father. "I think your father lost a lot when he married me," she said. "I even got the yacht."

Lita Grey claims Chaplin told her he *loved* only two of his wives: herself and Oona. It seems safe to conjecture that the feelings Chaplin and Paulette had for each other were genuine fondness rather than deep, passionate love. They retained this fondness for each other even after they divorced.

Charlie, Jr., noted that both his father and his ex had wonderful things to say about each other, and that they both joked about the settlement. Chaplin, Sr., told his son, "Your ex is a very lovely gal and a shrewd one. She took me for a little bit."

The probable settlement, everyone agreed, was around a million dollars, but Goddard has never confirmed or denied this. She acknowledged, however, that she had more than enough money and didn't have to work.

In the fall, Paulette was off to Europe with Anita Loos. The ladies had come up with a neat idea. *Look* magazine photographer Doreen Spooner would accompany them, and Anita would compile "Goddard's Guide" as a feature for the magazine—one week "Goddard's Guide to London," then "Goddard's Guide to Paris," etc.

Miss Loos' text recorded such lines as "Goddard feels that what you take with you is not so important as what you come back with. So Goddard's advice is to pack a few simple but flashy dresses and take your jewel case along—empty." In later articles, Goddard's advice included: "Find yourself a guide who will look things over from a fresher viewpoint. The ideal type would be some American in the oil business, preferably from Texas."

In still photographs, Paulette, now forty, looked very much as she always had. And Anita Loos concluded: "I always thought gentlemen preferred blondes until I traveled with Paulette."

Paulette spent much of the next year in Europe. Many of her Hollywood friends were there: John Huston, Anatole Litvak, John Steinbeck, Peter Viertel. Also stars Errol Flynn, Gene Tierney and Gene Kelly. An interesting development had taken place in the film business. Major studios were making films abroad to utilize funds frozen in Europe, and stars were willing to go to Europe because they would qualify for a tax break.

Paulette made a film in Europe that year, but not for a major studio. She had met the Danziger brothers, Eddie and Harry. They could put a deal together quickly. They allegedly asked Paulette, "What do you look best in?"

"A bathtub, bath towel and tights, in that order," she told them. (Paulette used to tell friends, "When in doubt, wear tights.")

Then the Danzigers came up with a script to highlight Paulette's costumes. The film co-starred ex–striptease queen Gypsy Rose Lee. Goddard and Lee were *Babes in Bagdad*. It was another quickie, this one shot (in Technicolor) in Spain. The two stars, both unusually bright women, became—and remained—good friends.

By this time, Goddard's business acumen was very well known. She dismissed it, saying, "Well, that's what people say about me, that I have a good business mind. But I don't think so. I don't even have an agent to take care of my finances, just an attorney. When I work in pictures, all I want, in addition to the specified salary, is a percentage of the picture. If the picture makes money, then I'm a good businesswoman. If it doesn't make money, then I'm a bad businesswoman." Some believe she took the percentage deals in lieu of the specified salary that small-time independents could not offer her.

Paulette still had her contract with Paramount, and she had been mentioned for a film with William Holden, *Beyond the Sunset*. And another called *Hurricane Williams*. Neither of these materialized for her. The latter was made as *Hurricane Smith* with Yvonne De Carlo.

In fact, Paulette would never work for Paramount again. Though it was not known at the time, this might have had less to do with her diminished draw at the box office than it did with politics.

Through the early nineteen-fifties, the House Un-American Activities Committee investigations of Hollywood were suddenly back in the headlines. Things had simmered down considerably in the late forties, but the Korean War had brought the "Communist danger" back into fearful focus. Although there was not an official blacklist other than the Hollywood Ten, there *was* an unofficial blacklist, even a "gray list." Many had been affected, including Paulette's friend John Garfield.

The studios and the unions were demanding loyalty oaths from employees and members. Everyone was nervous. People feared picking up a newspaper and reading what right-wing columnists like Walter Winchell, Ed Sullivan, Hedda Hopper and George Sokolsky might be saying. Naturally, there were a lot of lawyers involved. A veritable bureaucracy had grown up in the negotiations between studios, lawyers and the possible accused.

Paulette had obtained the services of top attorney Martin Gang, whose other clients included Norman Cousins, John Houseman and Burt Lancaster. According to *Naming Names,* Gang also represented people, including Sterling Hayden, Lloyd Bridges, Abe Burrows, Lee J. Cobb

184

and Larry Parks, who had gone before H.U.A.C. and informed on others.

Paramount, like all studios, was trying to clear everyone under contract to them. And the studio had demanded a letter from Paulette. She sent a letter, but Paramount found her comments "insufficient."

"This does not give us the kind of declaration that we would want from her," the Paramount people notified her lawyers.

What sort of declaration did they want?

"Namely, that she is not, and has never been, a Communist, and that her allegiance is to the United States."

Martin Gang eventually convinced Paramount executives to drop the matter. The studio had invested a lot of money in Goddard and might still derive some profit from the investment. Besides, noted Gang, "To ask her for any more than what is written here would only open a can of peas and she might get up on her high heels and kick."

It was assumed that this was a reference to the fact that Paramount wouldn't want the old Chaplin-Goddard relationship dredged up. Chaplin's battles with the government were still raging. He had completed another film, *Limelight,* in which he had cast Charlie, Jr., Syd and his children with Oona. After the film was screened in Hollywood, in August, Chaplin announced a planned vacation to Europe, sailing on the *Queen Elizabeth* in September of 1952. Although the government had issued Charlie a permit to return to the States (he had never become a citizen, and was still a British subject), once the *Queen* Elizabeth was at sea, the United States Attorney General announced that Chaplin's permit had been rescinded pending a hearing about his "fitness" to be readmitted.

Paulette was returning from Europe aboard the Holland-American liner *New Amsterdam.* It docked at six-thirty in the morning in Hoboken, New Jersey, and Paulette was besieged by reporters wanting a statement on the government's action against Chaplin.

"It's a matter for lawyers," said Paulette. "Those are legal matters I know nothing about." Goddard said Chaplin's work "speaks for him." When pressed about what she meant by that, she said, "Well, there is nothing greater on screen than Chaplin off screen." The baffled expressions on the reporters' faces prompted her to add, "That's pretty good, don't you think, so early in the morning?"

185

PAULETTE

Back in the States, Paulette was anxious to return to moviemaking. Her film career now entered a period of high activity and increasingly poor quality. In short order, she made three independent pictures. The first, *Vice Squad,* had some semblance of class. She would get co-star billing with Edward G. Robinson in this Levy-Gardner production for United Artists directed by Arnold Lavin.

Robinson was desperate to work—not for the money; he had plenty; but because he was being "graylisted" by the major studios for what they considered his dubious political affiliations. The *Vice Squad* producers were thrilled when Robinson agreed to do the picture for only $50,000, about one third of his normal salary. However, this was a huge amount considering the film's total budget was only $200,000.

Paulette's salary, on the other hand, seemed stupendous—she would receive $5,000 *per day.* The catch—they only needed her for three days of shooting. Thus, for $65,000, the producers had bought two genuine star names to place above the title.

Robinson played a big-city police captain and Paulette had a small but pivotal role as a local madam, although, in those days, she was described as head of an escort service. The part had a bit of glamour and Goddard flounced through it sexily dressed and wearing a lush mink coat. She was flatteringly photographed and her figure looked terrific.

Her next film was a programmer for Columbia, *Paris Model.* It was another of those episodic tales. In this case the connecting thread was a gown that is passed from owner to owner. Eva Gabor and Tom Conway were in one segment, Marilyn Maxwell was in another, and Paulette was in a segment with Leif Erickson.

Then came the absolute low point in her film career. The makeup and wardrobe tests alone on any of the pictures Paulette had done for De-Mille took longer than the entire shooting schedule of her next picture, *Sins of Jezebel.* This was a project straight out of a Patrick Dennis novel: a Hollywood "spectacle" to be shot in—was it possible?—four days! Even Belle Poitrine, in *Little Me,* would have been hard-pressed to comment.

For a woman who only six years earlier had co-starred with Gary Cooper in a $5 million epic, it must have been quite startling for Paulette to find herself involved in a project that, by her own admission, had a total budget of only $100,000.

But she told Hedda, "I used to say I'd rather have a short part with long eyelashes than a long part with short eyelashes. But I'm not that outspoken anymore."

For producer Sam Katzman, Goddard signed to do a project that, on paper, looked somewhat better than her recent films. It was a costume adventure called *The Charge of the Lancers,* and was to co-star Jean-Pierre Aumont.

The setting was the Crimean War, and for this picture Paulette insisted on a dialogue coach. Jean-Pierre Aumont has recalled that Goddard asked him, "with a shade of embarrassment," to work with her and the coach. He refused. According to Amount, "Our roles consisted mostly of looking professional when we climbed onto a horse and shouted 'charge' or 'giddyup'!"

One day on the set, director William Castle wondered why Paulette was taking so long with the scene. "What's the matter?" he asked. "You seem depressed."

It turned out, Aumont recalled, that Paulette's dialogue coach had been "forcing her to inject into her 'charge' and 'giddyup' as many pauses, thoughts and emotions as would be necessary to play Lady Macbeth." In later years, when Paulette could be more philosophical about this period and these films, she told a friend: "I dropped my bomb and I got out—fast."

In 1953, forty-two-year-old Paulette made her début on the new medium, television, in a segment of NBC's "Ford Theater." And the Goddard name was in the headlines once again when Burgess Meredith, who had remarried, now sued Paulette for $400,000, which he said was his share of their community property.

Goddard countersued, her suit testing the validity of their Mexican divorce, thereby opening questions on the status of his current marriage. It was all settled out of court.

Though the public was unaware of it, there finally was a new man in Paulette's private life. Their attraction for each other was immediate and sustaining. He was someone with an international literary reputation. He was a well-to-do, sophisticated and successful man drawn to women who shared his interest in travel, art and literature. His name had been linked with Dietrich's and Garbo's, and now he was charmed by Paulette Goddard.

PART

III

13

His life could have been the subject of one of his own novels or a tale by Hemingway. Erich Maria Remarque had been christened Erich Paul Remark in the city of Osnabrück, Germany, in 1898. He later adopted his mother's name as his middle name and changed the spelling of his last name. (His great-grandfather was French and had spelled his name Remarque.)

Erich had been brought up a Catholic. Although his family was poor, he had been given a good education and seemed gifted as both a musician and a writer. He served in the German Army during World War I, and although he never reached the front his experiences led him to write of the horrors of that war.

In postwar Berlin the young man, now a journalist, was part of the frenzy that engulfed the literary and artistic worlds on the Continent. He enjoyed living the high life and nightclubbed with people from the theatrical and film worlds. It was then that he met one of Germany's leading film actresses, chubby (at that time) Marlene Dietrich.

In 1929, when his novel *All Quiet on the Western Front* was published, Remarque became, almost overnight, an internationally known writer. Although there had been other successful novels about the Great

War—notably John Dos Passos' *Three Soldiers* (1921) and Heming-way's *A Farewell to Arms* (1929)—Remarque's novel captured readers because it was the story from the viewpoint of the common, conscripted soldier.

The success of his novel provided Remarque with money and status, and he became a favorite of the artistic set. Soon his antiwar novel was made into an American film, which also received worldwide acclaim. Remarque could easily have succumbed to the lures of a Hollywood contract. But he didn't. Unlike some popular authors of the period, he was disciplined and determined to master his craft. He chose to remain in Europe and continue as a novelist and short-story writer.

But the success of *All Quiet* and the subsequent film version made him a target for the Nazis. By 1931, he found he was being persecuted for his pacifist views and he fled to Switzerland. Remarque, who had married in 1927, and then divorced, now remarried his wife so that she too could remain in Switzerland. "I couldn't allow her to be sent back to Germany just because we weren't in love anymore," he said.

While young Paulette Goddard was cavorting in Hollywood in the spring of 1933, Remarque was a man in exile watching his country turn into a veritable insane asylum. In front of Berlin University, the Nazis burned all copies of Remarque's books and a print of the American film *All Quiet on the Western Front.* Throughout the thirties, however, Re-marque continued to write, employing themes—among others—that en-deavored to show that not all Germans were Nazis.

He divided his time between France and Switzerland. Then, on the eve of the Second World War, with his close friend Marlene Dietrich, who was visiting France, he set sail for America on the *Queen Mary.* (Remarque's wife made her way to the States too, but the two lived apart for years and were finally divorced in 1951.)

Remarque followed Dietrich to Hollywood and remained there for three years. He was popular in the film capital, where his work was well known. The ten-year-old *All Quiet on the Western Front* was still hailed as the classic antiwar film. Other Remarque novels, *The Road Back* and *Three Comrades,* had also been filmed. Shortly after his arrival in Hol-lywood, *So Ends Our Night,* based on his novel *Flotsam,* was made into a picture.

Remarque met many of Hollywood's greats, including Chaplin, but he did not meet Paulette at this time; she was out of Chaplin's orbit by then. During the war, Remarque wrote *Arch of Triumph,* and that novel too became an immediate success. It was generally agreed that the author had written the female character with Dietrich in mind, and people assumed she would play in the proposed film version. (She didn't. Ingrid Bergman got the role.)

Remarque had moved to New York in 1942. During the war, he suffered a grave trauma when he learned that one of his two sisters, in Germany, had been executed for treason by the Nazis. She had dared to voice her opinion that Germany was going to lose the war. Through this difficult time, it was undoubtedly friends like Dietrich who helped Remarque to withstand his pain.

His close relationship with Marlene continued until around 1946. According to some reports, it was a platonic relationship, and Remarque himself said that people arrived at the conclusion that they were in love because Dietrich "put me at the top of her ten-most-attractive-men list."

There seems ample evidence that they were lovers, however. In later years, Remarque told his friend British author Virginia Woolf that Dietrich had kept certain letters and he feared she might publish them after his death, embarrassing Paulette. Besides, he hated to have his private life made public.

Probably the desire to keep his privacy was what made Remarque attractive to women like Dietrich and Garbo. Both women were great listeners, and, at heart, homebodies. But the public perceived them as the height of allure, so that being seen with Dietrich or Garbo gave the author a mystique that further enhanced his already rather mysterious personality.

Remarque was an avid art collector and had been since his financial success in the late twenties. He collected paintings by van Gogh, Renoir, Degas, Cézanne, and was particularly interested in Egyptian and Chinese objets d'art. He was also a connoisseur of fine wine and good food, and those few people who knew him well described him as a man of wit.

After his friendship with Dietrich cooled, in the late forties, some claimed that it had ended because Remarque was never much of a physical lover. That he was, in fact, bored by the physical and more interested in the woman's mind.

193

PAULETTE

It has been said that he met Paulette in the late forties. They may have met in 1948 when both were in California. She herself said, "We met in a Hollywood flower shop and he sent me flowers. It was four years later when we ran into each other on Fifth Avenue."

In 1949 and 1950 Remarque was in Germany to research a novel he was writing. Then he returned to New York. The first reliable report of the Goddard-Remarque affair does not appear until the early fifties. By then, the fifty-four-year-old author had been living in the States off and on for twelve years and had become an American citizen. Since the end of the war, he had divided much of his time between New York, which he termed his favorite city, and his palatial home, the Casa Remarque, in Porto Ronco, Switzerland, on the shores of Lake Maggorie. He also liked Paris and spent a great deal of time there.

Anita Loos asserts that Remarque met Goddard at a flower shop on New York's Park Avenue. (Remarque lived on Park Avenue, at the corner of Fifty-seventh Street, in the fashionable Ritz Tower.) He was ordering flowers for his current lover. "He sent the flowers, but he asked Paulette to dine."

Paulette stated that after re-encountering Remarque while walking in New York, "He asked me to dinner the next Friday night. I had to break a date to go, but after that we always had dinner together."

While some say that Goddard and Remarque were inseparable from the moment they met, the facts do not bear this out. Though they did see each other, they traveled separately and continued their separate professional lives. Paulette did rent a villa in Switzerland, and also spent a great deal of time in Paris in the fifties. In fact, it now appears that Europe was her base of operation and she merely visited the States.

Paulette was still, by choice, a working girl. In England, she made another film, *The Unholy Four*. It was a mystery programmer and *The New York Times* subsequently hit the nail on the head when their reviewer wrote that if she did any more films like this, she would find herself picking up the pieces of a career.

Around this time she obviously began reassessing her priorities. Returning to Europe from one of her frequent trips to the States, she said, "I just turned down a movie offer from Hollywood to make this trip to Europe, and nowadays that's unique. Turning down films, I mean. But you see, I don't believe in sacrificing anything to make a movie." She still regretted making *The Crystal Ball* instead of joining Meredith in England back in 1942. "I decided a long time ago never to give up anything for *the* great part. *The* great part may never come along. And even if it does, it's no longer important after the run of the picture."

Many wondered how Goddard avoided, in these crucial years, a downhill slide rivaling those of her contemporaries (some of whom resembled a Tennessee Williams character from *Sweet Bird of Youth*). There was a simple answer. Paulette was a woman who had a realistic perspective on the fantasy industry that had luxuriously supported her for so many years.

In late August, 1954, Joseph Russell Levy died. Paulette Goddard's disgruntled father had apparently never forgiven his daughter, and he made it a point of leaving her one dollar in his will, with a stipulation that if she contested the will she wouldn't even receive the dollar. Reports on his estate ranged from a low of $3,000 to a high of $89,000. Paulette declared that she didn't want anything from a man she never knew.

Paulette's mother, Alta, was alive and well. They continued to be close and, according to Paulette, her mother was still a beauty and still known as "Legs" Goddard.

Paulette's affair with Remarque had, up to this point, been unpublicized. But now their private lives began making news. According to Elsa Maxwell, Goddard's love affair with Remarque was the talk of Hollywood, Paris, St. Moritz, London and Rome. In fact, noted Elsa, "Wherever you go, their romance is a conversation piece."

Maxwell focused in on what it was about Paulette that seemed to attract Remarque. "Before Paulette came into Erich's life he was a sick man who seemed bored with existence. Now he seems to be his old self again. Paulette lifts his dour German spirits like the cable cars they take up the mountains to watch the ski jumping."

Though Elsa failed to note it, this was what Goddard had done with Chaplin, back in the early days of their relationship. She had lifted Chaplin's spirits and enabled him to resume work and be productive.

Remarque was in a highly productive period of his career. In 1952, *Spark of Life* had been published in both English and German. It was dedicated to the author's sister Elfriede. Now, two years later, a new work, *A Time to Love and a Time to Die*, was another success. (The

German title was less romantic, *A Time to Live and a Time to Die*.) This book was dedicated to P.G.

These two novels, which concerned Germans in World War II, re-established Remarque as the leading literary commentator on the German experience during wartime. *Spark of Life* dealt with suffering and death in concentration camps. *A Time to Love and a Time to Die* was about a German youth fighting on the Russian Front. Remarque was hailed worldwide. And critics were quick to point out that, unlike his World War I novels, these novels were less pessimistic. They held a hint of optimism about Germany's future.

Remarque's own future seemed somewhat bright and optimistic, and no doubt P.G. had a great deal to do with it. The press noted that Remarque and Goddard had spent more time together during the past year than any other well-known unmarried couple. And so it began once more: Paulette Goddard, twenty years later, again making headlines for living with a man she loved without benefit of marriage.

Elsa Maxwell warned Remarque: "In Paulette, Erich, you have met your match. With good reason I call her my 'bronze butterfly.'"

Erich, suffice to say, was nobody's fool. Just as Chaplin's genius was evident in his films, and Gershwin's in his music, Remarque's sensitivity and intelligence shined forth in his writing. He was a man who literally could have had any woman he chose, regardless of age. Social convention wasn't against him, as it would have been for a woman: if Remarque had set his sights on a twenty-five-year-old, the world would have smiled its admiration; if a woman Remarque's age, however, had set her sights on a twenty-five-year-old man, she would have been a laughingstock.

The point is that Erich had a wide choice and he chose Paulette. And it wasn't because of youth and beauty. She was no longer young and her beauty was that of a mature woman with character lines in her face. She was hardly, at this stage, the physical embodiment of "the gamine" who had so magnetized Chaplin or the dazzling young femme fatale with whom Gershwin had fallen in love. Remarque fell in love with Paulette's mind, and her talent for making life a pleasure for the person she was with.

The love affair continued, but Paulette found opportunities to work as well. She divided her time between New York and the Continent and was active on television. Memories were stirred when NBC signed God-dard for a TV production of *The Women*. The 1939 George Cukor film could hardly be improved upon, but then, as now, television was recyc-ling proven material.

The cast included Shelley Winters, Ruth Hussey, Mary Astor, Nancy Olson, Cathleen Nesbitt, Pat Carroll and Nita Talbot. Mary Boland was re-creating her role as "the Countess," and she and Paulette were the only actresses from the original film. But Goddard wasn't re-creating "Miriam"; that part had gone to Valerie Bettis. Paulette played Roz Russell's role of "Sylvia," and one reviewer noted that Paulette "was a disappointment. She seemed more the impish tease than a frightening female."

Later in the year, Paulette was on the small screen again, in a "Bob Hope Special." The comedian had gathered some of his former screen leading ladies in a show that featured clips from the films they had done together.

There was talk of Anita Loos writing a TV series for Paulette, to be called *White-Collar Girl*. It never got off the ground. Goddard contin-ued to scotch rumors that she was engaged to Remarque, but columnists noted that she was often in New York only when Remarque was there.

In Europe, Paulette filmed several episodes of the "Errol Flynn The-atre," a TV series never shown in the United States. Actor Patrick Brock worked in the series, and has recalled, "She was pleasant and I liked her." He relates a character-revealing anecdote: "She had been allocated a very lovely, newly painted, glamorous dressing room. One day she was needed for a scene, and they couldn't find her anywhere. It was a serious holdup in this quick French shooting."

Brock had worked at the facility before and, as he said, "knew the layout well, so I elected to help in the search. I thought of the wardrobe room, as I knew she was friendly with the wardrobe mistress. So I climbed up the shaky, outside staircase, opened the shabby door and there she was, the very glamorous Paulette Goddard, dressing and mak-ing up behind a blanket on a line at a corner of the big untidy loft. 'Why,' I asked her, 'when you have that lovely dressing room?' 'Well, honey,' she replied, 'I'm superstitious and I hate the color green, so I just brought my things up here. I didn't want to cause any fuss.'"

Paulette was not temperamental and was easy to work with during

197

these TV years. But there were other problems. On another Flynn episode, it became apparent that Paulette was "too mature" for the closeups and was not convincingly portraying the young character.

Patrick Brock was there: "At this point most actresses might have taken flight and the part would have been recast, but not Paulette. With enormous courage, I thought, she did something quite different . . . She came back on the crowded silent set (bad news travels fast) where we all awaited her. She wore a gentle, more flattering dress and a very careful light makeup and her hair was redressed into a more wavy style with bangs.

"The set was cleared and she 'tested' for lighting and makeup." They used rice-paper filters and tiny spotlights. The cast returned and the show was refilmed.

In the States, Paulette filmed an episode of the series "On Trial" entitled *The Ghost of Devil's Island,* with Philip Reed. And with the usual Goddard bravado she announced that she was back to do a Broadway play and "two films for Paramount."

In Hollywood she saw old friends. "I want to see Cecil B. DeMille," she said. "I admire him more now than when he was younger. I still quote him. He feels the things that click in people. He's a remarkable man."

She told the Hollywood crowd that she enjoyed her nomadic life. "I've never had a permanent home, I have property, but no home. I have houses but no home. You see, I'm not ready to settle down. I have no roots anywhere. I love being wherever I happen to be." In short, she was a forty-six-year-old free spirit.

But, she was asked, where did she really *live?* "If I have a home at all," she said, "perhaps it is in Switzerland on Lake Locarno. I have some of my paintings there. But most of them are with my mother, here in Hollywood. I don't care for possessions, only for things I can pack." For a woman who didn't care for possessions, however, she had amassed a world-famous collection of art and jewelery.

Like all stars whose careers seemed behind them, the inevitable question arose. Would she write her memoirs? "I keep getting offers for my life story, but I'm too busy living it," she said. "I'll wait until I'm eighty. My mother is a little worried about my philosophy of life. 'What will you do when you're lonely at seventy?' she asks me. That's when I'll get the education she couldn't afford to give me."

Although Paulette was a prosperous woman able to indulge her whims—her passion for beautiful and expensive clothing remained unabated—it is amusing that, according to friends, she had an aversion to paying retail prices and would often shop at New York's Seventh Avenue wholesale houses. During this period, she began doing what other former movie stars often found themselves doing—public relations. In 1957, she announced: "I'm going on a three-week tour for a fashion house. I'm a sort of goodwill ambassador. I'm looking forward to it. Especially New Orleans. I love good food."

Her TV work continued. She played in an episode of "Ford Theater," *Singapore,* with Charles Korvin and Rex Reason. She said she loved doing television. "It's such a breakneck pace, you know. It's kiss and go with your leading men. You meet them in the morning and go right into a clinch. The filming is over before you get to know their last names. As for 'live' TV, it's like a première on Broadway that closes after the opening night." This from a woman who was so nervous in front of the cameras in her heyday that sometimes her upper lip trembled.

Goddard had never gone back to the stage after her 1950 summer stock fling. In fact, she had said: "I enjoy going to the theater, but I wouldn't want to participate in any of it. I saw Roz Russell in *Wonderful Town* and during the performance kept saying to myself, 'Isn't it wonderful she's working that hard.'"

However, Goddard was about to embark on another live theater production. Producer Robert Whitehead had offered her the lead in a national touring company of *The Waltz of the Toreadors.* Initially she told Whitehead, "In this play, I have to identify myself with a character that doesn't suit me—a spinster. If, however, you want me to do Moll Flanders . . ."

But Goddard later agreed to do the tour because "it was the best play in New York. I didn't demand a top role, and I didn't get it. I wanted to learn, and I couldn't have been luckier than to get Melvyn Douglas as leading man. He is such a fine actor and teacher. For the first time I came to know what timing meant—how to wait for the laughs and how to speak the lines to get more."

It was announced that Paulette had a highly unusual clause in her contract. Remarque, too, was in New York, preparing his play *The Last Station* for Broadway. And Paulette's clause stated that no matter where she might be, she would receive time off to attend the New York open-ing night of Remarque's play.

The play had already premièred in Berlin, and undoubtedly the author had gotten a taste for the theater. Now he was about to add another dimension to his illustrious career; he would enter the acting profession. Film director Douglas Sirk (also a German refugee) was doing the movie version of Remarque's recent hit novel, *A Time to Love and a Time to Die*. The script was co-written by Remarque and Sirk, although Remarque took no screen credit. Sirk convinced the author to portray a small but important character—the schoolmaster, Pehlman.

Remarque and Goddard continued to make news. In August, United Press announced that the couple would wed. The wire service said that Paulette had told friends she and Erich would be married at Christ-mastime in St. Moritz. The story continued: "Asked why she had waited so long to announce their plans, Miss Goddard said: 'I believe in five-year engagements.'"

Confusion arose. Other reports said they were already married. (The press coverage seemed to be a replay of the Goddard-Chaplin situation over two decades earlier.)

An article in *Variety* had called Paulette "Mrs. Remarque." Paulette subsequently told Sheilah Graham, "I can explain that. I was in Berlin for Erich's play, *The Last Station*. The Germans always describe a woman who has been married as Frau. The papers printed that Erich Remarque and Frau Paulette were in Berlin."

Sheilah accurately tabbed Paulette "The girl who is never at a loss for words." Remarque, on the other hand, was not as friendly or talkative as Paulette. When queried about a supposed cancellation of wedding plans, he tersely noted, "There's nothing to be canceled."

In the fall of that year, Paulette said, "I'll be married in the near future—before spring—right here in my home town, New York." When reporters pointed out that there had been announcements of her forthcoming wedding "about every six months during the past five years," Paulette said, "But not by me." She was parrying with the press just as she had in the nineteen-thirties. "The newspapers announce it," she claimed. "I just don't know how it happens."

Reporter Olga Curtis pressed her, "Did your fiancé ever ask you to set a date?" Paulette countered, "I never discussed it. Even with myself." And she added, "You reporters keep asking and I answer, don't I?"

PAULETTE

*   *   *

Paulette and Melvyn Douglas went on tour with *The Waltz of the Toreadors*. In Milwaukee, Goddard stated she would continue to tour with the play and then join its Broadway run. But she noted that she still had a contract with Paramount, "and if a suitable film role comes along . . ."

None did. In late 1957, the tour was in hiatus and Goddard returned to New York to spend Christmas Eve with Remarque. Supposedly she notified Whitehead that she was marrying Remarque and leaving the play the following month. However, there had been rumors of her leaving the play before that.

She returned to the tour and in January the show opened in Detroit. But after the Detroit run Paulette returned East and the marriage rumors again circulated.

She took an apartment on the fifteenth floor of the Ritz Tower and started plans to furnish it. Remarque's apartment was on the fourteenth floor. If they were planning marriage, friends reasoned, it would certainly be a European arrangement.

A reporter tried to get Remarque on the phone, and later printed: "To an inquiry about his coming nuptials, Remarque gave the shortest possible answer: he hung up." People who knew him say Remarque was horrified at this kind of intrusion into his private life. Moreover, a few of his friends, notably Dietrich, did not think Paulette was the right woman for him.

The image of Paulette as a "gold digger" was one the press kept intensifying. It was good copy to print such tales as her encounter with Jim Thompson, president of the Thai Silk Company of Bangkok. The story: They were having dinner together when she admired his silk suit. "I'll give it to you," he said, and took the suit off then and there. Paulette: "What was so touching about it was that this happened in my home, not his. Thompson said good night at three a.m. and walked out the door—in his shorts."

Goddard added to the gold-digger legend with sophisticated jokes. Once, when she was asked about a diamond necklace that contained many large stones, she stated: "I got it by getting engaged so often—I never give anything back."

There were many retold tales about her femme fatale reputation. One concerned an international playboy who wanted to send special flowers to Paulette and asked a friend of hers, "What is her favorite flower?" "Tell him I adore white violets," Paulette said when she was queried. "He'll never find any, so I won't have to bother thanking him." The man found a florist who filled his unusual order. When there was still no response from Paulette, her friend conjectured, "He would have done better to have sent white diamonds." An oft-quoted line of Goddard's was: "I don't accept flowers. I take nothing perishable."

When she was asked about a diamond engagement ring, she said, "That's in the safe-deposit box. I can't wear *all* my jewels!"

For twenty-five years, the public had been treated to tales of Goddard's gift-getting abilities. After she had definitely left the tour of *Toreadors,* people wanted to know if the new baguette-diamond ring Paulette was sporting signified a marriage. "Oh, that. I got that for Christmas but we just didn't have time to get the license."

But then, in late February, 1958, the news broke: Goddard and Remarque had finally wed. The couple had ostensibly sneaked off to Branford, Connecticut, and had been married in a short civil ceremony by Judge Cornelius T. Driscoll in his law offices. Another judge, McGregor Kilpatrick, had waived the five-day waiting period. For witnesses Paulette had brought along her two attorneys, Halsey Cowan and Robert Morris, and their wives.

The bride, her brunette hair in a stylish pageboy, looked happy and youthful. She wore a burgundy wool dress with a short, matching jacket with mink collar. Her accessories were brown suède pumps and a brown hat. She carried a full-length mink coat. Remarque was conservatively dressed in a double-breasted blue suit.

Paulette gave her age as forty-two. (She was at least forty-seven.) Remarque, accurately, gave his age as fifty-nine.

Word of the marriage quickly spread through downtown Branford, and by the time the couple emerged from the building there was a crowd of over three hundred waiting. Shockingly—at least to Remarque—there were suddenly dozens of reporters and photographers on the scene. Someone had leaked the secret plans. The literary lion wore a dour expression, but his new wife instantly sparkled for the cameras. She delighted in waving her left hand, which displayed a platinum wedding band set with diamonds, and she said: "I guess this makes it official. Anyway, I feel I've known Erich all my life."

PAULETTE

When pressed for their honeymoon plans, Remarque remained silent, but bubbly Paulette informed the press that they were staying in town at home and that they would keep both apartments. "When people work as hard as we do, and keep different hours, it is better to have separate apartments," she explained.

Would she continue to work, now that she was married again? Of course. She hadn't decided whether she would do a play, TV or radio, but she had no intention of retiring.

The couple had finally wed. But accounts noted that when they got into the Cowans' car to drive back to New York, Paulette sat in the front, Remarque in the rear.

Reporting on the wedding, a newspaper headline punned: PAULETTE, ERICH WED—IT'S NEARLY ALL QUIET.

The wedding-night party was held at Erich's apartment, and a special treat was the screening of a new movie. But this year Paulette Goddard wasn't the movie star in the family. The film, *A Time to Love and A Time to Die,* featured Erich.

After the movie's release it was Remarque, not the film's star, John Gavin, who received the acting plaudits. Still, Remarque had decided this was his first and last acting job. His writing was all-consuming; he remained as prolific as ever and was one of a few novelists artistically recognized *and* commercially successful.

Paulette and Erich continued to divide their time between New York, Paris and Switzerland. Remarque's latest novel was *The Black Obelisk,* and he was already deep into work on another.

As Madame Remarque, Paulette enjoyed a new social standing. But she was not quite ready to give up her career and, as they had previously, the couple spent a great deal of time apart.

Remarque, of course, was a celebrity in his own right. However, when he became Goddard's husband he began getting a different kind of publicity.

It was reported that in Paris one night he was in the Crazy Horse, a bar that was famous for its striptease artists. Supposedly, Remarque was buying one of the girls a drink when an obnoxious Texan kept interrupting their conversation. The story goes that the manager of the club ordered the girl to leave Remarque and join the party of Texans. As she tried to do so, Remarque grabbed her arm, claiming that he was a paying customer too. The girl joined the others. Remarque said something the Texans considered an insult and he found himself in the midst of a physical brawl. Now, it seemed, Remarque was fodder for the columnists too.

Paulette filmed an episode of "Adventures in Paradise" for ABC-TV. With Suzanne Pleshette and Gardner McKay, she starred in *The Lady from South Chicago*.

She also made a few appearances on inconsequential television programs, such as the CBS "Sam Levenson Show." She tested her allure on a young CBS page backstage. She stood in the doorway of her dressing room and gazed seductively at him. The page recalls: "She was posed in the doorway like an ad from one of her old films, one arm raised on the doorjamb, her other hand resting on her hip. Her head was lowered and her long-lashed eyes were gazing up. She was wearing a large heart-shaped ruby brooch at her waist."

After she appeared on camera, Paulette rushed backstage and asked anxiously, "How was I? Was I all right? How did I look?"

The page attempted to answer, but Paulette continued, "You have to be vivacious out there—you have to make your personality come through—"

The page assured her she had been wonderful.

Her desire to work led her back to the legitimate stage. With Reginald Gardiner, she did a production of *Laura* at the Coconut Grove Theater in Florida.

But after that she seemed content to be Madame Remarque. Her friends were skeptical when they heard that Goddard was learning to cook. She confirmed it, and said: "I can cook anything—Chinese, Spanish, Irish, French." But she firmly told them: "I will cook only for Erich." (Erich was used to having famous women, like Dietrich, cook for him.)

Although she was not working, Goddard's desire for publicity remained strong. (One is reminded of advertising genius David Ogilvy's comment, "Never read your own publicity—just measure it.") And Paulette was not impossible to reach, if a person was enterprising enough: P. Goddard was listed in the Manhattan telephone directory.

The public had an opportunity to learn what the closet of the girl who never gave anything back contained. In New York, en route to

Switzerland, she permitted photographers to pose her with her most re-cent purchases—American-made garments, "all of which," she pointed out, "add up to the price of one Paris couture purchase." Included were dresses by Ben Reig, Louis Feraud, Branwell, Tina Leser, Bill Blass, Jr. Sophisticates and several St. Laurent copies. Her accessories were from Elizabeth Arden. Last, but not least, there were drip-dry uniforms from Bloomingdale's for her French maid.

Now that she was Madame Remarque, and had evolved into a mem-ber of the international social set like her old friend Merle Oberon, Paulette seemed at times somewhat disdainful of her Hollywood con-temporaries, many of whom had been reduced to appearing in horror films. "I'm always slightly embarrassed to meet other actresses of my vintage," she said. "We have so little in common. They're all so dedi-cated, I find—so desperate."

She also noted, "Everything in Hollywood is now geriatrics. They're all retired, the people I once knew, and they're solely interested in stay-ing alive. They spend all their time out there in health-food shops. My mother is in her seventies and her sole enthusiasm is just survival. She sold her home and moved into the Bel Air Hotel because she doesn't want any of the responsibilities or tensions of running a home."

About her own years in Hollywood, she was totally unsentimental: "I lived in Hollywood long enough to learn to play tennis and become a star, but I never felt it was my home. I was never looking for a home, as a matter of fact." Although she maintained that her collection of bronze Egyptian cats was larger than the Metropolitan Museum's, she stated, "But I don't like to collect anything I can't pack."

Concerning her legendary allure and good looks, she observed: "If your point of view is right, your allure will take care of itself." Paulette's philosophy was "Leave yourself alone as much as possible. Don't worry—I never do; I'm too busy to remember things."

People noted Paulette and Remarque were separated a great deal in the early days of their marriage. Paulette explained: "We get on very well, I must say. I'm gregarious and he's sedentary; it works out fine."

It appeared that Goddard was finally happy in the sort of arrangement Chaplin had once wanted. She and Erich would lead their separate lives, sharing what they wanted of the other's society and coming together for the companionship they both craved. They created their own world together, one of candlelight dinners and romance. They were entering a new period in their lives; Paulette was nearly fifty, Remarque was in his sixties.

But naturally, in the Remarque marriage as in every marriage, each made concessions for the other. For example, Goddard was offered a TV series, "But, I didn't even discuss it with my husband. I just thought, No, it isn't right; I can't ask him to live in *Burbank*." Finally, Paulette Goddard was choosing the man over her career. However, now she could afford to be philosophical. She observed, "Luck plays far too great a part in an acting career for a career to be taken seriously."

Goddard wasn't the only member of the Remarque family sought for interviews. Occasionally, Remarque would agree to see a persistent reporter if he was assured that they would talk only about important matters.

At the Ritz Hotel in Paris, writer Joseph Barry persuaded the author to discuss a recent trip to Germany. After all, Remarque, along with Dietrich, Thomas Mann and a handful of others, represented a very select group of people. They were non-Jewish Germans who had opposed Hitler, left the country and renounced their German citizenship. So when a man like Remarque returned to visit postwar Germany, it was important news.

Remarque observed, "They really don't like to see us. We're an unpleasant reminder. There's even the irony that they think of us as deserters—we who were forced to flee."

Remarque reminisced that the Nazis had tried to discover a Jewish ancestor for him, and noted, "Unfortunately, there were none." And he lamented that even now the old people in Germany hadn't changed and the young people had been kept in ignorance about the past.

Goddard, who was at Remarque's side, interrupted. "Reporters asked me, 'What do you think of Munich, our wonderful city?' And I said, 'To be honest, it's provincial.'" And Goddard reiterated, "It is! And we should be honest with them."

Remarque concurred that culturally the Germans had "fallen back into provincialism." He lamented the loss of a cultural city like prewar Berlin. He discussed a play currently popular in Berlin about the Pope's refusing to help German Jews during the war. Remarque explained that the play was a hit because the Germans were looking for justification.

"If the Pope himself was guilty, how, they say, can you blame the little German?"

And Paulette offered her own opinion: "For the Germans, God is guilty." After many years, Goddard was again speaking out about social issues. People who thought of her as a clotheshorse, jewelry addict and international gadabout had forgotten that back in the forties she had voiced her social conscience.

In 1961, Remarque's novel *Heaven Has No Favorites* (dedicated to Paulette Goddard Remarque) was published. For the first time, the author received poor reviews.

(Years later, *Shadows in Paradise* was made into a film entitled *Bobby Deerfield*. Al Pacino played the title role and the picture bore little resemblance to Remarque's novel. As Sam Goldwyn might have noted, "The public stayed away in droves.")

In the early nineteen-sixties, Remarque suffered a heart attack, but he continued working undauntedly. He also wrote a screenplay, *The Last Ten Days,* adapted from a book by M. A. Musmanno, about the last ten days of Hitler's life. As Erich's health deteriorated, the Remarques began spending their summers in Switzerland and winters in Rome, instead of New York.

Italian film producer Franco Cristaldi talked with Goddard, now fifty-four, about doing a film. It was *Time of Indifference,* based on an Alberto Moravia novel. The cast was imposing: Rod Steiger, Claudia Cardinale, Shelley Winters. Paulette agreed to portray Cardinale's glamorous mother, an impoverished countess. She later said the film had been "a sort of tour de force for me. That's why I did the part."

Regarding future work, Goddard revealed, "There were always discussions—big discussions—in Europe someplace, and I'd say, 'That'll be fine, yes, that'll be fine,' and then I'd wait." The right script never came along. Paulette kept busy studying French and Italian. She studied Zen Buddhism for a while, and kept limber with ballet and dancing lessons.

In the winter of 1965, an avalanche destroyed part of the Remarque home in Switzerland. The major part of the damage was done to the garage and garden; none of the famed Remarque artworks were touched. That winter Paulette and Erich were set to sail to the United States, but

Paulette delayed the trip because she wanted to stay longer in Paris to shop for clothes. It turned out to be a fortunate delay; their ship encountered a heavy storm and was hit by a freak wave. The people who occupied the cabin the Remarques had originally reserved were seriously injured.

Around this time, amidst unprecedented publicity, Charlie Chaplin emerged from retirement and produced and directed the story he had written thirty years earlier for Paulette, *A Countess from Hong Kong.* The film starred Sophia Loren and Marlon Brando in the parts that had been created for Paulette and Gary Cooper.

Sadly, the master director had finally lost his touch, and the film was a turgid attempt at comedy and an unsuccessful venture. (MCA-Universal chairman Jules Stein, at the post-première party, quipped: "We should shelve the picture and release the party.")

Even though Paulette and Charlie were both living in Switzerland, she never saw him. "We live on different mountains," she said.

It must have been a blow to Paulette when, in 1968, Charlie, Jr., died. The carefree youth, the smiling boy she had watched grow up, had evolved into a disillusioned forty-three-year-old alcoholic.

These were trying years for Paulette. Remarque had a series of small heart attacks, but he continued to work. *The Night in Lisbon* was made into a movie for German television. Then his health deteriorated to the point where he entered the Saint Agnese Clinic in Locarno and around noon, on September 25, 1970, his heart collapsed and he died. Paulette was at his side.

The news of his death was flashed around the world. One of the literary giants of the twentieth century had succumbed. Paulette personally oversaw the funeral arrangements. A mass was held at the Roman Catholic church at Ronco, and Remarque was buried in the village cemetery, "overlooking the lake that he loved so much," said Paulette.

Goddard brought his finished, unedited novel to New York. With his publishers, Harcourt Brace Jovanovich, she discussed a title for the book. The working title had been *The New York Story,* but Paulette chose a new title, *Shadows in Paradise.* She noted, "It's his most personal, most powerful novel. It's about New York. Really it's about East Fifty-seventh Street, where we lived for years."

She even chose the jacket cover. It featured a bright picture of Central

Park. "It's the way he saw the city." Referring to the publisher's initial cover, she said, "The one they came up with first was too gloomy. You'd have been afraid to have it on your night table."

She had taken such a detailed interest, she said, "because it's really my book. He had no children. We had only each other."

Those few people who knew both Goddard and Remarque well say that only a man as European as Remarque could have truly understood and appreciated a woman like Paulette. With him, she had met her match. And with Remarque's death, Anita Loos conjectured: "Romance must have disappeared from her life forever."

14

Shortly after Remarque's death, Paulette said, "I never really counted on how it was all going to turn out." However, she also noted: "I bounce back. A year is like a weekend now, just like a moment, and as you get older it gets worse. But I never have missed anything and if I wanted to work more I could."

It was true. Friends were trying to lure her back to work, assuming it would help her forget the void in her life. The time couldn't have been better: a nostalgia boom had literally swept the country. The nation's disenchanted young people yearned for the beauty and fantasy of the old days, epitomized by Hollywood's films. Incredibly, the stars of those films were once again in big demand. The intervening decades had transformed most of the former gods and goddesses into puffy-eyed, sometimes unrecognizable shadows of their former selves. But interest in them was at an all-time high.

Goddard was, understandably, not exactly in a frame of mind to jump right on the bandwagon. When she first returned to New York, she stayed at a hotel. She did not want to stay at the Ritz Tower because their apartments there "held too many memories."

She did socialize a bit. She was at the Broadway première of *No, No,*

Nanette in early 1971. She saw old pals such as former co-star Joan Crawford. Crawford introduced her to Pete Rogers, who invited Paulette to pose for the famous Blackglama mink campaign, "What Becomes a Legend Most?" (Crawford had done it in 1969.) Paulette followed such other legends as Garland, Dietrich and Streisand, and posed for photographer Richard Avedon. Supposedly Paulette gave her mother the mink coat she recieved as payment, because Paulette "didn't wear black."

Sometime later, when Crawford suggested that she could introduce Paulette to an eligible tycoon, Goddard bristled. She told Joan, "I've never dated a businessman in my life." She had, of course, married one back in 1927.

Through the year, Paulette continued to wander from country to country. The past was once again her present when, late in the year, she returned to New York to publicize the reissue of *Modern Times*. The Lincoln Arts Theatre, on Fifty-seventh Street, was launching a Chaplin festival, and the girl who had been Charlie's quintessential gamine—the only one of his leading ladies who had gone on to a prestigious career of her own—was there. In white fur and diamonds, Paulette posed before a poster caricaturing the Little Tramp.

For *Modern Times* Paulette attended a New York Film Critics awards dinner. Another guest at the affair was a fast-rising young actress in the movie industry, Geraldine Chaplin, one of Charlie and Oona's beautiful children. Paulette and Miss Chaplin chatted amiably, and the young woman couldn't help but notice and admire Paulette's glittering diamond bracelets.

"Your father gave me those," said Paulette.

"He never gave me anything like that!" Miss Chaplin exclaimed.

Goddard inched back into New York social life. She and her friend Pamela Sherek lunched at La Côte Basque. Paulette let reporters know that she was a fan of New York's current mayor, good-looking John Lindsay. "He's better-looking than both Gary Cooper and John Wayne." And, in case people had forgotten, Paulette reminded them: "I ought to know—I worked as leading lady for both men."

She did return to work. Her friend Helen Hayes was doing a television movie with Mildred Natwick, called *The Snoop Sisters*. They'd be portraying two old sisters, mystery writers, who wind up, of course, solving cases that the police can't. It was being produced by MCA for

NBC. Leonard Stern was executive producer and director, and had written the screenplay from a story by Hugh Wheeler.

There was a role in the picture that seemed perfect for Paulette—a glamorous former movie queen who is murdered. Since it was a feature to launch a proposed series, the production values were good. The cast included Art Carney, Jill Clayburgh, Kent Smith, Craig Stevens, Fritz Weaver, Ed Flanders and Kurt Kaznar.

Paulette signed for the role. One of the plot points in *The Snoop Sisters* is that the murder of Paulette's character is linked to a scene from one of her old films. The sisters screen the film to discover the clue. For this segment the producers used a clip from the 1940 film *The Ghost Breakers,* a scene where the leggy young Goddard rushes down a staircase screaming. However, perhaps to placate Paulette's vanity about her age, or perhaps as a plot device, the clip was described as a scene from one of her 1946 films.

Later, Paulette complained that while her makeup and wardrobe tests for *Snoop Sisters* had been lit and photographed to her satisfaction, she was not happy with how she appeared in the final film. To date, this is the last time she has appeared on screen. Paulette claimed she had only done it because the project "tempted me," and she stated: "I won't do any more acting." *Variety,* however, reviewed her performance warmly: "Time has not lessened her electricity nor dimmed her star quality."

In 1972, Charlie Chaplin made news when he returned to the States to receive a special Oscar from the Academy of Motion Picture Arts and Sciences. He also stopped in New York City to attend a special tribute for him held at Philharmonic Hall. There was a post-screening reception and Paulette, bejeweled, was there. Chaplin and Goddard had not seen each other in years. Although both continued to spend most of their time in Switzerland, they still lived on "different mountains."

On one of her trips to and from Switzerland, Paulette brought back a copy of Remarque's play *Full Circle* and gave it to a writer to prepare for a possible American production. She assumed it would take some time to get the deal going, but as luck would have it things fell into place quickly.

She later explained that she had just flown to New York from Switzerland. "And very early, the very first morning I was here, I went out for a walk, to walk off my jet lag. And who do I see, walking down

Madison Avenue, but Otto Preminger—he's a great walker, you know, and I went over to him and I said, 'Otto. The play.' 'Ah, yes,' he said. 'Where is it?' So I told him Peter Stone was working on it. He called Peter and had lunch with him. . . . I thought it would take six months to get things moving. Instead, it took six days." And within six months the play had opened. Unfortunately, the closing notice went up quickly.

Shadows in Paradise had not been well received either. Most literary critics agreed that *Shadows* was not a fitting final product for such a good novelist. They noted that the posthumously published book was never really completed to Remarque's satisfaction, and they blamed the publisher for not editing out repetitions and triteness. Remarque was also criticized for being too graphic in his love scenes, something none of his previous novels had been.

The author had always used elements of his own life in his novels. In this story, which takes place in the nineteen-forties, the characters decide to go see a Paulette Goddard film. Although most of the story is set in New York, the hero also travels to Hollywood, and Greta Garbo and Dolores del Rio are mentioned in the text. Writing the book had occupied most of the last six years of Remarque's life. The theme of the book was that America turned out to be a false paradise for German refugees and those who try to return to Germany discover they cannot go back either. As in all his books, Remarque set forth his philosophy that in the final analysis each person stands alone.

Though past sixty, Paulette was given proof that she was still a femme fatale. When she was browsing around one of the Seventh Avenue showrooms where she liked to pick up designer dresses at bargain prices, a very rich old man, who was nationally known (he had recently been appointed to an important post by newly re-elected President Nixon), spied Goddard and tried for an introduction. He was obviously smitten, to the extent that he sent Goddard telegrams asking her to accept a post on the President's Council for Physical Fitness and literally begging her to call him for a date!

All this was happening while the Watergate scandal was in the headlines. Each day, members of Nixon's staff were testifying against the President. Paulette and her friends found it amusing that the bigwig Nixon supporter who was pursuing her ignored the possibility that he might be supplying the press with more material to embarrass the Administration. Naturally, Paulette had no intention of exposing her ardent admirer, but she quipped, concerning shredding machines—currently a hot topic of Watergate conversation—that a shredding machine was the last thing a girl should own.

By the mid-seventies, social life in the United States had changed drastically. During the years when Paulette had spent so much time abroad, America had seen the rise and fall of the beatnik and the coming and going of the flower children smoking their marijuana.

New York society was filled with moneyed but disillusioned baby boomers who were into cocaine, high tech, plastic and partying. The bizarre aspects of social life were now, if not sanctioned, certainly at least accepted. Bisexuality, transvestism, illegitimate children, orgies, drug parties—these were among the subjects people were reading about.

Probably the most outrageous celebrity that the seventies produced was artist and filmmaker Andy Warhol, who by that time was the undisputed leader of the underground movement in firm control of New York's trendsetters. *Vogue* magazine had asked Warhol to photograph his twelve favorite women. One of them was Paulette. "I was about to go away," she recalled. "I told him where he could find me." The Metropolitan Museum was having a special exhibit, the Gold Show. Warhol tracked Goddard down and from the minute they met there was instant rapport. Soon she was the momentary favorite of the Warhol group.

Paulette, in glamorous clothes and fabulous jewels, was seen everywhere with Andy. Although she had many fur coats, of every type, Paulette wore only white fox in the season of 1973–74. She said, "It was the winter of the white fox. I was always wrapped in it, whether it was long, short or just a stole." She called Warhol the white fox because of his alabaster skin and startling white hair.

Warhol made glowing comments about the star. "Paulette is still beautiful, she really is. She's very trim, her eyes are very blue, and her hair is still in the pageboy she's worn since *Modern Times*."

She, in turn, had glowing things to say about him. "He is the best audience I have ever found. I like to talk and he likes to listen." And she noted, "Actually, Andy quite fits into my pattern. I have always preferred creative men to the big, booming butter-and-egg type."

Warhol made an attempt to educate Paulette to current fashion. "At lunch once I said, 'Paulette, I've been meaning to tell you, it's not chic anymore to wear a lot of jewelry, because people get robbed so much. What's chic now is this art deco plastic stuff.' She took one look at it and said, 'You want me to give up my rubies and emeralds and diamonds for . . . this?'" Needless to say, she didn't.

Although Paulette had said she would never write her autobiography, it was now announced that Harcourt Brace Jovanovich had signed Goddard and Warhol to do Goddard's story. It would be called *HER: Paulette Talks to Andy Warhol*.

In the spirit of the times, Harcourt Brace threw an announcement party at a currently fashionable disco, the Factory. Paulette described her friend Andy as "a three-dimensional man." The artist-writer-entrepreneur always had his tape recorder and camera handy, and even before the announcement of the book Warhol had recorded much of the time he had spent with Goddard.

People in the industry eagerly awaited *HER*. They knew that Warhol was not one for puff pieces. He would encourage Paulette to present the inside story.

For more than a year, Goddard stayed in Warhol's orbit and the book was an ongoing project—as far as the public knew. But eventually there was another announcement. Goddard had insisted on returning the publisher's advance. The book deal was canceled. Officially, the reason given was artistic differences. Paulette Goddard was not interested in writing the kind of book that Warhol and the publishers had expected.

One of her friends noted that Paulette was *never* one for telling secrets. And Paulette herself said, almost with pride, "Warhol taped me for eighty hours and I wouldn't tell him anything."

There were other conjectures about why the honeymoon was over between Goddard and Warhol. Some sources allege that the sometime-filmmaker had suggested that Goddard invest in some of his projects. In any event, by late 1976, as quickly as she had re-entered the arena of publicity, she abruptly abandoned it.

Anita Loos remained Goddard's closest friend. The two women spoke at least once a day on the phone. Anita loved Paulette dearly; one of Diego Rivera's portraits of the star was a prized Loos possession, on loan from Paulette.

215

People still recognized Paulette Goddard as she walked briskly through the streets of Manhattan. Her mother was now living in her own apartment in town. A friend of Paulette's was present when Goddard and her mother were having a conversation over the telephone. Paulette became angry at something her mother told her and hung up, furious. Paulette explained to her puzzled friend that her mother (who was not too far from ninety) had just invested ten thousand dollars in a bond with a ten-year maturity!

Bernard Drew recalled meeting Paulette's mother as she was leaving Paulette's apartment one day. Drew and Paulette went to the window and watched the lady, who was wearing a bright red coat, walk home along Fifty-seventh Street.

Paulette, in a reflective mood, pointed to the horizon and told Drew that she could trace her early life from the view—Long Island, where she was born; Brooklyn, where she had spent part of her childhood; Broadway, where she had gotten her start.

Drew discussed with Paulette Elizabeth Taylor's film *Ash Wednesday,* a picture about a woman who gets a face-lift. He asked Goddard directly, "Will you have one?" Paulette told him, "No." She said she was afraid of the operation.

There certainly was no reason for Paulette to consider plastic surgery since she had no intention of returning to the screen.

The day after Christmas, 1977, Paulette Goddard was saddened, as were millions of others, at the news of Charlie Chaplin's death. (Her name was in the news briefly as one of the great comedian's ex-wives.) Chaplin had achieved immortality. His name, of course, has even entered the language, with the word "Chaplinesque" listed in modern dictionaries.

Chaplin's films are still shown in theaters across the world and are now on video tape as well. His two most popular films are *Modern Times,* his last silent, and *The Great Dictator,* his first talkie.

Shortly after Chaplin's funeral there was shocking news that his grave had been robbed and his body was being held for ransom. One of Goddard's friends reported: "She told me in Zurich that the kids who kidnapped Charlie Chaplin's body called her up and said, 'We have Charlie Chaplin's body.' Paulette said, "So what.' And hung up."

In the late seventies, Paulette established a scholarship program at

216

New York University with a gift of $25,000 to the School of the Arts. Twenty-five scholarships of a thousand dollars each were awarded to students in the fields of dance, directing, acting, drama, design and cinema studies.

Goddard was later given an award by N.Y.U. for her commitment and contributions to the university. She had donated Remarque's original manuscripts to N.Y.U., including *All Quiet on the Western Front* and *A Time to Love and a Time to Die*.

It seemed that the only time Goddard emerged from her private world, through the late seventies and early eighties, was to sell some of the extraordinary possessions she had collected.

In 1979 she sold part of her art collection, the Impressionists. "Owning these masterpieces has become a tremendous responsibility," she said, "because I travel so much. I think the public should have access to such great paintings and I'm tired of having them stored away in crates. I've been planning to sell them for some time."

The paintings, which included works by Cézanne, Monet and Degas, fetched more than $3.1 million, well over the $2.9 million estimate of the Sotheby Parke Bernet New York galleries. Paulette had twenty-nine artworks on sale out of a total of a hundred and nine that were up that day. Her paintings accounted for more than a third of the day's receipts.

While Sotheby's dealt with many famous and wealthy clients, there was no doubt that Paulette Goddard—swathed in a white fur coat and impeccably groomed—was someone special, as evidenced by the news photographers covering the event. However, Goddard received an unexpected and pleasant reminder of the impact her screen *persona* had delivered in its heyday when one of the young women employed at the gallery revealed a special reason for wanting to meet the former star. It seems the girl's stockbroker father had been a big fan of Goddard's—to the extent that he and his wife had named their daughter Paulette. Paulette Tavormina was introduced to Paulette Goddard and told her the story. The actress beamed, genuinely delighted at the compliment.

At the auction Goddard wore a piece of art, a Salvador Dalí brooch consisting of a pair of enamel red lips studded with diamonds. "Dalí designed it for me," she said. "I decided to wear it when I read that Man

Ray's painting of the giant red lips sold in this room on Monday night for $750,000."

Now that she had begun disposing of the Paulette Goddard Remarque Collection, would she miss the treasures? "Not a bit," she answered with a smile. She said she didn't feel so bad about selling them. But she added, on second thought, "Not yet, anyway."

She still possessed a collection of Braques and Modiglianis and a tremendous collection of pre-Columbian art. And she told the art world that she hoped to sell these "in the near future," and her jewels as well.

New York *Daily News* columnist Suzy reported that Paulette "strolled into Van Cleef and Arpels in New York with a diamond bracelet in her pocket and walked out with a check for $45,000. Years ago Erich had paid $10,000 for it."

While rumors continued to surface that there would be a major auction of Goddard's fabulous jewels, to date it has not taken place. Goddard did continue to sell her artworks. She eventually even sold two of her Diego Rivera paintings. *Young Woman with Sunflowers* sold for $242,000. *The Flower Vendor* brought in $429,000, reportedly the highest price ever paid for a Latin-American work. She did not sell Rivera's portraits of herself.

Not all Goddard's concerns were monetary. She was interested in preserving the memory of Remarque's contribution to literature, and she now donated his diaries for the years 1917–58 to the New York University Library.

For the past few years there have been disturbing rumors that Goddard suffers from ill health. Columnist Earl Wilson had reported in the mid-seventies that Paulette received unpleasant news from Happy Rockefeller's doctor—it was well known that Mrs. Rockefeller had suffered from breast cancer. But it was also well known that Paulette Goddard was not one to give in to unpleasant news; she was, and is, a fighter.

She has kept out of the public eye in recent years. She allows no photographs, and would not participate in a photo session for a recent book that flatteringly depicted former film stars in a then-and-now format. She did, however, phone to thank the author for sending her flowers—she told him that receiving them was "like a brief caress . . ."

She is rarely seen in New York, and as this book goes to press she spends most of her time abroad. Although out of sight, Paulette Goddard has certainly not been forgotten. She is one of the very few of her era who made the transition from celebrity and stardom to a successful and happy private life. It would appear that she has experienced most of the good things life has to offer: love, wealth, fame, accomplishment.

Only Paulette Goddard can say what life has taught her. But it seems certain that she has evolved from a girl who thought that money, jewels and movies were everything into a woman with a mellow outlook and a will not only to survive but to learn and grow continually. A note Goddard wrote to famed photographer Alfred Eisenstaedt offers insight into her philosophy: "Happiness is the absence of pain. 'Retouching' is the absence of beauty. Sayings of Goddard."

Her curiosity about people and places took her, not too long ago, to that exotic and mysterious place in New York known as Yonkers. Paulette had simply, spontaneously, boarded a bus, destination Yonkers, because she wanted to see what the place was like. (One wonders if the commuters aboard realized one of their fellow passengers was a world-famous woman whom many of them had read about, at one time or another, over the past half century.)

"You live in the present," Goddard once stated, "and you eliminate things that don't matter. You don't carry the burden of the past. I'm not impressed by the past very much. The past bores me, to tell you the truth; it really bores me. I don't remember many movies and certainly not my own." But movies will always provide a record of the beauty and vivaciousness of this unique woman. And her life has certainly been the stuff of which dreams are made.

She is indeed that *rara avis:* a one-of-a-kind American original.

FILMOGRAPHY

1. *The Girl Habit* (Paramount, 1931)
   Director: Edward Cline. Screenplay by Owen Davis and Gertrude Purcell.

   Cast: Charlie Ruggles, Tamara Geva, Sue Conroy, Margaret Dumont, Allen Jenkins, Donald Meek, Jean Ackerman, Paulette Goddard, Erica Newman, Norma Taylor

2. *The Mouthpiece* (Warner Brothers, 1932)
   Directors: James Flood and Elliott Nugent. Screenplay by Earl Baldwin. Based on the play by Frank J. Collins.

   Cast: Warren William, Sidney Fox, Aline MacMahon, Guy Kibbee, J. Carrol Naish, Jack LaRue, Paulette Goddard

3. *The Kid from Spain* (United Artists, 1932)
   Producer: Samuel Goldwyn. Director: Leo McCarey. Screenplay by William Anthony McGuire, Bert Kalmar and Harry Ruby.

   Cast: Eddie Cantor, Lyda Roberti, Robert Young, Noah Berry, J. Carrol Naish, Paulette Goddard, Betty Grable

4. *Modern Times* (United Artists, 1936)
   Produced, directed and written by Charles Chaplin.

221

Cast: Charles Chaplin, Paulette Goddard, Henry Bergman, Chester Conklin, Hank Mann, Louis Matheauz

5. *The Young in Heart* (United Artists, 1938)
Pruducer: David O. Selznick. Director: Richard Wallace. Screenplay by Paul Osborn and Charles Bennett.

Cast: Janet Gaynor, Roland Young, Billie Burke, Douglas Fairbanks, Jr., Richard Carlson, Minnie Dupree, Paulette Goddard, Henry Stephenson

6. *Dramatic School* (MGM, 1938)
Producer: Mervyn LeRoy. Director: Robert B. Sinclair. Screenplay by Ernst Vadja and Mary McCall.

Cast: Luise Rainer, Paulette Goddard, Alan Marshal, Lana Turner, Henry Stephenson, Genevieve Tobin, Gale Sondergaard, Melville Cooper, Virginia Grey, Ann Rutherford, Hans Conried

7. *The Women* (MGM, 1939)
Producer: Hunt Stomberg. Director: George Cukor. Based on the play by Clare Boothe Luce. Screenplay by Anita Loos and Jane Murphin.

Cast: Norma Shearer, Joan Crawford, Rosalind Russell, Mary Boland, Paulette Goddard, Joan Fontaine, Lucile Watson, Phyllis Povah, Virginia Weidler, Ruth Hussey, Margaret Dumont, Marjorie Main, Hedda Hopper, Aileen Pringle

8. *The Cat and the Canary* (Paramount, 1939)
Producer: Arthur Hornblow, Jr. Director: Elliott Nugent. Screenplay by Walter DeLeon and Lynn Starling.

Cast: Bob Hope, Paulette Goddard, John Beal, Douglass Montgomery, Gale Sondergaard, Elizabeth Patterson, Nudia Westman, George Zucco

9. *The Ghost Breakers* (Paramount, 1940)
Producer: Arthur Hornblow, Jr. Director: George Marshall. Screenplay by Walter DeLeon.

Cast: Bob Hope, Paulette Goddard, Richard Carlson, Paul Lukas, Anthony Quinn

10. *The Great Dictator* (United Artists, 1940)
Produced, directed and written by Charles Chaplin.

FILMOGRAPHY

Cast: Charles Chaplin, Paulette Goddard, Jack Oakie, Reginald Gardiner, Henry Daniell, Billy Gilbert, Carter DeHaven, Chester Conklin

11. *Northwest Mounted Police* (Paramount, 1940)
Produced and directed by Cecil B. DeMille. Executive Producer William LeBaron. Screenplay by Alan LeMay, Jesse Lasky, Jr., and C. Gardner Sullivan

Cast: Gary Cooper, Madeleine Carroll, Paulette Goddard, Preston Foster, Robert Preston, George Bancroft, Lynne Overman, Akim Tamiroff, Walter Hampden, Lon Chaney, Jr., Montague Love, Robert Ryan, Wallace Reid, Jr., Rod Cameron, Chief Thundercloud, Clara Blandick, Monte Blue

12. *Second Chorus* (Paramount, 1941)
Producer: Boris Morros. Director: H. C. Potter. Screenplay by Elaine Ryan and Ian McClellan Hunter.

Cast: Fred Astaire, Paulette Goddard, Burgess Meredith, Charles Butterworth, Artie Shaw and his band

13. *Pot o' Gold* (United Artists, 1941)
Producer: James Roosevelt. Director: George Marshall. Screenplay by Walter DeLeon.

Cast: James Stewart, Paulette Goddard, Horace Heidt, Charles Winninger

14. *Nothing but the Truth* (Paramount, 1941)
Producer: Arthur Hornblow, Jr. Director: Elliott Nugent. Screenplay by Don Hartman and Ken Englund.

15. *Hold Back the Dawn* (Paramount, 1941)
Producer: Arthur Hornblow, Jr. Director: Mitchell Leisen. Screenplay by Charles Brackett and Billy Wilder.

Cast: Charles Boyer, Olivia de Havilland, Paulette Goddard, Victor Francen, Walter Abel, Rosemary DeCamp

16. *The Lady Has Plans* (Paramount, 1942)
Producer: Fred Kohlmar. Director: Sidney Lanfield. Screenplay by Harry Tugend.

Cast: Ray Milland, Paulette Goddard, Roland Young, Albert Dekker, Margaret Hayes, Cecil Kellaway

17. *Reap the Wild Wind* (Paramount, 1942)
    Produced and directed by Cecil B. DeMille. Screenplay by Alan LeMay,
    Charles Bennett, Jesse Lasky, Jr.

    Cast: Ray Milland, John Wayne, Paulette Goddard, Raymond Massey,
    Robert Preston, Lynne Overman, Susan Hayward, Charles Bickford,
    Walter Hampden, Louise Beavers, Martha O'Driscoll, Hedda Hopper

18. *The Forest Rangers* (Paramount, 1942)
    Director: George Marshall. Screenplay by Harold Shumate.

    Cast: Fred MacMurray, Paulette Goddard, Susan Hayward, Lynne Over-
    man, Albert Dekker, Eugene Pallette, Regis Toomey, Rod Cameron

19. *Star Spangled Rhythm* (Paramount, 1942)
    Director: George Marshall. Screenplay by Harry Tugend.

    Cast: Betty Hutton, Eddie Bracken, Victor Moore, Anne Revere, Walter
    Abel, Cass Daley, MacDonald Carey. MC: Bob Hope. Guest stars: Wil-
    liam Bendix, Dorothy Lamour, Paulette Goddard, Veronica Lake,
    Arthur Treacher, Vera Zonina, Fred MacMurray, Franchot Tone, Ray
    Milland, Susan Hayward, Ernest Truex, Mary Martin, Dick Powell,
    Cecil B. DeMille, Preston Sturges, Alan Ladd, Katherine Dunham,
    Marjorie Reynolds, Bing Crosby, Robert Preston

20. *The Crystal Ball* (United Artists, 1942)
    Producer: Richard Blumenthal. Director: Elliott Nugent. Story by Steven
    Vas; adaptation by Virginia Van Upp.

    Cast: Ray Milland, Paulette Goddard, Gladys George, Virginia Field,
    Cecil Kellaway, William Bendix, Ernest Truex, Yvonne DeCarlo

21. *So Proudly We Hail* (Paramount, 1943)
    Produced and directed by Mark Sandrich. Screenplay by Allan Scott.

    Cast: Claudette Colbert, Paulette Goddard, Veronica Lake, George
    Reeves, Barbara Britton, Walter Abel, Yvonne DeCarlo.

22. *Standing Room Only* (Paramount, 1944)
    Director: Sidney Lanfield. Screenplay by Darrel Ware, Karl Tunberg.

    Cast: Paulette Goddard, Fred MacMurray, Edward Arnold, Roland Young,

Hillary Brooke, Anne Revere, Veda Ann Borg, Marie McDonald, Sig Arno

23. *I Love a Soldier* (Paramount, 1944)
Produced and directed by Mark Sandrich. Screenplay by Allan Scott.

Cast: Paulette Goddard, Sonny Tufts, Beulah Bondi, Mary Treen, Ann Doran, Marie McDonald, Barry Fitzgerald, Frank Albertson, Hugh Beaumont

24. *Duffy's Tavern* (Paramount, 1945)
Director: Hal Walker. Screenplay by Norman Panama and Melvin Frank.

Cast: Bing Crosby, Betty Hutton, Paulette Goddard, Alan Ladd, Dorothy Lamour, Eddie Bracken, Brian Donlevy, Sonny Tufts, Veronica Lake, Arturo De Cordova, Cass Daley, Diana Lynn, William Bendix, Joan Caulfield, Gail Russell, Helen Walker, Barry Fitzgerald, Victor Moore, Marjorie Reynolds, Barry Sullivan, Ed Gardner (as Duffy), Howard Da Silva, Billy De Wolfe, Walter Abel. Olga San Juan

25. *Kitty* (Paramount, 1946)
Producer: Karl Tunberg. Director: Mitchell Leisen. Screenplay by Darrell Ware and Karl Tunberg.

Cast: Paulette Goddard, Ray Milland, Patric Knowles, Reginald Owen, Cecil Kellaway, Constance Collier, Sara Allgood, Eric Blore, Mae Clarke

26. *The Diary of a Chambermaid* (United Artists, 1946)
Producers: Benedict Bogeaus, Burgess Meredith. Director: Jean Renoir. Screenplay by Burgess Meredith.

Cast: Paulette Goddard, Burgess Meredith, Hurd Hatfield, Francis Lederer, Judith Anderson, Florence Bates, Irene Ryan, Almira Sessions, Reginald Owen

27. *Suddenly It's Spring* (Paramount, 1947)
Producer: Claude Binyon. Director: Mitchell Leisen. Screenplay by Claude Binyon, P. J. Wolfson.

Cast: Paulette Goddard, Fred MacMurray, MacDonald Carey, Arleen Whelan

FILMOGRAPHY

28. *Variety Girl* (Paramount, 1947)
Producer: Daniel Dare. Director: George Marshall. Screenplay: Edmund Hartman, Frank Tashlin and Robert Welch.

Cast: Mary Hatcher, Olga San Juan, DeForest Kelley, William Demarest. Guest stars: Bing Crosby, Bob Hope, Gary Cooper, Ray Milland, Alan Ladd, Barbara Stanwyck, Paulette Goddard, Dorothy Lamour, Veronica Lake, Sonny Tufts, Joan Caulfield, William Holden, Lizabeth Scott, Burt Lancaster, Gail Russell, Diana Lynn, Sterling Hayden, Robert Preston, John Lund, William Bendix, Barry Fitzgerald, Cass Daley, Howard Da Silva, Billy De Wolfe, MacDonald Carey, Arleen Whelan, Mona Freeman, Cecil Kellaway, Virginia Field, Cecil B. DeMille, Mitchell Leisen, Spike Jones City Slickers, George Reeves, Wanda Hendrix

29. *Unconquered* (Paramount, 1947)
Produced and directed by Cecil B. DeMille. Screenplay by Charles Bennett, Fredric M. Frank and Jesse Lasky, Jr.

Cast: Gary Cooper, Paulette Goddard, Howard Da Silva, Boris Karloff, Cecil Kellaway, Ward Bond, Katharine DeMille, Henry Wilcoxon, Sir C. Aubrey Smith

30. *An Ideal Husband* (20th Century-Fox, 1948)
Produced and directed by Alexander Korda. Screenplay by Lajos Bir.

Cast: Paulette Goddard, Michael Wilding, Diana Wynyard, Glynis Johns, Constance Collier, Sir C. Aubrey Smith, Hugh Williams

31. *On Our Merry Way* (United Artists, 1948)
Producers: Benedict Bogeaus and Burgess Meredith. Directors: King Vidor and Leslie Fenton. Screenplay by Laurence Stallings.

Cast: Burgess Meredith, Paulette Goddard, Fred MacMurray, Hugh Herbert, James Stewart, Dorothy Lamour, Victor Moore, William Demarest

32. *Hazard* (Paramount, 1948)
Producer: Mel Epstein. Director: George Marshall. Screenplay by Arthur Sheekman.

Cast: Paulette Goddard, MacDonald Carey, Fred Clark, Maxie Rosenbloom

33. *Bride of Vengeance* (Paramount, 1949)
   Producer: Richard Maibaum. Director: Mitchell Leisen. Screenplay by
   Cyril Hume. Additional dialogue: Clemence Dane.

   Cast: Paulette Goddard, John Lund, MacDonald Carey, Albert Dekker,
   John Sutton, Raymond Burr

34. *Anna Lucasta* (Columbia, 1949)
   Producer: Philip Yordan. Director: Irving Rapper. Screenplay by Philip
   Yordan and Arthur Laurents.

   Cast: Paulette Goddard, William Bishop, Oscar Homolka, John Ireland,
   Broderick Crawford, Will Geer, Mary Wickes, Whit Bissell, Gale Page

35. *The Torch* (Eagle Lion, 1950)
   Producer: Bert Granet. Director: Emilio Fernandez. Screenplay by Inigo de
   Martino Noriega.

   Cast: Paulette Goddard, Pedro Armendariz, Gilbert Roland

36. *Babes in Bagdad* (United Artists, 1952)
   Producers: Edward J. Danziger and Harry Lee Danziger. Director: Edgar
   G. Ulmer. Screenplay by Felix Feist and Joe Anson.

   Cast: Paulette Goddard, Gypsy Rose Lee, Richard Ney, John Boles,
   Sebastian Cabot, Christopher Lee

37. *Vice Squad* (United Artists, 1953)
   Producers: Jules V. Levy and Arthur Gardner. Director: Arnold Laven.
   Screenplay by Lawrence Roman.

   Cast: Edward G. Robinson, Paulette Goddard, K. T. Stevens, Lee Van
   Cleef

38. *Paris Model* (Columbia, 1953)
   Producer: Albert Zugsmith. Director: Alfred E. Green. Screenplay by Robert Smith.

   Cast: Eva Gabor, Tom Conway, Marilyn Maxwell, Cecil Kellaway, Florence Bates, Paulette Goddard, Leif Erickson, Barbara Lawrence, Robert
   Hutton, Prince Michael Romanoff (as himself)

39. *Sins of Jezebel* (Lippert, 1953)
    Producer: Sigmund Neufeld. Director: Reginald LeBorg. Screenplay by
    Richard Landau.

    Cast: Paulette Goddard, George Nader, Eduard Franz

40. *Charge of the Lancers* (Columbia, 1954)
    Producer: Sam Katzman. Director: William Castle. Screenplay by Robert
    E. Kent.

    Cast: Paulette Goddard, Jean-Pierre Aumont, Richard Stapley, Karin
    Booth

41. *The Unholy Four* (Lippert, 1954)
    Producer: Michael Carreras. Director: Terence Fisher. Based on the novel
    by George Sanders. Screenplay by Michael Carreras.

    Cast: Paulette Goddard, William Sylvester, Patrick Holt, Paul Carpenter

42. *Time of Indifference* (Continental, 1965)
    Producer: Franco Cristaldi. Director: Francesco Marselli. Screenplay by
    Francesco Marselli.

    Cast: Rod Steiger, Claudia Cardinale, Shelley Winters, Paulette Goddard

INDEX

INDEX